The Woodworker's
ILLUSTRATED
ENCYCLOPEDIA

Graham McCulloch

POPULAR WOODWORKING BOOKS
CINCINNATI, OHIO
www.popularwoodworking.com

Read This Important Safety Notice

To prevent accidents, keep safety in mind while you work. Use the safety guards installed on power equipment; they are for your protection. When working on power equipment, keep fingers away from saw blades, wear safety goggles to prevent injuries from flying wood chips and sawdust, wear hearing protection and consider installing a dust vacuum to reduce the amount of airborne sawdust in your woodshop. Don't wear loose clothing, such as neckties or shirts with loose sleeves, or jewelry, such as rings, necklaces or bracelets, when working on power equipment. Tie back long hair to prevent it from getting caught in your equipment. People who are sensitive to certain chemicals should check the chemical content of any product before using it. The authors and editors who compiled this book have tried to make the contents as accurate and correct as possible. Plans, illustrations, photographs and text have been carefully checked. All instructions, plans and projects should be carefully read, studied and understood before beginning construction. Due to the variability of local conditions, construction materials, skill levels, etc., neither the author nor Popular Woodworking Books assumes any responsibility for any accidents, injuries, damages or other losses incurred resulting from the material presented in this book. Prices listed for supplies and equipment were current at the time of publication and are subject to change.

Distributed in Canada by Fraser Direct
100 Armstrong Avenue
Georgetown, Ontario L7G 5S4
Canada

Distributed in the U.K. and Europe by David & Charles
Brunel House
Newton Abbot
Devon TQ12 4PU
England
Tel: (+44) 1626 323200
Fax: (+44) 1626 323319
E-mail: postmaster@davidandcharles.co.uk

Distributed in Australia by Capricorn Link
P.O. Box 704
Windsor, NSW 2756
Australia

Visit our Web site at www.popularwoodworking.com or our consumer Web site at www.fwbookstore.com for information on more resources for woodworkers and other arts and crafts projects.

Other fine Popular Woodworking Books are available from your local bookstore or direct from the publisher.

12   11   10   09   08   5   4   3   2   1

Library of Congress Cataloging-in-Publication Data

McCulloch, Graham.
  The woodworker's illustrated encyclopedia / by Graham McCulloch.-- 1st ed.
      p. cm.
  ISBN-13: 978-1-55870-834-1 (pbk. : alk. paper)
  1. Woodwork--Encyclopedias. I. Title.
  TT180.M193 2008
  684'.0803--dc22

                                        2008015126

Acquisitions editor: David Thiel
Senior editor: Jim Stack
Interior designer: Geoff Raker
Cover designer: Brian Roeth
Production coordinator: Mark Griffin

Metric Conversion Chart

to convert	to	multiply by
Inches	Centimeters	2.54
Centimeters	Inches	0.4
Feet	Centimeters	30.5
Centimeters	Feet	0.03
Yards	Meters	0.9
Meters	Yards	1.1

About the Author

Graham McCulloch is an architectural designer by profession and a woodworker by passion. Graham's profession has taken him from commercial interior design to the designing and construction of trade show exhibits in Montreal and later Halifax, Nova Scotia, where he and his wife Gwen now live. Graham is a very young septuagenarian and is still passionate about woodworking. When not in his woodshop Graham is writing books and articles in a number of Canadian woodworking publications. He has a bi-weekly ShortCuts column on the world-wide web at www.shortcuts.ns.ca.

Acknowledgements

This is the part of the book, like at the Oscar Awards (absolutely no equation) I stand up in front of a microphone with a long list of notes and thank my producers and directors, family and friends.

Well, I don't have a lengthy list but there is no question that my wife is at the top of it. Thanks Gwen for putting up with me through the pressures of one more book.

Special thanks go to David Thiel, my editor for putting up with some (occasionally) pretty inane questions and for making sense of my writing. David was able to magically turn some of the photos into useable and definitive illustrations and to find those that were all but obscure.

Thanks also to the fine employees at Lee Valley Tools, Rockler and Freud for their valuable assistance with many of the images in this book.

Dedication

This book is dedicated to my three children and my (at this writing) five grandchildren. Perhaps one or more of them will catch the sawdust fever and enjoy woodworking as much as the old man.

INTRODUCTION

 hat is woodworking? That is a tough question in many respects because there are so many different disciplines to encompass in a simple one–two–or–three line definition. Yet, that is what this book is all about, isn't it? I've tossed this around and fretted about it throughout the writing of this book and I've decided, at the risk of sounding glib, that woodworking is the art, yes, the art of removing everything in a piece of wood that you don't want. It is the art of looking at a piece of wood and visualizing what is in there and then very carefully uncovering it. This can be done by turning the piece on a lathe, carving it, chipping away at it or, as many of us do as well, cutting it to fit as a small element in a bigger picture like a piece of furniture. So yes, woodworking is an art.

Since 1993 I have written three books on woodworking, mostly focusing on making this art easier to apply. The books offer shortcuts that help woodworkers ply their art, trade or hobby using self-made jigs that simplify some of those more complicated repetitive tasks.

For the past five or more years I have felt that there must be some sort of woodworking encyclopedia around to help woodworkers define the many idiosyncratic woodworking terms. Being unsuccessful in finding one, I decided that I should start compiling material for a future book.

An encyclopedia on as technical a subject as woodworking, however, would be difficult to produce with just words. It would be easy enough to describe a word like *cup* when defining the term in connection to wood defects. This is simply a board that is concave between the edges. However, as the adage goes, a picture is worth a thousand words. In an attempt to keep this book down to a reasonable number of words I did not assign a thousand or more of them to each definition. Instead, this encyclopedia is rife with pictures, both photos and illustrations.

I have endeavored to cover just about every woodworking term known to us woodworkers but, even after double, triple and quadruple checking, this is the best that I could come up with. There are 288 pages in this encyclopedia, 1,070 definitions, 1,158 pictures and close to 100 charts or text boxes. I hope you will keep this handy either in your shop or library as a reference book. In compiling this book I realized that even with over 60 years of woodworking experience there were many terms and words that I was unfamiliar with. I think you'll find that to be true as well.

It is inevitable that there are woodworking terms that have not made it into this encyclopedia, and I ask you, dear readers, to submit any that I have missed. These will be compiled and added to a later revised edition. Please send me an e-mail at graham@shortcuts.ns.ca with *Encyclopedia* in the subject heading.

The book is written not just for the U.S. market but for most English speaking countries as well. You will find the Union Jack, the Old Glory and the Maple Leaf flags scattered throughout the book; they make reference to terms that are specifically characteristic of that country. There is also one flag belonging to Finland for an age-old woodworking term that was, in fact, the name of the woodworking class that I took as a youngster in Montreal. It was in grade school that I was first introduced to woodworking.

You will, I hope, forgive my rather weak attempts at humor in the book. In the very long hours spent on my computer I needed some comic relief.

Warning Note. Some of the photographs or illustrations in this book may show the tools being used without the safety guards in place. This is done strictly for the clarity of the photo or illustration and should not be considered as a recommendation by the author or publisher. The author encourages that you use all recommended safety measures outlined by the various tool manufacturers.

As I got closer to the publisher's deadline I was putting in more hours on the book and, of course, felt somewhat pressured. This, I guess, is a normal thing for writers to feel, but it can have negative effects on those around them. So, now that the book is finished I must apologize to Gwen, my wife, and at the same time thank her. Gwen has put up with my long hours on the keyboard and my sometimes short temper. Gwen, this book is dedicated to you, my love. Thank you.

WARNINGS

Canadian, eh?

Properly British

Warning! May cause death or a rash

Fire, Fire

Good ol' U.S.A.

Finland? Really?

A (ay) – see also, eh — A Canadian expression usually followed by a question mark. I get to put this in because I'm the author and this is my book.

Abrasives (abray-zivs) — Any material used for grinding, smoothing or polishing such as sandpaper or other abrasive compounds.

Abrasive Compounds (abray-ziv kompounds) — Abrasive compounds are used for smoothing and polishing wood and other materials through lapping or rubbing. Abrasive compounds include emery, Carborundum, pumice and rottenstone and are usually sold in shaker-type containers. The very fine-grained powdery compounds are mixed with a lubricant such as water or kerosene

and rubbed on the wood finish with a ball of cheesecloth.

Abrasive Papers — See Sandpaper.

Abrasive Synthetics (sin-thet-ix) — Simulated steel wool made up of an abrasive embedded plastic wool in various grades of fineness that is used for smoothing after the application of water-based finishes. These are also available in sheets for hand use or in powered sanders. Norton, Sia and 3M are among the companies that manufacture them.

ACQ — An acronym for the chemical formulation used in pressure-treated wood. A is for amine, alkaline or ammoniacal (depending on the specific formulation). C is for copper azole, and Q is for quaternary, a biocide sometimes shortened to quat. Use extreme caution when handling and using ACQ. Carefully read all warnings.

Acrylic Solvent (a-krill-ik) — This is a water-thin liquid adhesive that is used for bonding edges and surfaces of acrylic sheet materials and some other types of plastics. The adhesive is usually applied with a medical syringe to pinpoint the application. The adhesive dries almost invisibly. Very little solvent is required to make a firm bond.

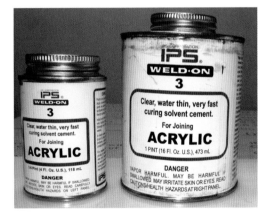

Adhesives (ad-he-sives) — See also Glue. These are materials (usually glues) that bond two or more similar or different materials together, either temporarily or permanently. These adhesives include Acrylic Solvent, Carpenter's Glue, Casein Glue, Contact Cement, Cyanoacrilate (Krazy Glue), Epoxy Resin, Hide Glue, Hot Glue, Marine Glue, Polyurethane

Adhesives, Rubber Cement, Urea
Resin and White Glue.

Adze (adz) — A woodworking tool
that dates back to about 3000 B.C. It
is used primarily for shaping, hew-
ing and carving wood for ships'
timbers or logs and beams for rustic
homes.

Air Cleaner — An electrically powered machine that filters dust-filled
air in a woodshop. A fan inside the
box-like machine draws in dusty
air, filters it and exhausts clean air.
These are usually installed near the
ceiling.

Air Compressor — A machine used to
compress air that is used to power
nailers, staplers, paint sprayers and
the like. An electric motor or gas
engine propels a piston that forces

Air Drying — This is a
method of drying wood
(boards) to stabilize
them for use in cabinetry
and construction. The
boards are rough-cut to
size and then stacked in
neat piles with stickers
between the layers. The
boards are left outside in
open–sided sheds until
they have reached the
desired moisture content.
The rule of thumb for air
drying is that it takes one
year for every one inch of
thickness for a board to
dry to a moisture content
(MC) of 14%. This will vary
depending on climatic
conditions.

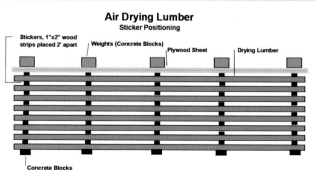

Air Drying Lumber
Sticker Positioning

Stickers, 1"x2" wood
strips placed 2' apart   Weights (Concrete Blocks)
                    Plywood Sheet   Drying Lumber

Concrete Blocks

air into a storage tank(s). One end of a hose is connected to the tank and the other end to the air tool. A regulator controls the air pressure.

Air Tools — See Pneumatic Tools.

Alcohol — The real stuff. This is not mixed with shellac flakes. It should be taken internally but not while working with sharp or powered tools.

Alcohol, Denatured — Also called Isopropyl Rubbing Alcohol, it is alcohol that has been made unfit for consumption. In fact, it is poisonous. Denatured alcohol is used to make shellac. Alcohol is mixed with shellac flakes, and the alcohol melts the flakes.

Alligation (al-i-gay-shun) — These are fine cracks that resemble alligator skin and that may appear in a primer-sealer coat. Alligation may result if there is grease, dirt or wax buildup on a surface, or when the application temperature is too low, or when the product is not thoroughly mixed.

Alligator Saw — See Keyhole Saw.

Aluminum Oxide (a-loo-min-um) — This is a synthetic mineral with a grey/brown appearance used as an abrasive grain. Aluminum oxide is particularly resistant to wear and is extremely durable. Ground aluminum oxide is used as a sandpaper grit.

Angle — The divergence of two straight lines measured in degrees.

45°

Angle Brace — A diagonal support to strengthen right angle frames or panels. The brace is usually glued and screwed to the frames.

Angle Square — See Speed Square.

Aniline Dye — See Wood Dyes.

Annual Growth Rings — The layer of wood growth developed by a tree in one year. These rings are seen in the end grain of lumber. The rings may be counted to determine the approximate age of the tree.

Antique Furniture — Furniture of any type that is over 100 years old.

Antiquing — A technique used to make a painted surface look older than it really is. The term usually refers to a thin glaze that is applied to a surface, allowing the undercoat to show through. A crackling finish may be applied as well, to give the appearance of age.

Antique Nail — Usually a round–headed nail with a plain or hammered finish that is used to fasten upholstery to a frame. The nail is decorative and designed to be exposed. They are generally ¾" – 1" in length.

Anvil — A large, heavy cast iron tool used for the hammering and shaping of heated steel as in the sizing of horseshoes. In woodworking the anvil is used for straightening nails, closing rivets, etc.

Apron — The upper frame of a table that supports the top and braces the legs.

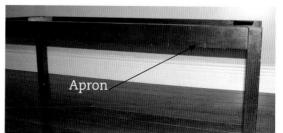

Apron

a

Apron Plane — Smaller than a block plane, this tool is designed to fit in a shop apron for quick touch-ups during construction and assembly.

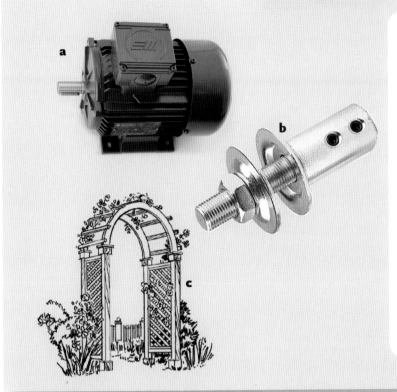

Arbor (ar-buhr) —
a) The rotating shaft of an electric motor that drives or powers tools.

b) A shaft that is driven by a motor that drives saw blades, router bits, sanders and other power tools.

c) A garden structure made of wood or other materials to support climbing vines or roses.

Ardox Nail — See Spiral Nail.

Arkansas® (ar-kan-saw) — This is a Norton trade name for a novaculite stone used for blade sharpening, honing and lapping.

Arts & Crafts Movement — A decorative wood furniture style that began in England during the late nineteenth century, where it was known as the Aesthetic Movement. Lead by William Morris, the movement rejected industrialization and encouraged fine craftsmanship and simplicity in design.

Assembly Time — Also called Open Assembly Time. The time lapse between the spreading of the glue on workpieces and when they must be assembled and clamped to attain the proper adhesion.

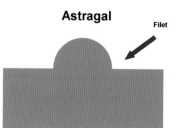

Astragal

Filet

Astragal — a) A vertical strip attached to the opening edge of one door in a pair, forming a jamb for the other door to close into. The astragal is an overlapping edge. b) A bead moulding with a filet on either side.

ATB — Alternate Top Bevel. This refers to the shape of the teeth on a common crosscut circular saw blade. The top edge of one tooth is ground to the left while the next is ground to the right.

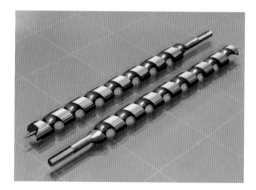

Auger (aw-gur) — See also Ship's Auger. The auger is thought to have been invented by Archimedes and named the Archimedes screw around 300 B.C. There are some records that show a likened device in the Hanging Gardens of Babylon 300 years earlier. The auger in its modern day design is used to drill holes in wood and is the forerunner of today's drill bit.

Auxiliary Fence — See Fence, Auxiliary.

Axe — See also Hatchet. The axe is probably one of the first hand tools invented and dates as far back as the Stone Age. The cavemen/cavewomen probably hunted animals with a spear-like weapon and then butchered them with an axe-like tool. Various forms of axes have appeared over the centuries as the tool has evolved into different shapes to suit the type of work at hand. The axe is primarily used for felling and limbing trees, for splitting firewood and by firefighters in gaining access to hot spots in burning buildings.

Awl — Also called a Scratch Awl or Bradawl — A pointed tool used to press an indent into wood to place a brad nail or to start wood screws. The tool is also used to scratch marking lines and is used like a pencil.

FUN facts

The axe has some notorious historical moments. When young George Washington's father asked him if it was he who cut down the cherry tree, he replied, "I cannot tell a lie, Pa, I cut down the cherry tree." These words are now deeply embedded in the historical lore of the United States. "Lizzie Borden took an axe and gave her mother 40 whacks, and when she saw what she had done she gave her father 41." Or so goes the limerick of the infamous Elizabeth Borden axe killings that occurred in Fall River, Massachusetts in August of 1892.

B — The first letter in a favourite Canadian beverage, Beer, which is consumed only after all the power tools are turned off and the woodworker has retired for the day.

Backer — The backer is a sacrificial board or piece of wood clamped or fastened to the back of your workpiece to prevent tear–out from a drill bit or saw blade.

Back Iron — See Cap Iron

Balancing — Veneer or laminate added to the back side of a veneered or laminated substrate to balance the tension caused by the gluing of veneer or laminate to the top surface.

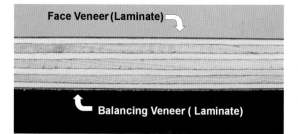

Face Veneer (Laminate)

Balancing Veneer (Laminate)

Dovetail

Dozuki (doe-zoo-key)

Gents

Offset

Tenon

Backsaw — See also Tenon Saw. A backsaw is any of several types of hand saws that has a stiffener on the top (back) edge of the tool and is designed for crosscutting freehand or with a jig such as a miter box. These may include a dovetail saw, a dozuki saw, a gent's saw, an offset saw or a tenon saw.

Ball and Claw Foot — See also Ball and Claw Leg. The foot of some chairs and other furniture that resembles a raptor's claw. This style of foot is found on Queen Anne and Chippendale styles of furniture.

Ball and Claw Leg — A form of cabriole leg, the foot of which appears to be shaped like a raptor's claw clasping a ball. This type of leg is generally found on Queen Anne and Chippendale style furniture.

 **Ball Catch** — See Ball Latch.

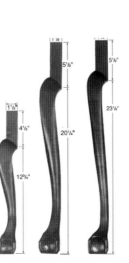

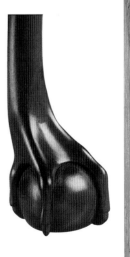

Ball Foot — See Bun Foot.

Ball Latch — An encapsulated ball in a housing with a spring. The case is recessed into the edge of a cabinet door. A receiving plate is fixed into the cabinet case.

Ball Peen (Pein) Hammer — See also Hammers. This tool is shaped like a regular hammer, but one end of the head is rounded and mushroom shaped. The rounded end is used to shape thin metal and to peen rivets in metal joints such as copper to make the metal joint more ductile. The tool is also known as an engineer's or machinist's hammer.

Baluster — (bal-us-ter) A baluster is a vertical shaft made from wood metal, stone or other materials that supports the coping of a parapet or the hand railing of a staircase.

Balustrade — (bal-us-trãd) This is a length of or a run of balusters capped with a hand rail that may or may not be part of a staircase.

 Banana Bar — See Caul.

Band Cramp — See Clamps, Strap.

Bandsaw Blades — See Blades, Bandsaw.

Banister — A synonym for a handrail.

Banjo — See also Lathe. You wouldn't want to strum this one; this is the heavy cast iron bracket on a lathe that supports the toolrest. The banjo slides along the bed rails and locks into position. The banjo allows the toolrest to be

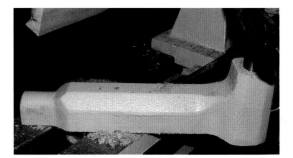

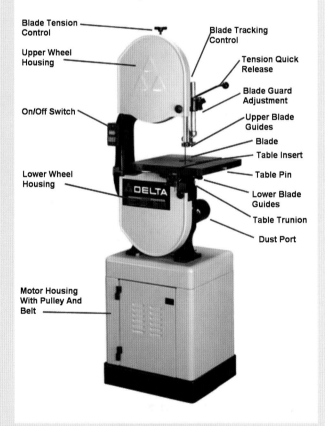

Anatomy of a Band Saw

Blade Tension Control

Blade Tracking Control

Upper Wheel Housing

Tension Quick Release

Blade Guard Adjustment

On/Off Switch

Upper Blade Guides

Blade

Table Insert

Lower Wheel Housing

Table Pin

Lower Blade Guides

Table Trunion

Dust Port

Motor Housing With Pulley And Belt

Band saw — The band saw was invented in 1808 by William Newberry and is now a necessary staple in a well-equipped woodshop. The tool consists of two or three rubber-tired wheels on which a steel strap-like saw blade runs. One of the wheels is driven by an electric motor. The band saw is used for cutting through wood or metal in either straight or curved patterns. The machine is also used for re-sawing and may be converted as a sanding machine. The larger two-wheel band saws are considered stationary tools but may be smaller as benchtop tools. Three-wheel band saws are generally benchtop tools. The three wheels allow for deeper (wider) board capacities but require more flexing of the saw blade and thus result in a shorter blade life. There are portable band saws available as well, but they are mostly used for metal work as in plumbing.

placed anywhere along the front of the lathe.

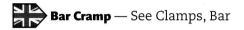 **Bar Cramp** — See Clamps, Bar

Bar Gauge — The bar gauge (pinch sticks) is a shop-made tool designed to measure the interior of workpieces like boxes and drawers and to verify that they are square.

Bar Gauge Heads — Bar gauge heads are the metal and plastic components that hold the bar gauge together. The shop-made hardwood sticks slide in their openings, and the heads lock the sticks in position.

Batten — In woodworking a batten is a piece of wood used to support or strengthen one or several boards that are edge-joined together. The batten generally runs perpendicular to the boards. A typical example is a board and batten door.

Battenboard — Similar to a sheet of plywood, but the core is comprised of solid wood strips that are edge-joined and may be up to 3" wide. The grain of the boards runs at right angles to the veneer surfaces.

Bark — The bark is the protective outer layer of woody plants such as trees. The bark is composed mainly of dead cells and is continuously added to from within.

Baseboard — Also known as skirting – A moulding that finishes off the bottom of a wall where it meets the floor. The baseboard covers the rough finish at the bottom of the plasterboard and the finished floor.

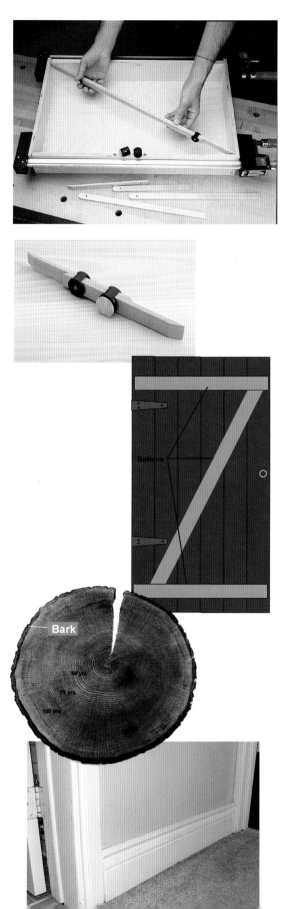

Battery History

1800 Voltaic Pile – Silver/Zinc
1836 Daniell Cell – Copper/Zinc
1859 Planté – Rechargeable Lead/Acid Cell
1869 Leclanché – Carbon/Zinc Wet Cell
1888 Gasser – Carbon/Zinc Dry Cell
1898 Commercial Flashlight D Cell
1899 Junger – Nickel Cadmium Cell
1946 Neumann – Sealed NiCad
1960s Alkaline, Rechargeable NiCad
1970s Lithium, Sealed Lead/Acid
1990 Nickel Metal Hydride (NiMH)
1991 Lithium ion (Li-ion)
1992 Rechargeable Alkaline
1999 Lithium ion Polymer

Batteries — According to the Collins Dictionary these are "two or more primary cells connected to provide a source of electricity." Today's woodworker is mostly concerned with rechargeable batteries that power his/her cordless tools. These batteries may be made from Nickel-Cadmium (Ni-Cad), Nickel Metal Hydride (NiMH) or Lithium-ion (Li-ion). Generally these batteries are made from individual low voltage cells that are wired together to make higher voltage battery packs in a compact case.

NiCad Batteries
+ Over 1,000 cycles, Simple Charging 1hr. or less, Able to Trickle Charge.
— Will Self-Discharge, As Power Drains Tool Slows Down.

NiMH Batteries
+ Higher Energy Density, Non-Toxic, Reduced Discharge Rate.
— Shorter Life Span, More Expensive +20%, Longer Charge Time.

Li-ion Batteries
+ Lightest Weight ½ of NiCad, 40% More Capacity, 2,000 Cycles, Little Self-Discharge.
— Power Drops Suddenly, More Expensive.

Bastard File — See File.

Bead — a) A decorative convex wood strip moulding. A bead may be formed as an add-on piece or formed directly onto the workpiece with a router or a shaper. b) As in a bead of caulk, a thin, round strip of caulk squeezed into a seam or joint.

Beadlock Joint — The Beadlock joint is also referred to as a loose mortise–and–tenon joint. A special jig is required to drill the mortises, and the tenons are sold by the foot. They are available in ⅜" and ½" sizes and make excellent joints.

Beading Tool — Beading or bead mouldings are made on a wood lathe or may also be made with a shaper head or a router bit.

⚑ **Bearings** — See Lead Bearings.

Bed — A woodshop is no place for one of these beds, you better see Lathe Bed.

Bed Rails — See Lathe.

⚑ **Beeswax** — a mixture of natural beehive wax blended with turpentine used as a polish for fine furniture and wooden bowls. Beeswax may be bought in solid blocks for self mixing or in a pre-mixed state. This is a traditional British finishing/polishing compound used in lathe turning.

Bee's Wing — A mottled appearance in the grain of some wood species such as this lacewood.

Belt Sander — The belt sander is an electrically powered machine that may be floor-mounted, bench-mounted or portable, depending on its size. The motor powers a drive wheel on which the sanding belt rides. An idler roller maintains the tension of the endless belt to prevent slippage and to keep the belt running straight. The stationary belt sander may have belts, 6" wide x 48" long or larger, the bench-top sander

belts are usually from 1" x 24" to 4" x 36" while the portable tools generally use belts that are 3" x 21".

Bench — (see also, workbench) A seat that may be with or without arms or a back and is usually longer than it is deep. It is a rustic form of seat designed for one or more people.

Bench Chisel — See Chisels

Bench Brush — An elongated brush with coarse bristles made for cleaning sawdust and wood shavings from a workbench. The Bench brush is about 12" long overall and made of wood. Some bench brushes have several rows of bristles making them thicker but basically the same elongated shape.

Bench Dogs — Wood or metal dowels or pegs fitted into the top of a workbench and a vise to secure a workpiece while working on it. The standard hole diameter for a round bench dog is ¾" or ¾" square for square dogs.

Bench Grinder — The bench grinder is an electrically powered motor with the arbor usually protruding from both ends. Grinding or sanding wheels of various substances (perhaps emery) are attached to the arbors. The bench grinder is used for sharpening and/or grinding and one wheel is usually coarser than the other.

Bench Hook — This is an aid for holding a workpiece securely while working on it. It is called a 'hook' because one end hooks to the edge of a work bench while the other end (the batten or stop) supports a

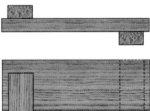

workpiece. The stop is usually made shorter than the width of the hook so that the stop will not interfere with any cutting operations.

Bench Plane — See also Plane, Hand. The bench plane is a hand plane used for the smoothing and removal of wood. There are many types of hand planes, but the bench plane is a general purpose tool and is based on the century–old Bailey pattern. The bench plane is available in several sizes (lengths).

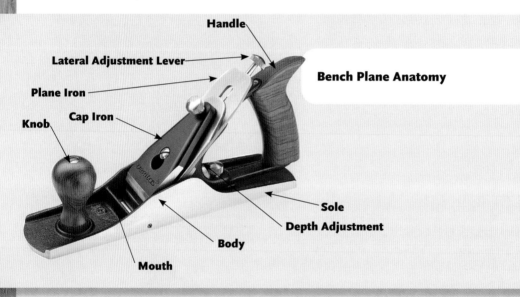

Handle

Lateral Adjustment Lever

Plane Iron

Knob

Cap Iron

Bench Plane Anatomy

Sole

Depth Adjustment

Body

Mouth

Bench Saw — a) A table saw that has been built into a workbench to provide the user with longer wings and outfeed surfaces. b) A bench-top table saw that may or may not be permanently fastened to a workbench.

Benchtop Tools — A term generally used for smaller power tools such as a belt/disc sander, drill press, grinder, jointer, lathe, scroll saw, table saw and the like. These power tools may offer most of the features found on

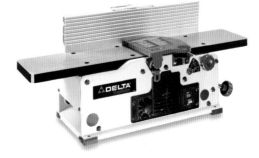

b

stationary machines but are built smaller for the woodworker with a small shop.

Bench Vise — See Vise, Bench.

Bending — See also Steam Bending, Kerfing. Bending or bent wood may or may not be a desirable effect for the woodworker. Sometimes, however, a project may call for the bending of plywood. This being the case there are some options available; flexible or bendable plywood is available with a soft core but may only be bent in one direction. Some plywood may be steamed to facilitate bending, or sawn part way through the plywood repeatedly with cuts one-inch apart or less, depending on the radius desired.

Bevel — An angle cut longitudinally on an edge of (usually) a board.

Bevel Chisel — See Chisels.

Bevel Cut — An angle cut by a table saw, compound miter saw or other cutting tool.

Bevel Gauge — See Sliding Bevel.

Bevel, Sliding — See Sliding Bevel.

Bi-Metal — This refers to a type of material used in the manufacturing of some types of saw blades such as bandsaw, hacksaw, jigsaw and hacksaw blades. A strip of harder and longer-lasting steel is welded to the softer metal body of the blade. The teeth are cut into the harder steel.

Bird's Eye — The term given to the eye-shaped markings in the grain of wood, mostly found in the wood of

FUN facts

TREE RUSTLING
In Quebec and New Brunswick thieves steal into maple sugar tree groves at night and with axes or machetes, quietly strip the bark off randomly chosen sugar maple (acer saccharum) trees. By doing this they can tell if the tree has a much-valued bird's eye pattern to it. They will then fell the tree and cut it into logs and later into boards for sale. A full tree of boards could yield as much as $10,000. The sad thing, though, is that the trees that are stripped and are not bird's eye will soon die. They will not produce any more Maple Syrup.

the sugar maple (acer saccharum) tree. The bird's eye pattern may be found in some other species as well, but it's not as common as in maple.

Bird's Mouth — A 'V'-shaped joint that resembles a bird's open beak. The joint is used in specific applications such as decorative openings or even bowl making.

Bird's Mouth Bit — A router bit shaped to produce a bird's mouth joint.

Biscuit — Small compressed and dried football-shaped wooden

b

wafers made from beechwood and used in joinery. Glue is applied to the biscuits and then they are inserted into matching oval slots made in the edges (or other areas) of boards. The slots are made by a biscuit joiner. The glue both swells in the slots and adheres the biscuits to make a secure joint. The biscuits are made in several sizes.

Biscuit Joiner — Also referred to as a plate joiner, this is a portable electric tool that powers a small cutting blade to make oval cuts into the edges (or other areas) of boards to facilitate biscuits.

Bits — See Drill Bits, Router Bits, Screwdriver Bits.

Blades

Bandsaw Blades — A bandsaw blade is cut and shaped from a thin, flat band of steel. The steel band is cut to the desired length and then the two ends are welded together to make a continuous loop. Bandsaw blades may be made of a variety of steel types including bi-metal and carbon, and may have carbide tipped teeth.

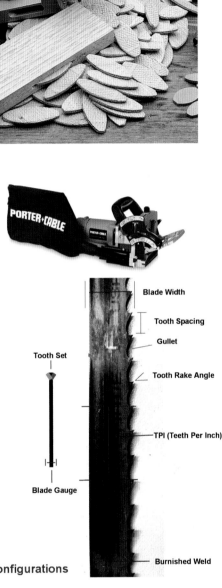

Blade Width

Tooth Spacing

Gullet

Tooth Set

Tooth Rake Angle

TPI (Teeth Per Inch)

Blade Gauge

Burnished Weld

Bandsaw Blade Configurations

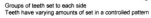

LENOX Set

Five tooth or seven tooth sequence (right, left, right, left, straight)
Uniform set angle

RAKER Set

Three tooth sequence (left, right, straight)
Uniform set angle

VARI-RAKER Set

Multi-tooth sequence depending on tooth pitch
Varying set angles
14/18 Vari-tooth has random wavy set

ALTERNATE Set

Every tooth set in an alternating sequence

WAVY Set

Groups of teeth set to each side
Teeth have varying amounts of set in a controlled pattern

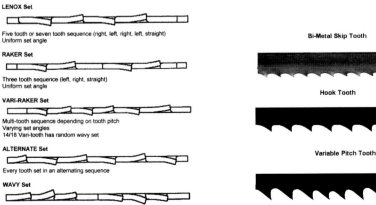

Bi-Metal Skip Tooth

Hook Tooth

Variable Pitch Tooth

FUN facts

In 1813 a Shaker-Sister by the name of Tabitha Babbitt was working at her spinning wheel and watching some men in a nearby sawmill. The men were struggling with a two-man pit saw that was being used to rip logs into lumber. She combined some of the elements of the spinning wheel, made a circular steel disc and cut sharp teeth on the perimeter. This was the first record of a circular saw blade in the US. Her religion prevented her from applying for a patent.

Sister Tabitha is also credited with inventing the cut nail. Apparently unknown to the good Sister, an Englishman named Samuel Miller apparently also invented the circular saw blade 33 years erlier in 1777.

Circular Saw Blades — See also Saw Blades.

Coping Saw Blades (kope-ing) — Coping saw blades and fret saw blades are very much the same in that they are both made for very fine cutting of wood and some metals and plastics. These saw blades all have small pins through the ends to facilitate installation in the saw frames.

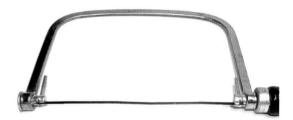

Jigsaw Blades — There are two types of commonly used jigsaw blades in use: the T–shank

and the U–shank (although the U–shank blades are becoming obsolete). Jigsaw blades are available in a number of types and tooth counts (tpi = teeth per inch) designed to cut various materials.

Jointer Blades — See Jointer Knives.

Fret Saw Blades — See Coping Saw Blades.

Reciprocal Saw Blades — Reciprocal (or reciprocating) saw blades have to be made to withstand rough treatment as they are used primarily in heavy construction and demolition. They must be able to withstand not just the cutting of wood materials but also hardwoods with nails or screws embedded in them.

Scroll Saw Blades — Scroll saw blades take on various forms and are much more versatile than

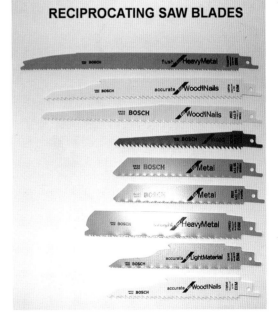

RECIPROCATING SAW BLADES

coping or fret saw blades as they do their work through an electrically powered saw. The fineness of the blade is determined by the tpi (teeth per inch) and the width of the blade. Scroll saw blades are available in skip tooth and reverse skip tooth for cutting in both the up and down directions. Spiral blades are also available for scrolling in all directions.

Plane Blades — See Plane Irons.

Planer Blades— See Thickness Planer Knives.

Blade Guard — See also Guards, Sawstop. This is a safety feature found on all wood-cutting machines that automatically or manually covers a rotating saw blade while it is in operation. The blade guard is designed to keep the operator's hands and fingers safely away from danger. With table saws many woodworkers remove these guards as they may hamper some woodworking operations. After-market table saw blade guards are available that are more versatile than those supplied with the saw.

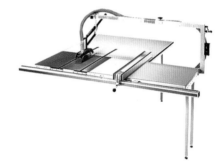

Blank — See Bowl Blank.

Blast Gate —The blast gate is a form of dam used in a dust collector to isolate particular sawdust-making machines in the workshop. A blast gate can be installed in the duct connected to each tool. The blast gate is opened only when that particular machine is in operation. Having only one gate open at a time in the dust collector provides better suction.

b

Bleached Oak — Oak that has been finished with bleaching so it appears paler than its natural color.

Bleaching — Back in the 1950s residential furniture in a bleached oak finish was in vogue. To attain this sometimes desirable finish (also known as pickling) the use of some chemicals is required. The careful application of a chlorine based chemical will remove some of the natural color and make wood paler. This process is generally applied on oak as in bleached oak. Using oxalic acid or a mixture of hydrogen peroxide with sodium hydroxide are other methods of bleaching. Dap® manufactures an oxalic acid based Wood Bleach product that will do an excellent job.

Blemish — Anything that mars the appearance of wood.

Blind Bolt — A method of locking one of a pair of cabinet doors. The blind sliding bolt is recessed into the edge or rear face of the door. A slide mechanism moves the bolt into a recess (hole) in the carcase of the cabinet to secure it. On smaller doors a single blind bolt would suffice, but larger doors would require two, one at the top and one at the bottom.

Blind Nailing — Nailing in such a way so that the nail will not be visible on the final work. A miniature chisel in a small hand plane device lifts a small portion of surface wood to allow a brad or finishing nail to be hammered into the workpiece. The shaving is then glued down.

Block Plane — See Plane.

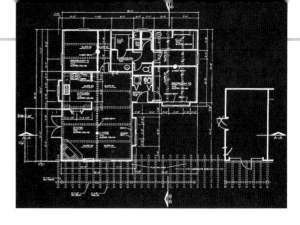

Blueprint — The blueprint isn't blue anymore. The blueprint is a printing of a designer's original drawing or plan. The blueprint is an obsolete method of reproduction.

Board — a) A flat piece of dimensional wood up to 2" thick. b) A generic term for a 6" or wider piece of wood.

Board Foot — A term used in calculating quantities of lumber. A board foot equals a board that is 12" x 12" x 1" thick. This is a nominal measurement.

Bolt — A threaded fastener with a head usually made of steel used with a nut and washers to connect two or more parts. A bolt may have many styles, partially threaded, fully threaded, hexagonal head, flat head, cap thread and many more specialized types.

Bond Strength — See Shear Strength.

Book Matching — The application of veneer sheets cut sequentially from the same tree in a mirror-image pattern.

Bore — a) To drill or to bore a hole into wood. b) The diameter of a hole. c) The hole in the center of a circular saw blade.

Bow — An undesirable bend formed in a board due to unequal surface stress.

Bowl Blanks — Blocks of wood of any species that have been dried and pre-cut to fit on a lathe for turning into bowls. Buying these can save the woodturner a lot of preparation time.

Bowls — In woodworking these are either decorative or utilitarian bowls that have been turned on a lathe. The pictured bowl was turned by Jamie Wolverton and was a category winner in a Canadian national competition.

Bow Saw — See Buck Saw.

Bowtie joint — See Butterfly Joint.

Box Nails — Similar to a common nail but thinner and in smaller sizes, usually ½" – 1½". The photo shows a) ½" box nail, b) 1 ¼" galvanized box nail, c) 1¼" box nail, d) 1½" coated box nail and e) a 4" common nail for comparison.

Box Joint — This is a joint that meshes rectangular tongues and provides more surface area for gluing. Freud makes a box joint cutter set that is comprised of two 8" circular saw blades. When placed on the arbor one way they produce ½" joints and when reversed they produce ⅜" joints.

Boxed Tenon — An L-shaped tenon used mainly as a vertical support joint.

Brace and Bit — The brace is the forerunner of today's corded or cordless drill. The origin of the brace goes back thousands of years. Today's version of the brace has a locking mechanism called a *chuck* that holds the bit. The bit, also called an *auger* or *ship's auger* has a screw-like tip that starts the auger into the wood to start the hole. The brace has a knurled control that allows the brace to drill in and to back up.

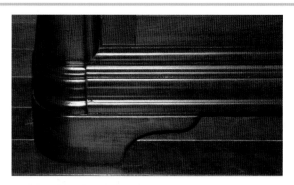

Bracket Foot — A scrolled and mitered cabinet foot commonly used on 18th century Chippendale style cabinetry. The bracket foot is made in two pieces in a mirror-like image and then joined.

Brad — A brad is a wire finishing nail formed from a finer gauge, usually 18 gauge, and with a finer head. Brads are generally available in lengths from ½" – 1¾".

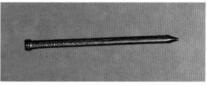

Bradawl — See Awl.

Brad Nailer — a) a pneumatic (air–driven) tool powered by an air compressor that drives 18 gauge wire nails. The tool is used for nailing mouldings and other fine details to cabinets or other woodwork. These brads are in strips of about 100 and are held together by a thin plastic film. The brads are loaded into the magazine of the tool, and when the trigger is squeezed a surge of compressed air drives a piston or hammer onto the head of the brad. A small dial controls the depth that the brad is driven into the wood. b) a small handheld tool that has a narrow steel tube with a piston in it that is spring–loaded. A brad (or finishing nail) is loaded into the tube, and the user positions it and then pushes on the handle to drive the brad into the workpiece.

a

b

Brazil Wax — An alternative name for Carnuba Wax.

Breakout — See Tear-Out.

Breast Drill — See Drill, Breast.

Bridle Joint — A joint used to facilitate a leg fastened to a horizontal member. It is sometimes used when a third or fifth leg is required to support a table or cabinet. Bridle joints can be used at the ends of both joining pieces, or along the length of one of the pieces as shown here at right.

Brush — See Bench Brush, Paintbrush.

Bubble Level — See Spirit Level.

Buck Saw — Also known as a bow saw, this is a saw used for cutting the limbs off trees and for felling small trees. The buck saw is a blade held in a wood or aluminum frame and tensioned with a threaded rod.

Bugle Head Screw — See Screws, Buglehead.

Bundle — Sheets of veneer cut from a log and arranged in sequential order. The bundle usually contains 24 or 32 leaves.

Bun Foot — A furniture foot found mostly on William and Mary style furniture. The Ball Foot is very similar but more rounded.

Bureau — See also Desk. Although somewhat vague in its definition, the bureau refers to a cabinet with drawers with a drop front writing desk. Pigeon-holes, more drawers and other small compartments are usually found behind the dropfront. The term *bureau* was used at the end of the 17th century, but prior to that it was referred to as an *escritoire* or secretary.

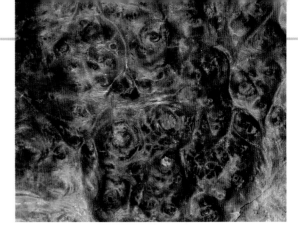

Burl — See also Underground Burl. A burl is found in various species of trees and is caused by small growths. When the tree is cut the burl produces much–desired swirls and patterns. Turners prize these burls for making interesting and decorative bowls.

Burn-In Stick — This is a stick of filler material used to repair surface damage on furniture. The stick end must be melted onto the damaged surface and then trimmed smooth. Also known as a lacquer or shellac stick.

Burr Edge

Burr — A burr is the undesirable fine wire–like edge that remains on a blade after sharpening. The burr is removed through honing.

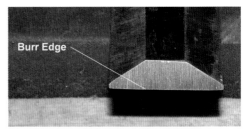

Butcher Block — The butcher block is a style of table used by butchers to cut meat and poultry in days gone by. The butcher block table was a very heavy table made up of many long blocks of maple, cherry or other hardwood. The blocks were glued together on their length so that the top surface was the end grain of the wood. In old butcher shops the tables were well cupped after years of chopping and cutting meat. Butcher block tables and cutting boards are still made in the same end grain fashion. The butcher block tables made now are not used for cutting raw meat.

Butcher Block Oil — See also Oils, Finishing. Butcher block oil is a nontoxic finishing oil that is safe to use on butcher block tables (as the name implies), but also on salad bowls, cutting boards and other wood products that come in contact with food.

Butler's Tray — A tray originally mounted on a folding stand that was popular in the late 18th and early 19th centuries. The butler's tray was rectangular in shape with rounded, folding edges or flaps. The end flaps had hand-grip cut into them. The edge flaps had special hinges on them that allowed them to be recessed and lay perfectly flat when opened. The butler's table has recently enjoyed a new popularity in North America.

Butterfly Joint — The butterfly joint is both a structural and decorative joint used mostly on tabletops. The joint is designed to add strength to a butt joint. The shape is that of a double dovetail to resemble butterfly wings. The butterfly itself is usually made from a wood that is contrasting to the tabletop itself. It is sometimes misnamed a bowtie joint.

Butt Chisel — See Chisels.

Butt Gauge — Usually found in a set of three, these have sharp edges on them and are designed to mark (and cut) positions for the installation of recessed butt hinges. This is a set of 3", 3½" and 4", the sizes of standard door hinges. The gauge is positioned at the edge of the door frame and then hammered evenly to make the cut marks. A mallet and chisel is used to finish the recess. This procedure is repeated on the door edge.

Butt Hinge — See also Hinge. A hinge is used to allow a door to swing. The butt hinge has two equal sides (flaps) joined by a hinge pin that allows free movement of the two pieces. Butt hinges are normally found on residential and commer-

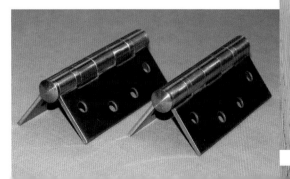

cial entry or interior doors as well as in some cabinetry applications. They are found in a variety of finishes and materials like brass or stainless steel. The butt hinge can be as small as ½" x ½" up to 6" x 6" and more.

Butt Joint — This is probably the weakest of all wood joints. The end of one piece of wood is joined to the face of another. The joint may be glued and/or screwed together, or it may use other types of mechanical fastening.

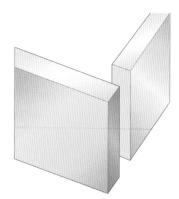

C-Clamp — See also Clamps. The C–clamp is a clamp that looks like the letter C and is generally made from cast aluminum, sheet steel or forged steel. C-clamps are made in various sizes including an elongated C and a deep C. The size of the C-clamp is determined by the opening or mouth of the C minus the swivel screw head. Pictured are a 1¼", an elongated 2¼", a deep 2½" and a 3¼" clamp.

Cabinet — A cabinet is a wooden box that may contain components such as shelves and/or dividers and is usually fully enclosed on five sides. The sixth side may be open or closed with hinged or sliding doors. A cabinet may be free-standing or attached to a wall or other structures such as kitchen cabinets.

37

Cabinetry — a) The art of building cabinets as furniture. b) The building of wooden furniture.

Cabinetmaker — A builder of furniture such as (but not restricted to) fine cabinets, like entertainment centers, bookcases and tables.

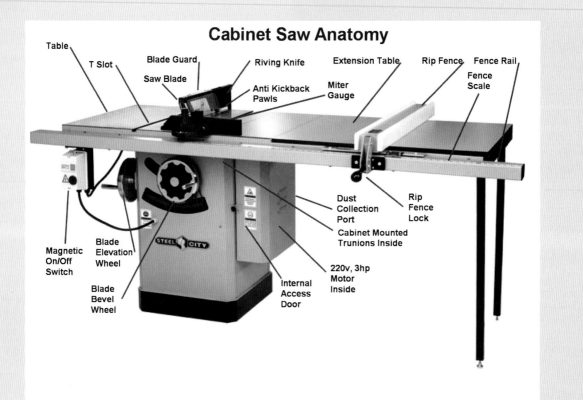

Cabinet Saw Anatomy

Table, T Slot, Blade Guard, Saw Blade, Riving Knife, Anti Kickback Pawls, Miter Gauge, Extension Table, Rip Fence, Fence Rail, Fence Scale, Magnetic On/Off Switch, Blade Elevation Wheel, Blade Bevel Wheel, Internal Access Door, Dust Collection Port, Rip Fence Lock, Cabinet Mounted Trunions Inside, 220v, 3hp Motor Inside

Cabinet Saw — The cabinet saw is typically a heavy–duty table saw powered by a 220 volt, 2hp – 3hp (or larger) motor mounted inside the cabinet. The cabinet saw has very heavy trunions and bearings that are mounted on the cabinet frame for strength and ease of alignment. Cabinet saws are made for 10" saw blades or 12" saw blades. The 10" models are the more popular. Cabinet saws are available with either left or right hand bevel models.

C

Cabriole Leg (kab-ree-ole) — A leg shape used on Queen Anne style furniture. The cabriole leg is characterized by graceful curves and a shape that resembles an animal leg. Unlike many standard shaped furniture legs, the cabriole leg can be only partially turned on a lathe.

Callipers — (Also spelled Calipers). A tool for measuring thicknesses and diameters. They consist of a pair of curved pivoting legs joined at the top. The sliding types of callipers can measure the outer and the interior walls of pipes. The interior pin of the sliding callipers is used for measuring depths. Some callipers are of the dial type and some are digital.

Cam clamp — The cam clamp is a hold-down clamp for us on a workbench. The post of the clamp fits into holes on the bench that are made for bench dogs.

Camber — A slight upward curve in wood that may or may not be desirable (as with the propeller at right). When undesired it is also called a bow, but when desired it is purposely made to prevent the board from becoming concave due to its own weight or the weight of what it is supporting.

Cambium (kam-bee-um) — The live, actively growing layer of a tree. The cambium is one cell thick and resides between the sapwood and the inner bark. It repeatedly divides itself to form new wood and causes the tree to grow and expand. The cambium is responsible for the annual growth rings of a tree.

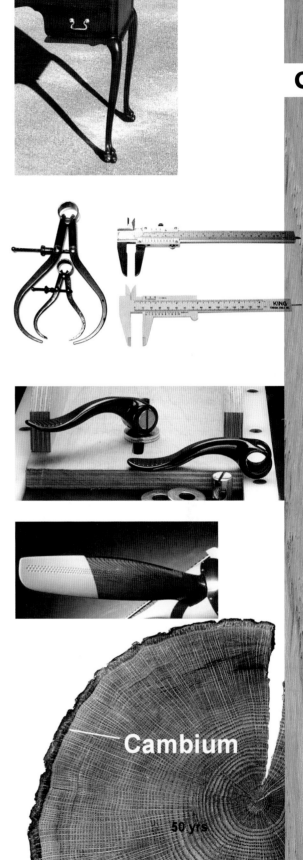

Cambium

50 yrs

Cant Hook — See Peavey.

Cantilever — An outward projection of a workpiece that is supported only at one end. An example is a cantilevered shelf that is supported only at the rear or with shelf L–brackets.

Cap Iron — See also Bench Plane. The cap iron is a steel plate that fits between the blade (iron) and the lever cap of a hand plane. The cap iron is curved at the bottom. It is designed to cleanly disperse wood shavings and to prevent wood from jamming in the plane's throat.

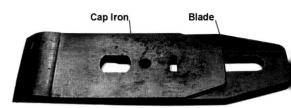

Cap Iron   Blade

Cap Nut — See Nut, Acorn.

Capital — The upper portion of a column, pilaster or pier that is widened for decorative or structural purposes to spread the weight of a load.

Carbide — See Tungsten Carbide.

Carbon Steel — Also known as High Carbon Steel. This is a material used to make wood chisels, plane irons and other woodworking and carving tools because it holds a keen edge longer than HSS (High Speed Steel).

Carborundum Powder (kar-bore-un-dum) — See also Abrasive Compounds. Carborundum is a trademark owned by Saint-Gobain Abrasives Inc. and is commonly referred to as a generic term for an abrasive. Carborundum is a blend of carbon, silicon and other minerals. The grains of these materials are ground to a specific size and blended as a powder which is used for smoothing and/or polishing unfinished or finished wood. The

C

powder is mixed with water or other lubricants and rubbed onto the workpiece with a ball of cheesecloth. Carborundum powder may also be used for lapping.

Carbide–Tipped Saw Blades — These are circular saw blades, band saw blades and some other saw blades that have tungsten carbide tips brazed or welded to the saw bodies. The carbide tip is shaped to a specific design for a particular purpose such as crosscutting. The tips are keenly sharpened.

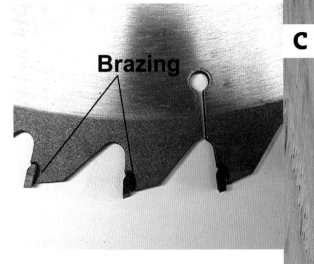
Brazing

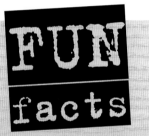

Carnuba Wax

Also known as Carnauba wax or Brazilian wax, this is the hardest of all natural waxes and is obtained from the leaves of a Brazilian palm tree (Copernicia prunifera). This tree is also known as the "Tree of Life".

The Carnauba palm grows in South America, Ceylon and equatorial Africa, but the wax is extracted only in Brazil where the tree is in abundance. The Brazilian palm reaches heights of 25 – 30' but may attain a height of 50'.

It is during the hot months of summer that the tree exudes the wax that protects it from dehydration. In the fall months, native workers remove a maximum of 20 fronds from each tree. They are dried in the sun and then thrashed to remove the wax.

Carnauba wax is expensive. It is used in the production of cosmetics, pharmaceuticals, the automobile industry and, of course, as a natural finish in woodworking. Carnauba is an excellent substitute for beeswax and in its pure form is safe to use as a finish on salad bowls.

Carcase (kar-kass) — See also Cabinet. The body of a piece of furniture with a box-like shape.

Carpenter — See also Carpentry. A tradesperson who practices carpentry.

Carpenter's Glue — Also known as Yellow Glue. Carpenter's glue is aliphatic resin-based glue that has an open time of 5 – 7 minutes. Carpenter's glue can be cleaned up (while still wet) with water or (when dry), with mineral spirits. Freezing will not harm the glue, but apply it at room temperature. Carpenter's glue has a sheer strength of over 3,500 lbs.

Carpentry — The art or profession of working with wood in the construction industry. A carpenter may work in the structural and/or finishing areas of the industry.

Carriage Bolt — A convex round-headed bolt used in the assembly of wood components when the bolt head will be exposed to view. The head of the carriage bolt is smooth and has a much larger diameter than the bolt and therefore acts as a washer to prevent it from penetrating or tearing into the wood. The shoulder of the carriage bolt is squared just below the head to prevent the bolt from turning when the nut is tightened.

Carving — See also Sculpting. The art of shaping wood with sharp carving knives or chisels. Carving may be two or three dimensional. Intarsia, marquetry and specialties such as wildlife carving are examples of the art. Carving by Alan Dorey.

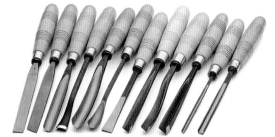

Carving Knives — These are specialized knives (or chisels) shaped for specific use in the various forms of the art of wood carving. Carving knives are usually sold in sets.

Case Hardened — An undesired effect in wood caused by poor seasoning. Typically, kiln drying is done too quickly on a board and the outer surface is hardened while the inner core is still moist. This can cause a very dangerous situation when the board is sawn. Sawing suddenly and dangerously releases the stress.

Casein Glue — See Glue.

Casters — (or Castors) These are small rubber or plastic wheels attached to a (usually) swivel base. They are designed to make heavy furniture easier to move. They are attached to the furniture through various methods such as a plate, screw or pin.

Catalyst (kat-a-list) — A substance that causes a chemical reaction such as when a joint is misted with water prior to applying polyurethane glue. The water is the catalyst that makes this glue work better.

Cat's Paw — a) A steel rod with a claw on one or both ends used for removing set common or finishing nails. b) Small round mark in wood that resembles a cat's paw print.

Caul (kawl) — a) A curved batten or board used to apply equal pressure across a large flat area such as when applying glued veneer or trim to a substrate. The caul is made of a hardwood species,

has an arched edge and a straight edge. b) Plywood or other flat material used to press veneer with equal pressure onto a substrate. Also known as a banana bar.

Caulk (kaw-lk) — A sealant applied to joints to seal the joint and prevent the penetration of water or moisture. Caulk is sold in tubes of various sizes including those with cone-shaped tops and tubes. Caulk is applied as a bead through the use of a caulking gun that has a trigger–activated piston that forces the caulk out of the tube.

Caulking Gun — The caulking gun is a tool used to apply caulk. The tube is placed into the channel of the gun, the tip of the caulk tube is cut on an angle, the inner seal is perforated and the trigger is squeezed. Squeezing of the trigger moves a piston on the gun forward, thus forcing the caulk out of the opening in the tip. The caulk comes out of the tube in a bead that is forced into a corner or joint to seal it tight.

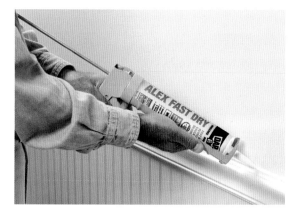

cc — This is the symbol or abbreviation for center–to–center in referring to certain spacing of wood members. For example if the specifications call for 4" stiles placed 18" cc, it means that the centers of the stiles must be 18" apart. Or, that same distance can be measured from either the leading edges or trailing edges of the two stiles.

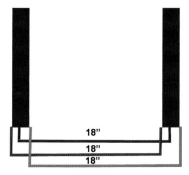

CCA — Chromated Copper Arsenate. A wood preservative containing arsenic that is no longer in use due to the dangers of the chemistry. CCA was treated much like the tobacco industry treated cigarettes. It was denied that CCA was poisonous to humans and the environment.

Cement — See Adhesives, Glue.

Centimeter — Centimetre. See Conversion Tables at the back of the book.

Center Finder — Centre Finder. a) A square, box-shaped jig with a knife edge running diagonally from corner to corner. A dowel is set tight into the corner and over the knife edge. The top of the dowel is tapped, rotated 90° and tapped again. The center of the dowel is where the two cut marks merge. b) A tool similar to a ruler that measures from its middle out to the edges. The center-finding rule is helpful in finding the centers of board widths.

a

b

Center Punch — Centre Punch The center punch is an aid for installing hinges. The center punch is 3" long and is made to find the precise centers of the hinge screw holes. The tool has a rounded end that fits into the hinge screw hole recess. A spring-loaded, pointed pin is then struck with a hammer to leave a starting mark for the screw. The brass center punch is 6" long and spring–loaded. The user pushes the tool into the positioned hinge screw hole and it then "fires" a point to make a screw starter hole. Other center punch tools are simply hardened steel with a point at one end that are tapped with a hammer to make an impression.

Chair Nail — See Antique Nail.

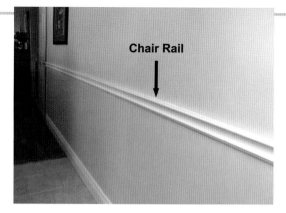

Chair Rail

Chair Rail — A shaped moulding fitted horizontally on a wall, 32" to 36" above the floor. The chair rail is parallel to the floor and is designed to prevent marring of the wall due to abrasion from the back of a chair. A chair rail is often used as a finishing cap for wainscotting.

Chalk — A white or colored powder used in Chalk Lines.

Chalk Line — A tool that provides a straight line over a long surface. The chalk line is an enclosed reel of polyester or cotton string. The string has a clip on the end of it that protrudes through a hole in one end of the enclosure or case. The enclosure is filled with chalk powder (white, red or blue) that adheres to the string as it unwinds out of the case. The clip end of the string is hooked to one edge of the flat surface (plywood sheet for example), drawn taut and then 'snapped'. The snapping provides a straight chalk line across the surface.

Chamfer (cham-fur) — A softening of a sharp edge such as the top edge of a table or cabinet. The chamfer may be a slight bevel made with a hand plane, router or other cutting tool.

Chase Mortise — This is a repair mortise that may require additional bracing or support. A stub tenon is placed in a normal mortise on one side (shown_, and a normal mortise is cut on the other. This allows the stub tenon to be maneuvered into it.

Chatter Marks — A series of undesirable repetitive rib-like marks left on a sanded or planed wood surface. These may be caused by too much

C

or too little roller pressure on both a thickness planer and surface sander.

Check — Checks are undesirable cracks in the ends or other areas of boards which are generally caused by the uncontrolled and rapid drying of the wood.

Tenon Cheeks

Cheek — The narrow area below the tenon in a mortise–and–tenon joint. The workpiece with the mortise butts against the cheek and shoulder.

Chinese Nails — See Corrugated Fasteners.

Chip Board — See Particle Board.

Chip Carving — This is a type of wood carving in which a sharp knife is used to remove small chips from a board in a single piece to form a pattern. Photo courtesy of sherpe.com

Chip Carving Knives — These are shaped knives designed for the chip carving artist. The knives are very sharp, and their wooden handles may be short and shaped to fit in the palm of the hand or longer for more leverage. The knife blade shapes are straight gouge, fishtail gouge, veiner, V–tool, skew and chisel. They are all available in various sizes and are numbered accordingly.

Chippendale — Thomas Chippendale 1719 – 1779. Chippendale was a cabinetmaker who worked in the mid-Georgian, English Rococo and Neoclassical styles. Chippendale was the first cabinetmaker to publish his designs in a book entitled *The Gentleman and*

Cabinet–Maker's Director. He published three editions, and by 1762 his designs began to hint at Neoclassicism. Chippendale's signature is the cabriole leg design.

Chisel — A chisel is a hand tool comprising of a narrow blade with a tang or a socket fitted into a long, round handle. The blade is tapered to a sharp edge and is used to remove or shape wood. The blades are made in various shapes and thicknesses designed for specific purposes. The following are some of the most popular chisel styles and their purpose. Chisels are used by striking the top of the handle with a wooden mallet. Hand chisels are different from turning chisels in that the handles and blades are shorter.

Bench — The bench chisel is the most conventional chisel with a 30° blade and beveled edges. The beveled edges allow the user to get close into corners.

Bevel Edged — Bevel edged chisels allow the woodworker to work more closely to edges and corners. Beveled edges may be available in most chisel styles.

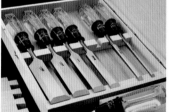

Butt — The butt chisel is a shorter chisel used mostly in carpentry for such tasks as mortising door hinges. The butt hinge generally has tang handles and a 30° bevel.

Corner — This hand tool is designed to square off rounded mortised corners made by a router. The chisel is made into a 90° angle and has 30° bevels.

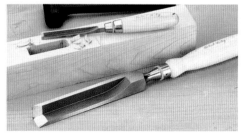

C

Cranked — Cranked chisels are a type of paring chisel with a bend in the blade. This chisel shape allows for more clearance in paring and is not designed for striking.

Firmer — The firmer chisel is about the same length as a bench chisel but considerably thicker and may be square edged or beveled. The firmer chisel may be used for paring or striking. This is a good tool for hollowing out.

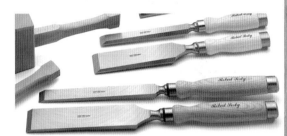

Framing — As a heavyweight, the Framing chisel is longer and wider and has beveled edges with a 20° to 25° bevel blade. As the name suggests this chisel is used in rough construction and is struck with a mallet.

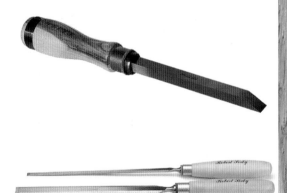

Mortise (more-tiss) — The mortise chisel is used to make mortises and tenons. It has squared edges and is struck. The tool was used to make mortise–and–tenon joints in widow sashes.

Paring — These chisels are longer and thinner than bench chisels with only a 20° to 25° beveled blade. They are used by pattern makers and for carving in soft woods. They are not designed to be struck.

Skew — The skew chisel has an angled blade designed to cut and/ or clean up tenons. Its sharp angle allows the user to get into tight corners. The blade has squared edges and a 30° bevel.

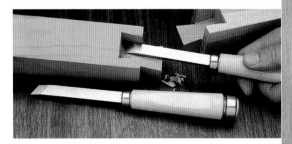

Chop Saw — See Miter Saw

Chromated Copper Arsenate — See CCA.

Chuck — See also Lathe Chuck. The chuck is found on a brace and bit, drill press, corded drill or cordless drill to hold and lock the drill bit in place for drilling. As the chuck is rotated the the jaws open or close allowing for various sizes of bits. The chuck pictured at the lower left is for a brace that uses square, tapered bit ends; the others are for conventional drill bits.

Jacobs Chuck
At the turn of the 20th century A. I. Jacobs invented the first three-jaw drill bit chuck. The chuck is still known as the Jacobs Chuck. Jacobs formed the The Jacobs® Chuck Mfg. Co. in 1902.

Circle Cutter — This is a dangerous tool to work with as the spinning bar and cutter bit are almost invisible. The circle cutter is for just that — cutting large circles in wood. The bar can be adjusted laterally; the cutting bit can be adjusted vertically or placed in different positions. The circle cutter can cut smooth wheels or cut circles leaving the inner edge clean. The circle cutter must be securely mounted in a drill press to use.

Circular Saw — See also Table Saw. A circular saw is an electrically or battery powered tool that uses a motor to drive a circular saw blade. The first of these are credited to Porter-Cable circa 1928. The company's first circular saw was driven with a worm gear, but that was soon taken over with a helical drive. Since 1928, the circular saw has undergone many improvements offering the user stronger motors, more versatility, laser assistance, accurate depth and miter sawing, adjustable handles and cordless options. The worm drive has not disappeared; there are many woodworkers who still prefer it. In the earlier years shortly after World War II, Skil Tools touted their circular saw as a skil saw. That nickname has become a generic name for the tool.

Pictured from top to bottom: Circa 1928 Porter-Cable, Bosch new, Skil Laser Saw, Bosch Worm-drive, Milwaukee adjustable handle and the DeWalt 36volt Lithium-ion cordless

Clamp — The clamp is one of the most versatile tools found in any well-equipped woodshop. The clamp is used to secure workpieces while they are being glued, to secure projects to a workbench while they are worked on or even as temporary fasteners. Clamps are found in various styles, shapes and forms for general or specific job applications.

 **Band** — See Strap Clamp.

Bar — A clamp that uses a rectangular steel bar between the jaws of a clamp. One jaw is in a fixed

position and one is movable. The movable jaw slides along the bar and locks at the desired position. A hand crank or squeeze lever tightens the clamp. Some of these bar clamps may have a removable back jaw that can be reversed to make a spreader.

Bench (Toggle) — The bench or toggle clamp is fixed to the surface of a workbench and is used as a hold–down clamp to secure workpieces while working on them.

C — These clamps are usually made of cast iron or formed steel and in the shape of the letter C. There are many styles and sizes of C–clamps available, with some specifically job-designed.

Corner — Similar in purpose to Right-Angle clamps but usually used in low profile workpieces. There are many styles available: screw tightening, strap tightening and others.

Frame — A type of clamp that is comprised of right angle blocks that threaded rods are fed through to secure the four corners of a frame at right angles.

G — The G–clamp is the British equivalent of the C–clamp, just a different way of looking at it.

Hand — The hand clamp is designed to compress workpieces with one hand. They are made so that the average hand can apply over 100 pounds of clamping pressure to the work.

Hand Screw — Probably the first style of woodworking clamp, the hand screw may be adjusted to clamp projects of various sizes and shapes. The threaded screws are independently closed or opened.

Parallel Jaw — The K–clamp made by Bessey is a revolutionary design for a bar clamp. It has parallel clamping surfaces and sits flat on a workbench to help prevent buckling or cupping. Many manufacturers now offer similar clamps.

Pipe — The pipe clamp is extremely useful because only the head and tail parts are purchased as a package. The woodworker then buys lengths of threaded black pipe that fit into the clamp parts. The lengths purchased may vary, but the wise woodworker will buy the pipe in 2' lengths and then purchase a quantity of threaded connectors to make any size desired.

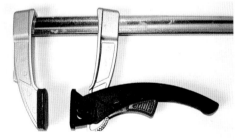

Ratchet — Also known as an F–clamp, this type of bar clamp uses a form of ratchet to lock the hand lever of the clamp. Some have a lever for tightening and some use a hand-tightened screw.

Right-Angle — See also Clamps, Corner. The right-angle clamp is designed to maintain box or frame corners at 90° while gluing up.

Spring — Spring clamps are designed for glue–up work that only requires light pressure. The clamp is like a modified clothespin,

which, by the way, is also a form of clamp.

Strap — Usually a nylon web strap that feeds through a ratchet mechanism that tightens the strap around irregular-shaped workpieces. This is best used on circular projects such as table edges.

Toggle — See Clamp, Bench.

Web — See Clamp, Strap.

Wheel — This is one clamp that you don't want used on your ve-hicle and it sure can't be used in woodworking.

Clamping Time — The time required to keep a glue joint clamped before the glue has set and cured. The clamping time is usually stated clearly on the label of the glue con-tainer.

Claw Hammer —See Hammer, Claw.

Classical English Furniture — Time Line

Date	Style	Designers
1485 – 1553	Early Tudor	
1554 – 1602	Late Tudor, Elizabethan	
1603 – 1648	Jacobean	
1649 – 1659	Commonwealth	
1660 – 1687	Restoration	
1688 – 1701	William & Mary	Gerret Jensen
1702 – 1713	Queen Anne	Daniel Marot
1714 – 1759	Georgian	William Kent
1760 – 1819	Mid/Late Georgian/Regency	Thomas Chippendale
1820 – 1836	Regency	
1837 – 1900	Victorian	William Morris
1901 —	Edwardian/ Arts & Crafts	William Morris

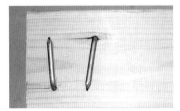

C

Clear — A term used for wood that is practically free of defects. A very small number of tight knots are permissible.

Clinching — The bending of the pointed end of a nail after it has protruded through boards to fully secure them.

Closed Coat — Sandpaper that is completely covered with abrasive particles. This type of sandpaper is used for hand sanding only as it will easily clog when used for power sanding.

Clear Coat

A term used for the final coats of clear wood finishes such as lacquer, polyurethane, shellac, varnish, and others.

Coach Bolt — See Carriage Bolt.

Cogged Joint — A joint used to prevent lateral movement.

Column — See also Side Bar. A vertical structural element that supports the weight of a structure. In architecture the column goes back to 2,600 B.C. and beyond. Illustrated on the following page are the Roman prder of columns.

Collet (kawl-et) — A split sleeve used to firmly grasp a bit, as in a router.

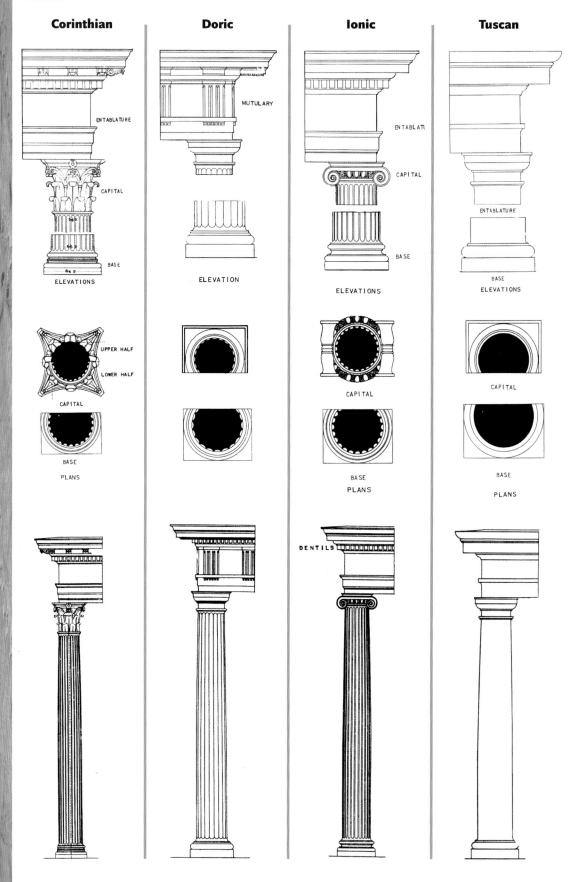

Corinthian

ENTABLATURE

CAPITAL

BASE

ELEVATIONS

UPPER HALF

LOWER HALF

CAPITAL

BASE

PLANS

Doric

MUTULARY

ELEVATION

Ionic

ENTABLATU

CAPITAL

BASE

ELEVATIONS

CAPITAL

BASE

PLANS

DENTILS

Tuscan

ENTABLATURE

BASE

BASE
ELEVATIONS

CAPITAL

BASE

PLANS

C

Colonial Style — An early American architectural and decorative furniture style. This style was brought to the eastern states by settlers from Europe, particularly England. As furniture took up a lot of space aboard the sailing ships, cargoes were limited to passengers and essential provisions. However, by the beginning of the 18th century fine furniture making began to re-emerge as an artistic endeavor. Craftsmen began to reproduce the styles remembered or passed down from ancestral homelands. This basic and functional style featured a minimum of ornamentation but later became more elaborate.

Comb — A comb-like painting tool used in strié (stree ay) finishing. See Combing.

Combing — See also Comb. This is any painting style that involves marking narrow lines of color on a surface. The technique is also known as strié (stree-ay) or dragging. Techniques that specifically imitate wood are called wood-graining techniques.

Comb Joint — See Box Joint.

Combination Machine — A woodworking machine that can be adapted to perform a number of common woodworking functions such as sawing, routing and turning. Shopsmith is one brand of this type of machine.

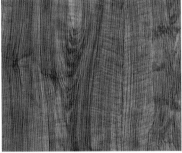

Combination Square — A sliding type of square that measures 90° and 45° angles and usually contains a bubble level and a scribe point.

Combination Wrench — A wrench with an open end and a box or closed end.

Commode — See Dry Sink.

Common Lumber — Lumber with obvious defects. This generally refers to dimensional lumber (eg., lumber cut to standard sizes).

Common Nail — See Nail.

Commonwealth Furniture — 1649-1659 A war between King Charles I and the British Parliament greatly influencee the furniture designs of the time. Parliament won the war and was dominated by religious zealots and puritans led by Oliver Cromwell. Thus, the style was also known as Puritan and Cromwellian.

Compass — When most people hear the word compass, the first thing that comes to mind is a device to determine direction. In woodworking, however, a compass is used for drawing or cutting circles. A compass for drawing circles can usually be found in an architects geometry set. An acrylic compass attaches to the base of a router. A sliding pin allows the user to adjust the pin to cut the desired circle diameter.

Compass Plane — See Planes, Compass.

Compound Miter — The compound miter is a saw cut that uses both the vertical plane and the horizontal plane.

Compund Mitre

Horizontal Plane

Mitre Angles

Vertical Plane

Bevel Angles

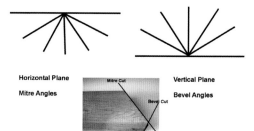

Compound Miter Saw — See also Miter Saw. Either a corded, cordless or hand powered wood cutting saw that can cut both bevels and miters simultaneously.

Compressor — See Air Compressor.

Concave — An inward curving shape such as the inside of a spoon.

Conditioner — A liquid applied to wood to equalize the absorption of stains or other finishes in the more porous species of wood, such as pine and poplar.

Conifer — The term usually used for evergreen trees. These trees do not shed their leaves (needles) in the winter.

Contact Cement — See also Adhesives. A rubber-based glue that permanently bonds on contact. The glue is applied to both surfaces to be joined, allowed to partially dry and then pressed together.

Contraction — The shrinkage of wood due to the extraction of moisture. As wood dries it loses its moisture content until it reaches its equilibrium. However, in areas with very

Contractor's Saw — The contractor's saw is a table saw that is built lighter than cabinet saws so that they may be somewhat easier to transport and set up on a job site. The contractor's saw usually has an outboard 1.5hp, 110-volt motor and drives the saw blade with 'V' belts or they may be direct powered. Lighter weight trunions are mounted from the underside of the saw table. The contractor's saw is mounted on an open, sheet steel leg base. Some are equipped with a folding aluminum base with wheels.

Contractor's Saw Anatomy

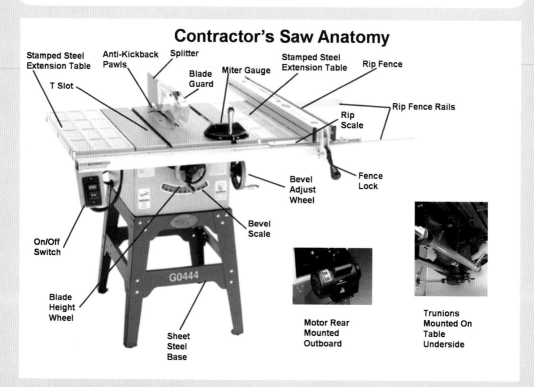

low humidity the wood may continue to contract. The woodworker should make provision for this event in the construction of workpieces.

Convex — An outward curving shape somewhat like my beer belly.

Cooper — The cooper is a dying member of the woodworking profession. A cooper makes wooden barrels. The use of plastics and other synthetic materials creates little call for wooden barrels today. The exception to this is in the aging of some wines and even beers. Wooden

barrels are still extensively used in the storing and aging of cognac, and a very specific oak wood is used to fabricate them. French Limousin oak is used exclusively to store Remy Martin Grand Cru. At a price upwards of $1,500 per bottle, a barrel would be worth over a quarter million dollars. The French cooper is well paid. There are four types of coopers. One specializes in "dry" or "slack" barrels that are made to store dry goods such as nails and cereals. Another makes "drytight" barrels, which are made to keep moisture out. These can contain flour, gunpowder and the like. The "white cooper" makes straight-staved barrels to be used as wash tubs, buckets and butter churns. The "wet" or "tight" cooper makes barrels that contain liquids like wine, rum and even liquids under pressure such as beer.

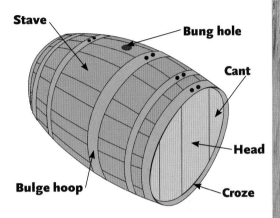

Stave — Bung hole — Cant — Head — Croze — Bulge hoop

Coopered Joint — This is a butt joint that is angled and used to make staves that make up a barrel. The joint is never glued. Instead a steel strap usually holds all of the staves together.

Coopers' Croze — A Coopers' croze (krowz) is a specialized tool used to cut a groove into the top inside of a barrel where the barrel head or top fits. A sharp chisel-like blade fitted into the crozes does the cutting. The croze is adjustable to suit individual barrel types.

Cope and Stick Joint — This is a tightly-fitting shaped joint performed not by a coping saw, but with a pair of mating router bits. This joint is where the rail meets the stile on a cabinet door.

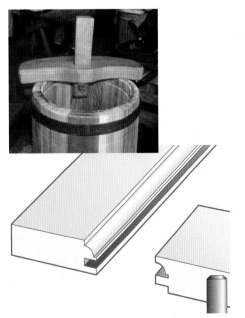

Coping (kope-ing) — a)Being able to put up with my poor writing. b) Using a coping saw to cut a matching shape such as in tightly fitting the mitered corner of a crown moulding.

Coping Saw — See also Fret Saw, Jigsaw, Scroll Saw. This is a hand saw with a round handle and a U–shaped metal frame. The frame is tensioned to hold fine toothed coping saw blades tightly. The blade may be removed and inserted into a starter hole to make an inside cut.

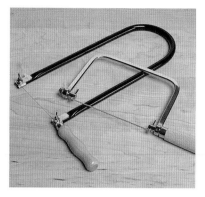

Corbel — An architectural term for a corner bracket or brace used to support a cornice or pediment. These are quite intricate in detail and are hand-carved. Also a support detail used in Arts & Crafts furniture.

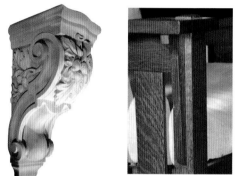

Core Box Bit — See Cove Bit.

Cord — A form of measurement that refers to firewood or logs. A cord is a stack of wood measuring four feet in height, four feet in width and eight feet in length.

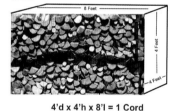

4'd x 4'h x 8'l = 1 Cord

Cordless Tools — Generally referred to as portable electric power tools. Includes drill/drivers, circular saws, and other tools that rely on rechargeable batteries as a power source.

Corner Brace — Used in cabinet making, the corner brace is used under a tabletop to secure the top to the table aprons. Note that the screws securing the top are in slots that allow for the expansion and contraction of the table top.

Corner Chisel — See Chisels.

C

Corner Clamp — See Clamp, Corner.

Cornice — See also Crown Moulding. A decorative moulded plaster or
carved wood moulding around the
perimeter of a ceiling.

Corrugated Joint Fastener —
This is a wide steel fastener
with one sharp edge used to fasten
joints, such as miters in picture
frames or screen doors. As the
fastener is hammered in it draws
the joint tighter. They are available
in various lengths (depths) ⅜", ½"
and ⅝".

Counter Bore — a) The act of pre-
boring or drilling a hole for a wood
screw or, more often, a lag screw or
bolt. b) The counterbore is a 3-in-
1 drill bit that drills a hole for the
threads of a screw, a larger hole for
the shoulder of the screw, and cuts a
tapered or flat recess to countersink
the screw head. Counterbores are
found in sizes to match the most
common wood screw sizes. Some
manufacturers have all-in-one counterbore tools that, when flipped, can
also hold a screwdriver bit.

Counter Sink — a) Recessing the head
of a wood screw so that it is flush
or below the surface of a workpiece.
b) A cutting bit that drills a shallow
tapered hole into which the head of
a wood screw fits so that the head
is either flush with the surface or
recessed below the surface.

Cove — See also Cove Bit, Cove
Moulding. A concave rounded inter-
section of a joint. The purpose of a
cove is to soften the sharpness of a
right angle joint.

Cove Bit — See also Router Bits. A router bit (or Core Box Bit) that has a rounded cutting edge to make Cove Molding and other decorative pieces.

Cove Moulding — A concave moulding that is usually used as a transition between a vertical and horizontal surface.

Craftsman Furniture — See Mission Furniture

Cranked Chisel — See Chisels.

Cramps — These are either pains in the sides or the British term for what we call clamps.

Crazing — This is a series or network of fine cracks in a varnish or lacquer finish due to age or excessive sunlight exposure. Humans wrinkle, furniture crazes.

Creosote (kree-oh-sote) — A liquid that is brushed or sprayed on wood to preserve and protect it when used outside or below grade.

Crescent Wrench — See Wrenches, Crescent.

Crocus Cloth (crow-cuss) — A medium weight cloth that is coated with iron-oxide and is used as a finishing or polishing medium with thinned linseed oil. The very fine texture polishes and removes dust flecks on clear coats.

Crook — An undesirable defect in a board that is laterally bent along its length.

Crosscutting — Cutting wood with a saw perpendicular to the direction of the grain. For best results the correct saw or saw blade should be used to minimize tear-out.

Crosscut Saw — See also Hand Saws. a) A hand saw that has teeth set for the purpose of cutting boards perpendicular to the wood grain. b) A one-man or two-man saw used for felling trees and cutting them into logs. The crosscut saw is three feet long or longer (with some longer than eight feet) and is used for cutting down trees with huge trunk diameters.

 **Cross Garnet** — See T–Hinge.

Crotch — The V–joint of a tree where it has separated into a second trunk. The wood from this crotch forms a very interesting pattern that wood turner's desire. This is also referred to as crotch swirl.

Crown Moulding — A decorative moulding attached to a wall at ceiling height, usually used in conjunction with paneled walls. A crown moulding may also be used to cap off a tall cabinet.

Crown Molding

Cup — An undesirable convex or concave bend across the width of a board.

Cupping — See Cup.

Curl — The grain pattern produced in wood when sawn at the junction of a branch and the stem of the tree.

Curly Maple — See Fiddleback Maple.

Cut — a) A term used in determining the ratio mix of denatured alcohol with shellac as a spit coat or a finish. A ½ cut is two parts alcohol and one part shellac. b) The act of dividing

FUN facts

Cubit

A somewhat controversial form of measurement used by the world's first boat builder.

Way back when God was talking to people, he chose (democratically by tender) the Noah Ship Yards to build a boat. It was immediately apparent that God himself drew up the plans for this; it was to be 300 cubits long, 50 cubits wide and 30 cubits high. Translated into today's measurements it would be 450 feet (137.16 meters) long, 75 feet (23 meters) wide and 45 feet (14 meters) high. Now, that's based on the idea that back then one cubit measured the distance from the tip of the elbow to the tip of the middle finger, or today, roughly 18".

Noah entreth the Ark. Gen: 7.

And ye Lord said unto Noah, come thou & all thy house into ye Ark, etc. v. 1. Of every cleane beast take by seavens, etc. v. 2. Of beasts that are not cleane & of foules and of every thing that creepeth, etc. v. 8. there went in two and two, etc. ver: 9.

However, if one believes science over the bible, Noah would have walked around with his knuckles dragging on the ground. This certainly would add another 6" (15cm) to the length of the cubit.

And of course, this brings up another conundrum. What did Noah use as a tape measure? Furthermore, how did he mill the wood for the boat? What did he cut the boards with and, of course, how did he fasten all these boards together? God specified that the boat (He called it an ark) have three chambers in it, and that the chambers be three stories high. What's a story? A door was to be built low on one side. I guess Noah must have known what a door was.

a board or other material into two or more pieces with a sharp cutting tool such as a knife or a saw.

Cut List — (also Cutting List) A list that woodworkers use before setting out to build a piece of furniture. The cut list is taken off the plan or blueprint. It is a specific list of the sizes and types (species) of boards and other components to be used. The cut list is helpful in ordering the necessary materials for the furniture piece and for determining the costs.

Project: Dining Table						
#	Part	Thickness	Width	Length	Material	Comments
4	Legs	1-1/2"	1-1/2"	27"	Maple	
2	Rails	3/4"	2-1/2"	60"	Maple	Tenons both ends
2	Rails	3/4"	2-1/2"	30"	Maple	Tenons both ends
1	Top	3/4"	34"	64"	Maple	

Cut Nails — These are handmade nails that are tapered and have sharp edges and a sharp point. Cut nails have a higher holding strength than wire nails. Cut nails were used in general construction, not in finishing work. Larger versions are commonly seen holding railroad tracks to ties (⊞⇒ sleepers). The sizes can vary from ¾" all the way up to spikes of 10" or longer.

Cut-Off Saw — See Miter Saw.

⊞⇒ **Cutters** — See Router Bits.

Cutting Board — A board made up of laminated hardwood pieces used in the home kitchen as a safe surface for chopping and dicing foods. Special food-safe oil is used to preserve the cutting board. These oils may be walnut or butcher block.

Cutting Tool — Any tool with a sharp edge or sharp teeth designed to cut, slice, hew, carve or chisel wood.

Cyanoacrilate Glue (sigh-anno-ak-rill-ate) — See also Glue. Also known as Krazy Glue, this glue will bond most dissimilar products together as long as they fit tightly together. It is also known for gluing fingers and other body parts together.

Dado (day-doe) — a) A rectangular groove in a board or other workpiece. b) A decorative lower portion of an interior wall (also known as a wainscotting) with a chair rail moulding capping off the top edge. c) In classical architecture, the plain pedestal area of a column between the base and the column. A dado may be cut by hand with chisels, with a router or with a table saw using a dado set.

Dado Plane — (day-doe) See Router Plane.

Dado Set (day-doe) — A set of saw blades mounted on the arbor of a table saw in a specific configuration. The set consists of a left outside blade and a right outside blade. Chippers of various thicknesses are

placed between these to make the desired width of the dado. In addition, most of the better quality dado sets include a set of shims in a variety of thicknesses to fine tune the width of the dado. The better quality sets will have 24 carbide–tipped teeth with four tooth chippers.

Dado Wobble Blade — This is a wobble blade that is set on a special hub that sets the circular blade on an angle. With the rotation of the saw's arbour, the blade wobbles. The angle of the blade may be adjusted to vary the width of the dado that the blade cuts. The wobble blade does not provide a finished dado as the blade does not give the dado a flat bottom. This is due to the arc of the blade.

 **Danish Oil** — See also Linseed Oil, Oil, Finishing, Tung Oil. Danish oil is a clear polymerized linseed oil wood finish used to protect the wood and enhance its appearance. Danish oil may be a blend of linseed oil, lacquer and solvents and is wiped on the surface and rubbed in. This process is repeated until the desired appearance is achieved. Caution: Rags used to apply Danish oil may spontaneously combust. Allow cloths to dry out doors on a clothes line.

Debarking — This is a step in the milling process of logs. Before the logs can be cut into boards the bark of the logs must be removed. This is done by rotating the logs on a spiral auger-type roller.

Deciduous Trees — Trees that shed their leaves or foliage annually. These trees are commonly referred to as hardwood.

Deck Screws — See also Screws. Deck screws are rust and chemical resistant screws specifically manufactured for screwing deck boards to the frame of a deck or patio. They are designed to withstand the weather and the corrosion effects of pressure–treated wood.

Delamination — The process in which the layers (or laminates) of plywood or veneers start to come unglued.

Demilune Table —(deh-mee-loon) This is a half-round (in French, demi-lune means half moon) table designed mostly for use in entry ways as a space saver. The top often hinges to open to a full table.

Denatured Alcohol — See Alcohol, Denatured.

Density — Density is a term that re-

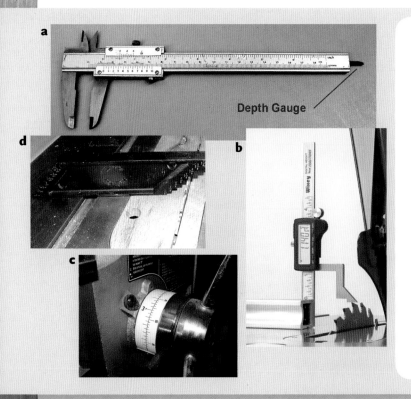

Depth Gauge

Depth Gauge — A tool or instrument used to determine the depth of a hole, saw kerf or other recess. A depth gauge is found as a pin on (a) vernier callipers. A depth gauge may be used to set the (b) height of a table saw blade, the protrusion of a router bit from the router base or table or for the (c) depth that a drill bit penetrates. (d) Another version of a depth gauge that may be used on a table saw, router or drill press.

fers to the hardness of a given wood species and is referred to as weight per cubic foot of dried wood.

Dentils — These are decorative rectangular blocks with spaces between them that may be found immediately below a cornice or crown moulding. Decorative dentils may also be found on fireplace mantles.

Depth Stop — See also Drill Stop. Any mechanical device used to control how deep a tool penetrates into wood. Depth stops are found on

Desk

It is not known for certain when the first wooden desk was built but it appears to have been built for writing for accommodating a stand-up scribe. The first desks had sloping writing surfaces. Some were built simply as sloped top boxes with a hinged writing surface. The interiors were storage areas for quills, inks, paper and other materials. The desk later evolved into a tall cabinet with a drop-down front called an escritoire or secretary.

By this time the height of the writing desk had become a standard 29" – 30". The desk soon became a large and elaborate piece of furniture with a very large writing surface supported by two pedestals and a wide center drawer. The pedestals contained either drawers or cabinets with doors and shelves inside.

circular saws, drill presses and compound miter (⛨➡ mitre) saws.

Detail Sander — See also Profile Sander. An electrically powered orbital sander that can accommodate a number of various (usually) hard rubber contours to which sandpaper strips are attached. These contours are designed to fit into coves or round-overs and corners. In addition to these shapes, a detail sander also has various flat sanding pads that allow the user to sand in tight corners. Some, like the Fein Multimaster tool pictured, have additional accessories for cutting or grinding.

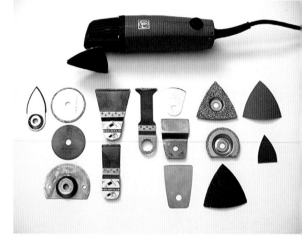

De-Waxed Shellac — See also Shellac. A shellac product that has had all traces of its wax content removed. This refinement makes the product more receptive to other finishes such as lacquers. De-waxed shellac is used as a constituent in French polishing.

Digital Fence Read-Out — A digital fence read-out is an after-market tool that attaches to a table saw rip fence. A LCD (Liquid Crystal Diode) read-out shows the precise position of the fence in relation to the saw blade. The readout displays measurements in both fractions and millimeters.

Dimensional Lumber — Usually softwood that has been cut to standard sizes and used in residential and commercial construction. May also be referred to as 2x4s 2x6s, etc.

Disc Sander — A disc sander is a sanding machine that turns a circular pad to which a sanding disc is attached. The sanding disc may be

d

attached to a handheld sander that facilitates 5" – 6" diameter discs or 6" – 12" discs that fit on a stationary disc sander.

Distressing — A finishing process that adds dents, scratches, burns and other indications of wear and age for decorative purposes. Tools that accomplish distressing are chains, awls, hammers, screwdrivers and blow torches.

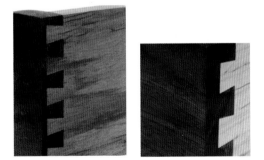

Double Lapped Dovetail — This joinery is used to achieve the strength of a dovetail joint but without its appearance. Both pieces have a lap, but one is allowed to show a different wood species.

Dovetail — A dovetail is a form of wood joinery that is noted for both its utility and beauty. The dovetail is noted for its strength and is commonly used to attach drawer fronts to the sides. A series of pins interlock with tails that are either hand–cut or machine made. See also dovetail jig.

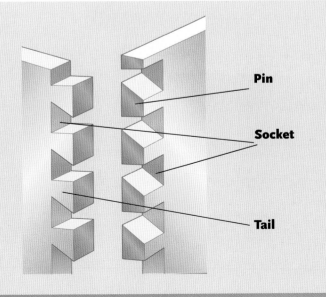

Pin

Socket

Tail

Dovetail Anatomy — The dovetail joint consists of three components as pictured: the pins, tails and sockets.

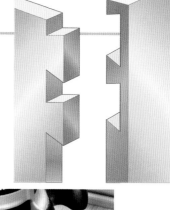

Dovetail, Half Blind — The half blind dovetail is a lapped joint that gives a drawer front a clean finish but shows the dovetail joinery on the drawer sides.

Dovetail Jig — The dovetail jig is a tool that, along with a router, allows the woodworker to make dovetail joints of various configurations. The jig usually clamps two workpieces into it, and the router, equipped with a dovetail bit, cuts both the pins and the tails simultaneously.

Dovetail Key — See Butterfly Joint.

Dovetail Router Bit — The dovetail router bit is used in conjunction with a router to fashion dovetail joints. A router bushing guides the router bit through the router jig templates.

Dovetail Saw — See also Backsaw, Hand Saw. The dovetail (or gent's) saw is a thin bladed, fine-toothed handsaw with 18 – 22 teeth per inch and a round handle. The dovetail saw is meant for cutting both the pins and tails of through dovetails with no tear-out.

FUN facts

The dovetail joint dates back to the first dynasty of ancient Egypt and has been found in furniture that was entombed with mummies from that era. The dovetail joint has also been found in the tombs of classical Chinese emperors.

d

Dovetail, Sliding — A sliding dovetail is somewhat looser than normal dovetails may be used as a drawer slide in lieu of a metal drawer glide.

Dovetail, Through — The through dovetail allows both the pins and the tails to be visible on the drawer front and the drawer sides. This joint is more commonly found on decorative or utility boxes such as humidors.

Dowel — See also Plugs. A round, long piece of wood as in a wooden rod, available in a variety of diameters and lengths, but usually 1" or less.

Dowel Center — A tool or jig used to position the center of a dowel as in dowel joints. The jig is made in a number of diameters to match the most common dowel sizes. To use the dowel center you first drill a hole in one half of the workpiece. Insert the appropriate dowel center into the hole and then align the other half of the workpiece over the center. Apply pressure to make a mark for the mating hole. Drill a hole of the same size where it is marked and then glue and insert the dowel in the two holes.

Dowel Cutter — The dowel cutter is a hollow tool that is mounted in a drill. A square piece of wood is fed into the tapered hole of the cutter. It is then rotated, and the knife produces an accurate length of dowel.

Dowel Jig — This is a tool used to align two or more pieces of wood for the purpose of joining them with dowels. The jig will perfectly align the pieces for drilling the appropri-

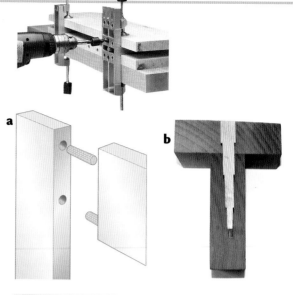

ate–sized hole in which to fit the dowels.

Dowel Joint — a) A form of joinery, the dowel joint uses short dowels inserted into matching sized holes to make a tight joint for two or more pieces of wood. The dowels are scribed to allow glue to penetrate into the tight fitting holes. b) A variation of the conventional dowel is the Miller Dowel, a tapered, stepped dowel.

Dowel Threader — The dowel threader is a tool that can cut screw threads on hardwood or softwood dowels. The purpose of this is you can make your own bench vises or clamps. To make these you simply clamp the dowel tightly and turn the arms of the threader to make the threads the desired length. A similar mating tool will cut female threads. With this one you have to start with a pre-drilled hole.

Dozuki Saw — (doe-zoo-kee) A Japanese saw that is used for fine detail cutting. The blade of the saw is very thin. Therefore, the teeth are configured to cut on the pull stroke rather than the push. The dozuki saw is particularly suitable for hand cutting dovetails.

Drawknife — A very sharp straight or curved blade with handles on either end. As the name implies it is used in a drawing or pulling motion to debark logs and to rough-shape them for additional work, rustic furniture or log cabins.

Drawer — A box-like unit with an open top that is fitted into a cabinet and is meant to contain a variety of

objects. It is designed to open for access and close for concealment.

Drawer Glide — (or Slides) Metal rails that are attached to the drawer sides (or sometimes the drawer bottom) and the cabinet frame. These may be fitted with wheels or ball bearings and allow the drawer to partially or fully open.

Drawer Lock Router Bit — This is a router bit that does two jobs at the same time. By changing the router setup, this bit cuts both the sides and ends of a drawer box at 45° and simultaneously cuts a joint that locks the pieces together. Repeated opening and closing motions put a lot of strain on a drawer, and the joint created by this bit provides a very strong connection.

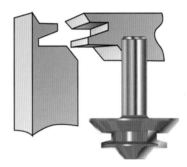

Drawer Knobs —See Drawer Pulls.

Drawer Pulls — Knobs or grips used to open and close drawers. They can be made of many different materials, such as wood, brass or steel, and are available in an extensive variety of shapes and sizes.

Drawer Runner — See Drawer Glide.

Drawer Slide — See Drawer Glide.

Dremel Motor Tool — (dreh-mul) In 1935 Albert J. Dremel invented the handheld motor tool that has become an essential part of almost every woodworker's tool cabinet. It has many copies but the Dremel has maintained its dominant status. The tool is used for everything from cutting and carving to grinding, polishing, drilling and sanding.

Dressed Lumber — Lumber that has been planed smooth on all four surfaces.

Dried Wood — This term refers to wood that has been either air dried or kiln dried to a moisture content (MC) of 12%.

Drill

Breast — A hand drill does not offer very much leverage when drilling into hardwood. The breast drill allows the user to place the top of the drill against his/her chest or shoulder to push on it while turning the hand crank wheel.

Hand — See also Brace and Bit, Yankee Screwdriver. A hand drill predates the now commonly used corded and cordless power drills. A hand crank wheel is geared to turn the shaft of the drill, to which a chuck is attached. The drill bit is installed into the chuck. There are a number of styles of hand drills, but the tool has almost reached obsolescence.

Portable, Corded — Corded electric drills date back to the 1930s and had a maximum drill bit size of ⅜". The electric drill has been greatly improved over the years. Now, the norm for a home workshop is a drill with a ½" bit capacity. All the current models have variable speed controls and reverse switches. Many also have torque controls, a hammer-drill feature and two or three speed ranges as well.

Portable, Cordless — The cordless drill is powered by a rechargeable battery and offers all of the ad-

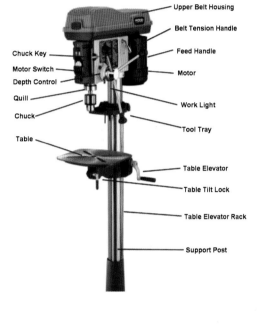

d

vantages of a corded tool without the electrical cord. Cordless drills are available in voltages from 3.6v to 36v, from palm-sized tools to large two-handed hammer drills.

Drill Press — An essential tool in a well equipped woodshop, the drill press does not just drill and bore holes but may also double as a drum sander. The size of a drill press is determined by half the distance between the center of the drill press chuck and the edge of the support post. The drill press is available as either a benchtop tool or as a fixed (or stationary) tool. The drill press is generally a multi-speed tool, and the speeds are increased or reduced by means of adjusting drive belts found in the upper housing. However, there are drill presses available that offer belt-free speed adjustment. Features to look for in a drill press are table size, chuck capacity, tilting/rotating table, work light, quill travel, motor size and number of speeds.

Drill Press, Radial Arm — See Radial Arm Drill Press.

Drill Press Anatomy

Upper Belt Housing
Belt Tension Handle
Feed Handle
Chuck Key
Motor Switch
Motor
Depth Control
Quill
Work Light
Chuck
Tool Tray
Table
Table Elevator
Table Tilt Lock
Table Elevator Rack
Support Post

FUN facts

In the 1950s Porter-Cable developed what is thought to be the first cordless drill. This was a bulky tool, and the user had to wear the battery pack on his/her belt. It was a very basic drill with a single speed and was powered by an Eveready Nickel Cadmium rechargeable battery pack. The cordless drill is by far the best selling of all of the cordless tools available.

Drill Bits — There are a great variety of drill bits used in woodworking. For general hole drilling into either hardwood or softwood the woodworker's choice is a twist drill, which has deep helical grooves from the point along the shank. There are a number of finishes that improve the efficiency of a drill bit, such as black cobalt, bronze, chromium and titanium. The standard twist drill bit now has a split point that starts the hole more cleanly. Slightly raised, sharpened helical edges also help to keep the bit cooler and improve the wood ejection.

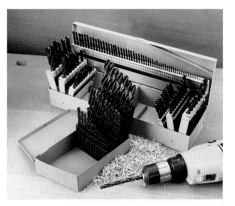

Around-The-Corner Drill Bit — See also Spade Bit. This spade-type drill bit is able to change direction within the hole it is boring due to its rounded cutting edges. Pictured is an example of what it can do, and the bit itself, made by Vermont American.

Brad Point — The brad point drill bit is a modified twist drill. The sharp point starts the hole more accurately while the side flanges cut cleaner. There have been some modifications to the brad point but none seem to cut better than the original.

Concrete — This is a bit that is made to bore small holes in concrete. The tip of the bit is made from tungsten carbide, and the shank is a double helix for cooling and rapid material removal.

Expansive — The expansive bit (or adjustable bit) is a modified spade bit that is used for drilling larger holes in wood. At its widest setting the expansive bit will drill

a hole 1½" in diameter. The main advantage of the expansive bit is that it is fully adjustable.

Forstner — Flat–bottomed holes are desired for the installation of clock mechanisms, and the forstner bit provides just that. Those that have been modified with carbide side cutters are designed for the installation of European hinges. Other modifications include a lead screw that draws the bit into the wood. These are made for the construction industry to feed conduit and wiring through studs and joists.

High Speed Steel — This is very hard steel used in just about all drill bits. Some, however, have additional coatings for durability and extended sharpness.

Ship Auger — According to the Nautical Dictionary: A large and extremely long drilling bit used by a shipwright to bore boltholes in the keel of a wooden boat. The Ship auger is a double helical shape with a lead screw point that helps to draw in the bit. The double helix design causes less friction in the hole and helps to remove the waste. Ship augers are usually found only in larger lengths and diameters.

Step — Step drill bits are made for specific purposes. The tapered one has steps spaced at ⅟₁₆" increments and is made for drilling into sheet metal for various sizes of connectors. A custom step drill is made for a specific type of dowel joinery while another is used for drilling pocket holes.

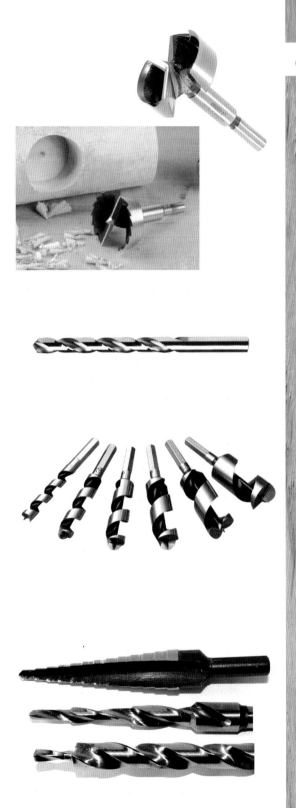

Spade — The spade bit is a flat bit used for drilling rough holes as in construction. They were generally considered throw-away drill bits, but some new hybrids are much more expensive and are meant to last longer and are able to be re-sharpened. On some, a lead screw has been added to aggressively draw in the bit for faster drilling. Wide helix grooves have been added for fast material ejection. Another type has rounded edges that allow the drill bit to change directions in the drill hole.

Pictured, from top to bottom: Milwaukee Spade Bit, Ridgid Speedbore, Vermont American Around-The-Corner bit.

Tapered — See Drill Bits - Step Drill

Twist — A twist drill is a standard drill bit found in conventional fraction sizes. A useful set of twist drills includes 29 bits in sizes ranging from 1/16" to 1/2" in 1/16" increments. Bits larger than 3/8" diameters have reduced shank sizes, usually 3/8".

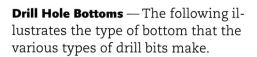

Drill Hole Bottoms — The following illustrates the type of bottom that the various types of drill bits make.

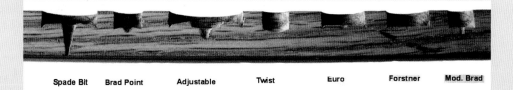

| Spade Bit | Brad Point | Adjustable | Twist | Euro | Forstner | Mod. Brad |

d

Drill Stand — A drill stand is a tool that allows the woodworker to convert a corded or cordless electric drill into a drill press. The drill fits into a pocket on the stand and is secured by a metal clamp. The drill is raised and lowered through a set of rack and pinion gears.

Drill Stops — Metal rings in varied diameters that slide onto drill bit shanks and are secured by set screws. The purpose of the drill stop is to limit the depth that a drill bit can penetrate the workpiece. They are usually sold in sets of six to fit all 29 standard fractional bit sizes.

Drum Sander — See also Surface Sander.

Pneumatic — (new-mat-ik) An air-filled drum sander that is quite versatile in that it will soft sand contoured workpieces without digging in or burning. By reducing the amount of air in the drum you can add a chamfered edge if desired. The drums are of varied sizes but usually 4" diameter x 8" long. The drum sleeves are available in standard grit sizes.

Solid Core — Solid core drum sanders are usually made of hard rubber and have a threaded arbour core. These are available from ¼" up to 2" in diameter and may be installed on a hand motor tool or drill press. The sandpaper sleeve is mounted on the rubber drum and the screw of the arbour is tightened, thus compressing the drum securing the sleeve.

 Drunken Saw — See, Dado, Wobble Blade.

Drying Wood — See also Air Drying. For woodworking it is most desirable to use dried wood as it is more stable and will remain straight and true. Drying both hardwood and softwood may be done by kiln (oven) or by air. With oven drying care must be taken to control the drying rate. Drying wood too fast may cause cracking or splitting. There are published schedules for various wood species. Lumber must be properly stacked with air circulation spaces and stickers placed equally throughout the stack. Air drying wood takes, on average, one year for every inch of thickness to bring the moisture content (MC) to approximately 15%.

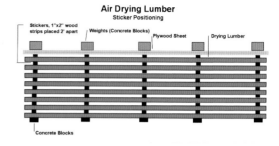

Air Drying Lumber
Sticker Positioning

Stickers, 1"x2" wood strips placed 2' apart | Weights (Concrete Blocks) | Plywood Sheet | Drying Lumber

Concrete Blocks

Dry Lumber — Lumber that has been dried to a moisture content of 19% or lower by air dry or kiln dry methods. Hardwoods are considered dry at 10%.

Dry Rot — A fungus that attacks the cells of timbers in home construction and ship building.

Dry Sink — Years before the three-piece bathroom (four-piece in some areas) and well before the shower massage, Pilgrims used a dry sink. The dry sink, also known as a commode, was a low cabinet with doors. Within the doors were shelves for soaps and personal items. There might be a towel rack on the side of the cabinet, and there were usually splash boards surrounding three sides of the top. Some had large holes cut into the top to facilitate a porcelain wash bowl. The dry sink was usually made from pine due to its prevalence in the New England states.

Drywall Saw — See Keyhole Saw.

Duct — See also Ductwork. In reference to woodworking a duct is used in conjunction with dust collectors. The duct or ductwork is made of metal or plastic tubes that are connected to stationary woodworking tools for carrying sawdust to the dust collector.

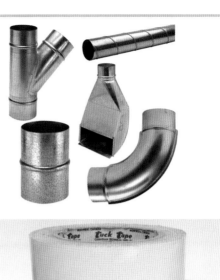

Duct Tape — The real stuff. Duct tape is a cloth-backed adhesive tape that is so called because it was first designed to seal the joints of air ducts. The original duct tape was grey in color to blend in with the metal of the ductwork. It was later discovered that the tape was an excellent mending product and was therefore produced in a variety of colors.

Ductwork — See Duct.

FUN facts

Aristotle

Duct Tape

A cloth–backed adhesive tape rumoured to be discovered by the famous Greek tycoon, Aristotle Duct in A.D. 1042. Ari discovered this by accident while walking through clear-cut pine trees on the way to his newly constructed subdivision. Apparently, some pine tar stuck to the hem of his Armani–designed toga. At the same time, the strap on his Florsheim sandal broke. Ari tore the tar covered hem from his toga and used it to repair the sandal strap. He immediately asked Armani to produce rolls of this tape in a variety of colors. Ari's contemporary, Archimedes, was building some sluices that leaked water terribly, and Ari's new tape came to the rescue. The rest is history. It was through great difficulty that the author was able to obtain this autographed photo of the reclusive Duct.

Duplex Nail — A nail with two heads. Although this may seem a little weird at first, a sober second thought will realize its value. The duplex nail is used as a temporary fastener, and the second head makes it easier to remove. The nail is driven in up to the bottom of the first head only.

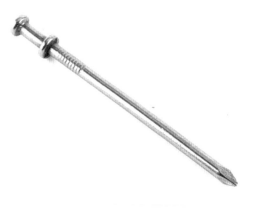

Durite® (doo-rite) — See also Sandpaper. A Norton trademark for silicon carbide sandpaper products.

Dust Board — A horizontal fixed member found between drawers on a cabinet. The purpose of a dust board is to to stop items in a lower drawer from preventing the upper drawer to open.

Dust Collector — A dust collector is similar to a vacuum cleaner in that it gathers sawdust from your woodworking tools through a ductwork system and disposes of it in containers. There are portable systems that connect to a single power tool or large dust collectors that can connect to all your stationary tools. Blast gates are connected to each power tool to allow the central dust collection system to work at that tool. These systems do not remove all the sawdust created but are a major help for a healthier woodshop.

Dust Filter — The dust filter is an important part of a shop vacuum and a shop air cleaner as it keeps the dust out of the shop air. There are a number of types of dust filters, but the most efficient are the hepa filters as they filter 99.8% of all particulates out of the air that passes through them. These are pleated filters, and

it is said that they are more efficient when they have some dust in them (but not enough to clog them). The most damaging dust for shop vacuums is gyproc dust but the hepa filter eliminates this.

Dust Mask — See also Respirator. Many wood species can be toxic and can cause respiratory problems or seriously aggravate existing respiratory illnesses such as asthma. See also Toxic Wood Species. Wearing an appropriate dust mask in a woodshop will help prevent the woodworker from breathing in these toxic sawdust particles. Pictured are several type. Their efficacy is based on the seal of the mask to your face and the type of filter in the mask. A bearded individual should wear a full face mask/ventilator. You should buy your mask at a safety supply store so you can purchase the appropriate filter.

Dutchman — A wood patch used to repair woodworking that can't be easily replaced. The dutchman can be created to precisely match the surrounding area, or can be a decorative accent shape when an exact match isn't possible (as shown). For example, if part of a window sill is rotten and it is too costly or laborious to fully replace, then you can cut out the rot and fit a Dutchman to match. Photo courtesy of Staples-Cabinetmakers.com

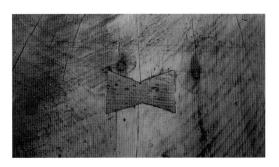

Dying — See Wood Dyes.

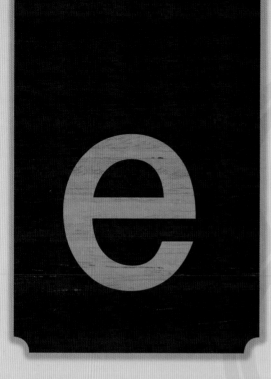

Earlywood — If you look closely at an annual ring on a tree's cross section you will see that the inner portion is somewhat lighter in color than the outer portion. The lighter color is spring wood or earlywood. The darker portion is summer wood or latewood.

Ebonizing — (ebb-on-ize-ing) This is the process of making a lesser wood species appear to be ebony. The most common way of doing this is to choose a tight-grained species and then use a black aniline dye or oil stain to blacken the wood. Normal clear coating is then used to protect the finish.

Edge Guide — An edge guide is usually a metal contraption that attaches to a woodworking tool and keeps the tool running parallel to the edge of the workpiece. The edge guide is laterally adjustable so that the user can vary its position. Tools that commonly use an edge guide are a router, circular saw, portable oscillating spindle sander and planer.

e

Edge Joinery — See Joinery.

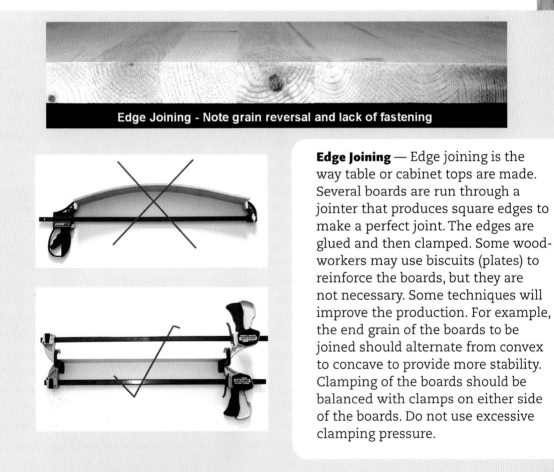

Edge Joining - Note grain reversal and lack of fastening

Edge Joining — Edge joining is the way table or cabinet tops are made. Several boards are run through a jointer that produces square edges to make a perfect joint. The edges are glued and then clamped. Some woodworkers may use biscuits (plates) to reinforce the boards, but they are not necessary. Some techniques will improve the production. For example, the end grain of the boards to be joined should alternate from convex to concave to provide more stability. Clamping of the boards should be balanced with clamps on either side of the boards. Do not use excessive clamping pressure.

Edge Jointing — See also Edge Joining. The process of making the edges of a board straight and square. This process is usually performed on a jointer.

FUN facts

Edwardian Furniture — 1901 —

At the death of Queen Victoria of England, King Edward VII was crowned. Furniture design became very eclectic in style that included rococo styles as well as Arts & Crafts designs by William Morris. Some furniture was almost mediaeval with dark and heavy woods. Art Nouveau appeared as did a reappearance of French and English 18th century design. Chairs and sofas were well stuffed and upholstered in flowery chintz.

Edge Trimmer — See Laminate Trimmer.

Eh — An identifiably Canadian expression as in, "That must be maple eh?"

Elevation — In the making of blueprints or plans for a project like a coffee table, the designer draws the plans as views from the top of the cabinet (called the plan view) and from the side or front (called the elevation view). The elevation view shows the front, back and both sides.

Emery — A natural mineral with a black appearance that is crushed and used as an abrasive grain.

Emery Cloth — A tightly woven cloth material coated on one side with emery grain and available in a variety of grit sizes.

Emery Paper — As above, but the emery is adhered to a strong paper backing.

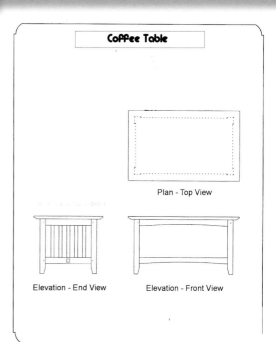

Coffee Table

Plan - Top View

Elevation - End View

Elevation - Front View

Enamel — A high gloss oil-based or solvent–based finish to which a color pigment has been added. Due to its relatively slow drying, brush marks level out. The surface being enamelled (painted) must be clean and dry.

e

End Cut Preservative — a) This may be any number of products that are meant to seal the ends of newly cut boards (🏴󠁧󠁢󠁥󠁮󠁧󠁿➡ timbers) as they air dry or kiln dry. This is done to prevent the rapid draining of moisture. If the moisture in green wood dries too quickly the boards tend to check and split. Latex enamel may be brushed or rolled on. Some wood mills use coloured paints to identify the species being dried.

b) End cut preservative (see creosote) is used on pressure–treated wood after being cut for use. Creosote or other preservatives will maintain the integrity of the pressure treatment.

FUN facts

Elizabethan Furniture – 1554 - 1602
Elizabeth I was the daughter of Henry VIII, and she reigned during the good fortunes of England. She was noted for her love of theatre and art. She will be remembered for clothing and hair styles but most noted for the furniture style during her reign on the throne.

Fred Roe

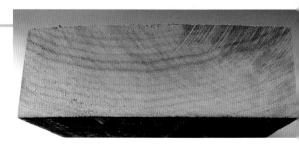

End Grain — This is the wood grain that is exposed after you have made a crosscut on a piece of wood.

End Matched — End matched wood solids or veneers are a form of bookmatching, but the boards or veneer sheets are mated end-to-end. There are two ways of end matching: the architectural end match and the continuous end match. The architectural match has the grain points facing each other while the continuous is a slip match pattern.

Epoxy Resin — Epoxy resin is one part of a two-part adhesive or wood filler. Epoxy adhesive is known as universal glue and is usually mixed by the user immediately prior to use. The glue is mixed 50-50 with epoxy hardener, and it dries in minutes after use. It will totally cure within 24 hours. Epoxy fillers are used to fill defects in wood, such as the voids found on some grades of plywood. This type of epoxy is found as sticks, with the outer skin being the hardener. The user then tears off the

desired amount, hand mixes it and applies it as required.

Equilibrium — In woodworking, this term is used when the moisture content of a board neither gains nor releases moisture from or into the surrounding air.

Equilateral Triangle — A triangle with all sides of equal length and all three angles being 60°.

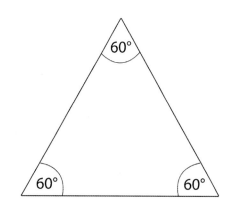

Escritoire — (ess-kree-twar) See Bureau.

Escutcheon — (ess-kut-chun) A decorative and/or utilitarian plate surrounding a keyhole, door knob, cabinet, drawer pull or other. An escutcheon may be made of many materials including brass, copper, steel, wood and others. The escutcheon protects the finish of wear areas on cabinetry.

Etagere — (ay-taj-air) An open shelf unit with several shelves meant to display knick-knacks or collectibles originating in the Victorian furniture era.

Expanding Bit — See Drill Bits, Expansive Bit.

Expansion Bolt — A bolt that is used to anchor lumber to masonry. The outer jacket of an expansion bolt expands to grip the side walls of a pilot hole due to wedge pressure at its base or the wedge force of a bolt screwed into it.

 Expansive Bolt — See Expansion Bolt.

e

Face Edge — The face edge is a reference edge, the edge of a board that has been straightened and squared to the face of the board. Woodworkers will generally make a mark on this edge similar to the face mark.

Face Jointing — The process of making the face of a board straight and square. This may be achieved through the use of a jointer or thickness planer.

Face Mark — The pencil mark put on the face or edge surface of a piece of wood denoting the face and edge that are going to be used in your project.

Face Plate — A circular or disc-like piece of castiron used to fasten bowl blanks in order to turn them on a lathe. The face of the face plate has holes drilled in it to facilitate screws used to secure the workpiece. A threaded hole in the back is used to attach the plate to the lathe mandrel. They are available in a variety of diameters.

Face Side — Similar to the face edge in that it is the surface of choice for your workpiece, has been planed and is square with the face edge.

Face Veneer — Veneer that has been chosen for its appearance, not for its strength.

Facing — An edge of hardwood, plain or decorated, that is put on a softwood shelf or table edge both for aesthetic and durability purposes. The width of the facing will be identical to the shelf thickness.

Facing

False Fence — See Fence, Auxiliary.

Fasteners — See Nails, Screws, Staples, etc.

Fastening — The act of connecting two or more materials together either permanently or temporarily through the use of adhesives or mechanical means.

Faux Finishing — (foe) Faux is French for *false* meaning an imitation finish.

f

Faux finishing may resemble a wood grain or textures that resemble fabrics. Faux finishing is done using a varied assortment of tools designed for this purpose.

Featherboard — No birds or foul are harmed in the making of a featherboard. A featherboard is used as a horizontal or vertical (or both) support that forces a board snug to the table and to the saw fence when ripping. This may also be used to keep the board flat on the saw table in the same operation. Or it may be used on a router table or band saw for the same purpose. The featherboard locks into the T-slot on tool tabletops.

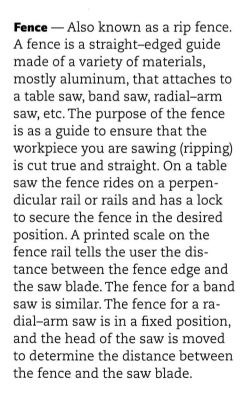

Fence — Also known as a rip fence. A fence is a straight–edged guide made of a variety of materials, mostly aluminum, that attaches to a table saw, band saw, radial–arm saw, etc. The purpose of the fence is as a guide to ensure that the workpiece you are sawing (ripping) is cut true and straight. On a table saw the fence rides on a perpendicular rail or rails and has a lock to secure the fence in the desired position. A printed scale on the fence rail tells the user the distance between the fence edge and the saw blade. The fence for a band saw is similar. The fence for a radial–arm saw is in a fixed position, and the head of the saw is moved to determine the distance between the fence and the saw blade.

f

Fence, Auxiliary — An auxiliary fence or false fence is used when the saw blade must be flush to the fence face. The auxiliary fence is generally a sacrificial length of plywood or other species similar in width and length to the actual fence. It is clamped to the actual fence and the blade is often cut into the fence.

Fence, Split — The split fence is used on a router table when using it as a jointer and for some other operations. One side (usually the right side) of the fence is set back to the amount of material that is to be removed as it passes through the router bit. The other side (usually the left side) is adjusted forward and flush with the face of the workpiece after the removal of the stock.

FUN facts

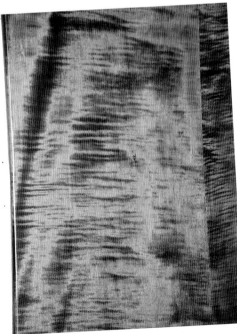

Fiddleback Maple

Fiddleback maple is one of the most prized hardwoods. It is also known as flame maple, tiger maple and curly maple and is used in the making of stringed musical instruments, not just for appearance but also for its tonal qualities.

The fiddleback phenomenon is also occasionally found in other wood species such as walnut, koa, ash and some others.

Fiddleback exhibits a visual phenomenon termed *chatoyancy* in the lapidarian world. Viewed from one angle the stripes appear to be dark, but when that angle is changed those same stripes appear to be quite light.

Even with today's technology, botanists are unable to determine what causes the fiddleback pattern.

Ferrule — (fehr-rule) A metal (usually brass, copper or steel) band or reinforcement used to connect different materials together, such as a chisel's tang to a wooden handle, bristles to a paintbrush handle, a sureform to a wooden handle, an eraser to the end of a pencil, and many more.

Fiberboard — (🇬🇧 fibreboard) A relatively soft, engineered sheet material made from sawdust and cellulose products. The raw materials are compressed with heat and adhesives and are formed into sheets that are cut to standard sizes, like 4' x 8'. Unlike medium density fiberboard (MDF) this could be termed low density fiberboard. It has also been referred to as Tentest, a trade name. Fiberboard may be used as a tack or memo board that is covered with a fabric material.

Fielded Panel — See also 🇬🇧 Raised Panel. The panel found in a raised panel cabinet or entry door. The panel is generally slightly smaller than the frame it sits in to allow for expansion/contraction.

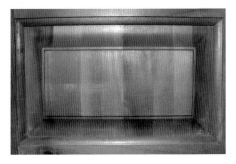

Files — See side bar, See also Rasps.

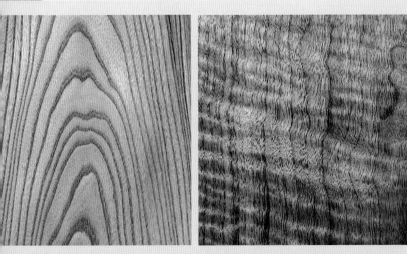

Figure — This is a distinct grain pattern usually found in flat cut wood. Some species are more highly figured than others. Figuring may also be found due to coloring, defects and parasites.

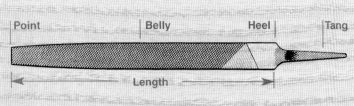

Point | Belly | Heel | Tang

Length

Filing: A Story

The hand file is thought to have been discovered in 1090 B.C. as recorded in the Bible during King Saul's reign. It was a couple thousand years later that files were cut by a machine that was invented by Leonardo da Vinci. However, the first commercially-made, machine-cut files were made by the French-man Chopitel in 1750.

The teeth of a file are made by a rapidly recip-rocating chisel that strikes successive blows to the file blank. The hardened chisel cuts into the soft blank, displacing and raising the steel in the desired tooth structure. The file is then tempered, cleaned and oiled to prevent rusting.

The hand file is a multi-purpose tool that can be used for smoothing, grinding, sharpening and material removal in a multitude of materials like wood, steel or plastic.

The file is available in various shapes and in various cuts or grades, such as coarse, second–cut and smooth. There is also the bastard-cut which is somewhere between the second–cut and the smooth, hence its name.

The four-in-hand is a unique file that is half-round in shape and has two rasp surfaces and two double-cut file surfaces.

Four-in-hand

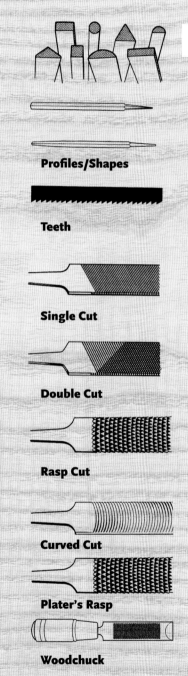

f

Profiles/Shapes

Teeth

Single Cut

Double Cut

Rasp Cut

Curved Cut

Plater's Rasp

Woodchuck

Filigree — See also Fretwork. Filigree, in general terms, is the intricate lace-like detailing in woodworking. However, the term is more commonly used in jewellery making or in fancy wrought iron work like that found in the French Quarter of New Orleans.

Filler — See also Grain Filling, Wood Filler. A synthetic paste material that fills the open pores in wood species such as oak, elm and others. Filler does as its name suggests; it fills in the hollows of open-grained wood and provides a smoother finish.

Filling — See Grain Filling.

Fillister Plane — See Hand Planes.

Finger — This is the part of the anatomy that woodworkers should make every effort to retain. Woodworkers can perform their art much more efficiently if they can count to five on hands that are firmly attached to their bodyies. **Use safety gear!**

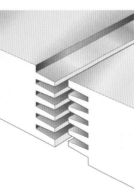

Finger Joint — The use of finger jointing can be an economic wood saver. For non-structural (horizontal) uses, finger–jointed wood makes use of normally unusable lengths of wood and joins them together. The finger joints provide a larger gluing area for higher strength. Finger joints may be found in mouldings that are paint grade. The finger joints may be made with a special router bit.

Finish — The final applications of protective and/or decorative materials to wood. The finish is usually brushed, sprayed or rubbed on.

FUN facts

A Penny Nail For Your Thoughts

The origin of the penny system for measuring nails is not without controversy. Some say the term goes back to the days of the fiddler Nero or even before. The designation *d* is an abbreviation of *denarius*, the ancient Roman equivalent of a penny. It was thought that much later the reference to pennyweight was the cost of 100 nails of a particular size. Thus, seven denarii would buy 100 2¼" nails. Even later and in England, that rule withstood the test of time. The denarius equivalent became the penny, but it still had the *d* designation. This is because it was the weight of an Anglo-Norman penny signified as dwt (pennyweight) and then simply abbreviated to *d*.

To further complicate things, another theory is that 1,000 four-penny nails weighed four pounds.

The penny system is still in effect in the U.S. but in Canada and England the inch system prevails. However, in the U.S. the penny system refers only to nails used for wood-to-wood situations. A roofing nail, for example, is measured by the inch.

Finishing Nail — (🏴 lost head nail, oval Nail) See also Nail.

Finishing Nail

The finishing nail is a wire nail with a small head and is designed to be used in areas where the nail head must be hidden. The finishing nail is thicker than a brad nail and is available in longer lengths. The length of a finishing nail is measured only on the shank and does not include the head. The diameter (gauge) of the finishing nail shank varies by its length.

The head of a finishing nail has a small indentation on the top to facilitate the use of a nailset to recess the top of the nail into a workpiece.

Size	Length	Gauge	Number/Lb.	Size	Length	Gauge	Number/Lb.
2d	1"	16.5	1,351	8d	2½"	12.5	189
3d	1¼"	25.5	807	9d	2¾"	12.5	172
4d	1½"	15	584	10d	3"	11.5	121
5d	1¾"	15	500	12d	3¼"	11.5	113
6d	2"	13	309	16d	3½"	11	90
7d	2¼"	13	238	20D	4"	10	62

Finishing Sander — See also Orbital Sander. An electrically or pneumatically powered flat surfaced sander that moves in a very small orbital pattern to remove small amounts of material. The finishing sander is used after rough sanding that removes surface wood fibers. The finishing sander is usually a machine with a larger flat sanding surface that utilizes one half of a sheet of sandpaper and has a speed of 10,000 orbits per minute (OPM). Other finishing sanders also have a flat sanding surface but are smaller in size and use a quarter of a sheet of sandpaper. These have speeds of 14,000 OPMs. There are other types as well, with their own designation, such as random orbital sanders.

Firmer Chisel — See Chisel, Firmer.

Firsts — This describes the best quality lumber. A similar term used is Firsts and Seconds (FAS) to describe the best available lumber.

Fish Glue — This is a specialized type of adhesive made from isinglass that is extracted from the belly of a sturgeon. Fish glue is used primarily in the building of pianos, and is used to cement leather and cloth to wood.

Fish Plates — See also ⊞ Gusset. These are braces that join wooden structural beams end-to-end. The fish plates are securely fastened through the use of lag or carriage bolts and nuts.

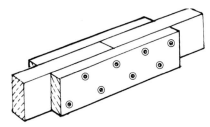

Flake Board — See also Particle Board. Flake board and similar sheet wood products, like particle board, all have one thing in common, and that is the conserving of forest prod-

ucts by utilizing waste wood chips and fast-growing wood species. They vary by the size of the particles, the compression and the alignment of the particles. Flake board is usually used as a substrate for veneers.

Flap Disc — An abrasive product of angled flaps of fabric-backed sandpaper that is cemented to a phenolic resin backing plate used to aggressively remove materials, such as in stripping the finish off wood or the removal of rust from metal. As the flap disc is used, it continuously exposes a fresh abrasive surface. The flap disc is attached to the arbor of a right angle or bench grinder.

f

Flap Wheel Sander — A wheel composed of abrasive strips mounted perpendicular to the hub. The flap wheel is designed to fit on a motor-driven arbour such as a bench grinder or even a drill press or portable drill. This tool is used for sanding mouldings and other irregular wood shapes. The flap wheel sander is also used for smoothing metal and for the removal of rust. As the flap wheel wears, it continuously exposes fresh abrasive. The flap wheel sander is available in a variety of grit sizes and several diameters from 1" and up to 8".

Flap Stay — See Lid Stay.

Flat Sawn — See Flat Cut.

Flexible Curve — A long, 24" or 36" rubber-coated flexible tool designed for making free hand curves. The flexible curve bends freely in a horizontal plane and lays flat. The tool is designed to draw the curves and then later cut them.

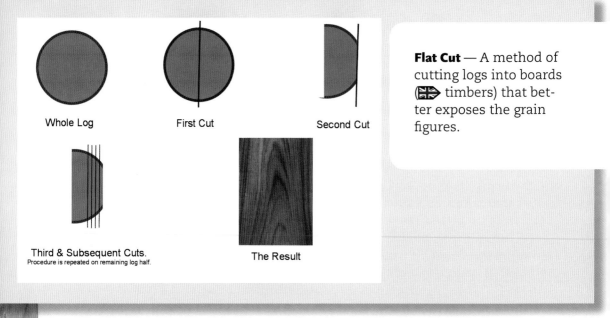

Whole Log   First Cut   Second Cut

Third & Subsequent Cuts.
Procedure is repeated on remaining log half.

The Result

Flat Cut — A method of cutting logs into boards (🇬🇧 timbers) that better exposes the grain figures.

Flex Shaft — This is an enclosed steel cable attached at one end to a motor and at the other end to a hand-piece. The motor is usually hung on a bracket close to the work place. The hand-piece contains a collet that holds any of a number of cutting, drilling, sanding or grinding tools (bits). The motor of the flex shaft generally has a foot pedal attached that controls its speed. This is an excellent tool for woodcarvers.

Flitch — The veneer leaves or sheets that are produced from one log and remain in the sequence in which they are cut. This allows the woodworker to easily bookmatch the veneers.

Flush — A term describing two surfaces that are level with each other.

Flush-Cut Saw — See also Offset Saw. The flush-cut saw is used for trimming off the tops of exposed dowels or other wood components that are to be trimmed flush with the surface of a workpiece.

Flute — A concave or convex shape in a moulding, pilaster or column.

Folding Rule — A ruler made of hardwood with brass joint fittings that folds into a compact size, usually 8"-12" in length. The folding rule is made in various lengths up to 8'. Some have a sliding portion that acts as a bar gauge for inside measuring. Since the invention of the tape measure, the folding rule is almost obsolete.

Foot — It's what you walk on, and there are twelve inches in one.

Fore Plane — See Plane.

Fork Chuck — Also known as a 🇬🇧 spur end, this is used in the head stock of a lathe to grasp the workpiece for working between centers when lathe turning.

Forstner Bit — See Drill Bits, Forstner.

Four-In-Hand — See Files

Frame — The interior support pieces for a cabinet that consist of solid wood or plywood members. The outer sides, bottoms and tops are fastened to the frame to form a finished cabinet.

Frame Clamp — See Clamps.

French Cleat — A way of fastening cabinets to a wall without having to screw the backs directly to the wall. The advantage is that the cabinets lay flush against the wall and are easily removable if required. This method does require advance planning as the back of the cabinet needs to be recessed.

Fork Chuck

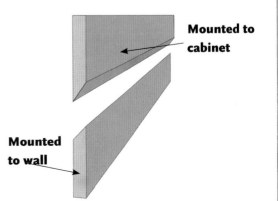

Mounted to cabinet

Mounted to wall

f

French Polish — Generally a term used to apply a high gloss finish to furniture and other wood products. It is not a specific product. French polishing is a method of applying and rubbing many layers or coats of shellac on the wood surface, with a durable oil being used in the final layer. The shellac and oil is applied with a pad, consisting of an outer layer of cheesecloth covering a cotton wad. French polishing is a very labor-intensive process and provides a deep, high-gloss finish. The finish, however, is not very durable. The process is still used but mostly by luthiers.

Fretsaw — See Coping Saw, Jigsaw, Scroll Saw.

Fretwork — Also called scrollwork, this is the intricate filigree that is hand cut with a fret saw or scroll saw.

Frog — See Hand Plane Anatomy.

Fuming — A process in which wood is made darker in color by the fumes of aqua ammonia. Furniture or wood is placed in an airtight tent or enclosure with an open bowl of aqua ammonia. The fumes emitted by the ammonia react with the natural tannin of the wood and cause it to change to a darker colour. Fuming was first introduced by Gustav Stickley because the process accentuates the medulary ray pattern in quarter-cut oak. It is generally rumoured that the process was discovered many years ago when some oak lumber was stored for some time in a barn. The urine from cows and horses caused the oak to change color.

G-Cramp — See Clamps, C.

Galvanize — This is the electrochemical bonding of zinc to steel or iron. The purpose of this is to prevent rust from forming on fasteners and other products when used outdoors.

Gang Nail — See Nail Plate Connector.

Garnet — A natural mineral with a red/brown appearance used as an abrasive grain.

Garnet Paper — See also Abrasives, Sandpaper. Garnet paper is sandpaper covered with garnet of various grit sizes. Garnet paper is used primarily for hand sanding as it is not as hard as some of the synthetic materials used in power sanding.

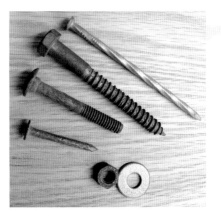

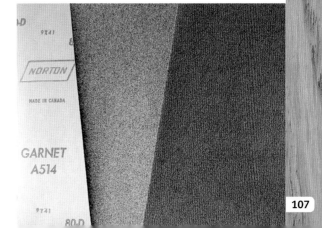

Gel Stain — This is an oil-based wood stain that has a thick consistency. Because of this consistency the stain will not run or drip. Gel stains do not cause lap marks, and they don't raise the wood grain. Gel stains provide twice the coverage of conventional liquid oil stains. They can be applied to non-porous materials and grained to provide a faux finish. The stain should be applied by brush or sponge and then wiped off with a dry cloth. Caution: Used cloths may spontaneously combust. Dry cloths by hanging outdoors.

FUN facts

Georgian Furniture

The Georgian period is divided into three eras: Early Georgian (1745 – 1780), Mid Georgian (1730 – 1750's) and Late Georgian (1750 – 1830). Designers who were prevalent in the Late Georgian period include Chippendale (1745 – 1780), Hepplewhite (1760 – 1790), Adam (1760 – 1792) and Sheraton (1790 – 1806). The importation of mahogany from Cuba and Honduras had a great influence on the designs. It was easier to carve than walnut and thus was responsible for the reappearance of delicate carvings in furniture. Thomas Chippendale designed lighter furniture using his cabriole leg designs. George Hepplewhite was best known for his chair back designs like shield, hoped heart and oval. Robert Adam brought simple, classical designs of the Greek and Roman styles to England. Thomas Sheraton preferred straight, simple lines to his furniture designs, and hand carving basically disappeared. He also liked mechanical components like a tambour door or folding desk.

Gent's Saw — See also Backsaw. Unlike regular back saws, the gent's saw has a round hardwood handle and is used primarily for cutting dovetails. The tooth set is slight, and the tooth count is high.

Gimbals — A contrivance with a ring or base on an axis that permits a tool to remain horizontal even when its support has been tipped. Gimbals are found in self-levelling tools like laser levels.

g

Gimlet — A screw-tipped tool for starting screw holes in wood or other materials. A gimlet is particularly useful for starting short screws in awkward situations. And, if you are finished woodworking for the day, a gin gimlet might be refreshing.

Girth — The diameter of a tree measured at 1.5 meters above the ground.

Glue — See also Adhesives. Although synonymous with the terms *cement* and *adhesive*, the term *glue*, in this writer's opinion, refers to products like Hide Glue and Fish Glue. *Adhesives* refers to synthetics like polyvinylacetate (PVA) and *cements* refers to products such as contact cement and ceramic tile cement.

Glue Blocks — Glue blocks are not used much any more, but they can add considerable strength to a frame. The glue block is generally triangular in shape and fits into the corner of a butt joint. Glue is added to the block and it is then screwed into the frame. The glue block also helps to keep the corners square.

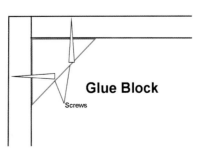

Glue Block

Screws

Glue Gun — This is not really a gun but a tool that heats glue sticks and extrudes the melted glue through various types of tips onto the workpieces that are to be glued together.

Glue Joint — Any wood joint held together with glue.

Glue Line — The sometimes visible line that appears when two (or more) boards are glued together.

Glue Line

Glue Laminated Timber — Timbers of great length, breadth and strength may be produced by gluing many timbers together. Finger joints are used to join the ends, and the joints are staggered as the plies are added. This very same process can be achieved for both cabinet work and major architectural construction.

Glue Sticks — Dowel-like rods of hardened adhesive that are used in a glue gun that melts the sticks and extrudes the hot liquid. Glue sticks are available in various lengths and diameters as well as glue types. Glue sticks (hot melt glue) are generally not considered effective for woodworking.

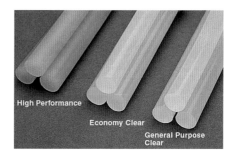

High Performance

Economy Clear

General Purpose Clear

Gorilla Glue — Gorilla Glue, because of its specific merits, deserves a separate listing. Gorilla Glue is a modified form of polyurethane glue that will glue just about anything to anything else. Gorilla Glue is waterproof when cured which means it may be used below the waterline. Gorilla Glue requires moisture as a catalyst to curing, so it is best to mist both glue surfaces lightly with water.

Glue — The Sticky On Stickum

Assuming that the project you are building will be used inside then products like Franklin Titebond, LePage's Carpenter's Glue or WeldBond are the right choices. These are synthetic (polymer) glues, yellowish in color and creamy in texture. They provide the best adhesion properties for most interior woodworking projects. They allow moderate set-up (10 minutes or so) times and can be handled after about six hours. Best though is 24 hrs until final curing. Squeeze-out should be wiped up immediately with a damp cloth. For projects that will be exposed to the weather, 'weather-proof' adhesives should be used. These will keep your project together through rain, sleet or snow but will fail if immersed in water for any length of time. These adhesives include Titebond ll, Titebond lll, WeldBond and LePage's Outdoor Wood Glue. In addition, polyurethane adhesives fall under the 'weather-proof' category. For use below the waterline there are waterproof adhesives such as most two-part epoxies, Gorilla Glue, Titebond lll and WeldBond.

Adhesive Types

Non-Permanent: Double-face Tape; Rubber Cement; Hot-Melt Glue (most); Spray Adhesives (some)

Permanent : These will have a shear strength in excess of 3,000 lbs, an open time of 3 – 20 minutes and clean up with water or mineral spirits.

    White Glue — Polyvinyl Acetate (PVA) – 3 – 5 min.- water clean-up
    WeldBond — Secret Formula – 3 – 5 min. – water clean-up
    Titebond II — weatherproof, PVA – 5 – 7 min. – water clean-up
    Yellow Glue — Aliphatic Resin (AR) – 5 – 7 min. – water clean-up
    Hide Glue (Liquid) — 10 – 15 min. – mineral spirits clean-up
    Contact Cement — Requires special solvent (hazardous) for clean-up.

Specialty Glues

    Liquid nails — Construction adhesive for installing wood panelling.
    Cyanoacrylate — Crazy Glue, bonds instantly, requires a perfect fit.
    Titebond Molding Glue — PVA – sets in 3 – 5 minutes, wider nail spacing.
    Hot-Melt Glue — For temporary wood fastening, usually used for crafts.

Gouge — A steel chisel-like tool with a concave blade used in lathe turning or in woodcarving. These gouges are usually made from high speed steel and must be kept very sharp to cut smoothly.

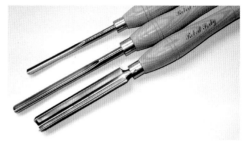

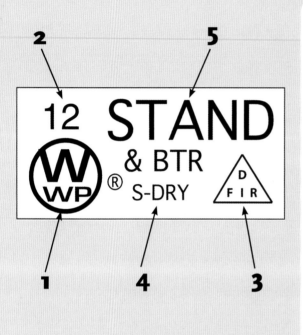

The Lumber Grade Stamp
A grade stamp shows: (1) the registered symbol of the certified agency; (2) the mill identification number; (3) the species or species group; (4) the seasoned condition; and (5) the grade name or number. In the illustration, this grade stamp states that the lumber is certified by the Western Wood Products Association, from Mill 12 (which can be found in the WWPA membership directory); is from a coniferous tree (also known as softwood – Spruce-Pine-Fir); was graded according to National Lumber Grades Authority rules; is kiln–dried and heat treated (19 % or less moisture content); and is of standard grade.

Grade — See also Grading. In woodworking terms, grade refers to the quality of both softwoods and hardwoods. Softwoods in Canada and in the U.S. require that the mill producing the lumber identify each board with a grade stamp.

Grading — A process by which wood is sorted or classified by either industry associations or governments to control and rate its quality. In softwood, the mill places a quality stamp on every board it produces.

Grain — a) The striated or lined patterns found on the surface of boards. b) A substance usually ground into granules and used for the removal of material as in abrasives.
c) A substance ground into granules and pressed under high pressure and heat into shapes for the purpose of producing sharpening stones or wheels.

Grain Filling — Some wood species, oak and mahogany for example, have very porous grains that require filling in order for the wood to have a smooth finish. This can be accomplished by rubbing the wood with an abrasive such as pumice mixed with linseed oil which levels and fills in these pores. A similar result may be achieved with the use of commercial grain fillers. These fillers are available in many colors to match the wood species that you are working with.

Greek Order — See Columns.

Green Wood — Freshly cut unseasoned lumber with free water remaining in the cells. Green wood usually has a moisture content above the fiber saturation point of 25 – 30%.

Grinding — This is , perhaps, the first step in sharpening tools. Through the use of a grinding wheel on a bench grinder, the woodworker removes flaws and nicks from chisels, gouges and irons prior to the finer honing of the blades.

CAMI Grade	FEPA P-Grade	Grit	Description	Average particle size in microns (inches)	Notes
		4 ½	COARSE	1842 (.07174)	
	P12			1815	
	P16			1324	
16		4		1320 (.05148)	Removing rust, old paint
30		2 ½		638 (.02488)	
	P30			642 (.02426)	
36		2		535 (.02087)	
	P36			538 (.02044)	
40		1 ½		428 (.01669)	
	P40			425 (.01601)	
50		1		351 (.01271)	
	P50			336 (.01271)	
60		½		268 (.01045)	
	P60			269 (.01014)	
	P80		MEDIUM	201 (.00768)	
80		0		192 (.00749)	Finishing rough lumber
	P100			162 (.00608)	
100		2/0		141 (.05500)	
	P120			125 (.00495)	
120		3/0		116 (.00452)	
	P150		FINE	100 (.00378)	
150		4/0		93 (.00363)	
180		5/0		78 (.00304)	Final grit prior to finish
	P180			82	
220		6/0	VERY FINE	66 (.00257)	
	P220			68 (.00254)	
	P240			58.5 (.00230)	
240		7/0		53.5 (.00209)	
	P280			52.2 (.00204)	
	P320			46.2 (.00180)	
280		8/0	EXTRA FINE	44 (.00172)	
320		9/0		36 (.00140)	
	P400			35.0 (.00137)	
	P500			30.2 (.00120)	
360				28.8 (.00112)	
	P600			25.8 (.00100)	
400		10/0		23.6 (.00092)	Final grit prior to finish
	P800			21.8 (.00085)	
500			SUPER FINE	19.7 (.00077)	
	P1000			18.3 (.00071)	
600				16.0 (.00062)	
	P1200			15.3 (.00060)	
	P1500			12.6	Higher grades, primarily for automotive work
800				12.2 (.00048)	
	P2000			10.3	
1000				9.2 (.00036)	For lapping/rubbing out finish (French Polishing)
	P2500			10.3	
1200				6.5 (.00026)	
1500				3.0	
2000				1.0	

Grit Size — See the chart on page 114. For many years there has been confusion for the woodworker when purchasing sandpaper. There are three different systems used to determine the grit. There is the Ought system, such as 4 Ought, written as 4/0 and equal to 150 grit. There is the Grit system as outlined in the chart at left. And there is the Descriptive system, a loosely structured system that simply describes the sandpaper as coarse, medium, fine, very fine, extra fine and super fine. Now, the P system is becoming the standard as it more accurately describes the grit sizes.

Groove — See also Dado. In Tongue and Groove, the groove is usually a rectangular recess in which the

Garnet Sandpaper under Microscope

FUN facts

It is said that the only True Grit was that possessed by the late John Wayne. However, the woodworker's true grit refers to the size of a grain of abrasive used in sandpaper, honing stones and grinding wheels.

There are two common standards for grading sandpaper: the Coated Abrasive Manufactureres Institute (CAMI) in North America and the Federation of European Producers of Abrasives (FEPA) in Europe and England. Worldwide, the FEPA system now seems to be the standard.

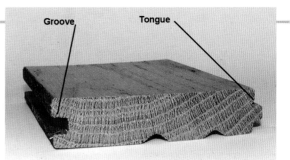

Groove　Tongue

tongue will fit. A groove may be also cut to allow a panel to fit into it or to accommodate a track for sliding doors.

Grout — A mortar-type substance that, when mixed with water, is applied into the joints of ceramic, slate, marble or terra–cotta tiles to seal them after installation. The grout is applied with a rubber float to ensure that the grout mix is totally embedded in the joints. A damp sponge is then used to smooth the grout in the joints. When dry, a damp sponge, moistened with a mix of vinegar and water, is used to remove the haze.

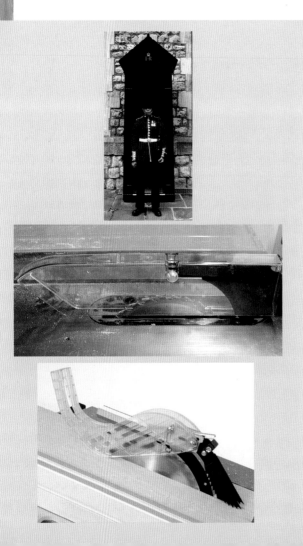

Guard — a) You may need one in your shop if it's in a high crime area. b) The guards that we are referring to, however, are not the armed sort but rather the power tool safety sort. Guards are put on power tools for the user's safety and are designed to keep the operator's body parts safe from injury. The table saw guard is an example of a safety guard, but its traditional poor design prompts many woodworkers to remove it. The traditional table saw blade often gets in the way and hinders visibility. Other power tools have more convenient guards. c) More recently, due to new safety standards, the table saw blade guard has finally shown improvements. Bosch has produced a split blade guard that allows the user to make cuts closer to the blade while still maintaining safety. The riving knife and anti-kickback pawls remain functional as well.

Growth Rings — See Annual Rings.

Guide Bushing — (Or Router Bushing) Guide bushings are used in conjunction with a router to follow a template such as those found on a dovetail jig which is used to make dovetail joints. The guide bushings, usually made of brass, fit on the router's base plate. The shank of the router bit fits into the opening.

g

Guide Bush — See Guide Bushing.

Gullet — The concave space between the teeth of a saw blade. The gullet is purposely spaced and sized for specific blade types. The purpose of the gullet is to both remove the sawdust and to cool the blade by reducing the friction.

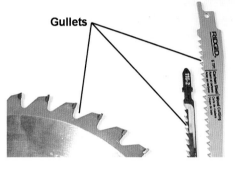

Gullets

Gum — Random spots or lines, usually black, sometimes found in black cherry boards or veneer. The gum is a natural secretion in some wood species.

Gusset — A wood (or metal) plate attached to both ends of a joint to reinforce it.

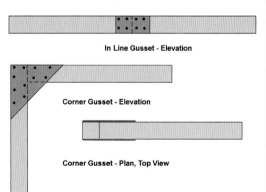

In Line Gusset - Elevation

Corner Gusset - Elevation

Corner Gusset - Plan, Top View

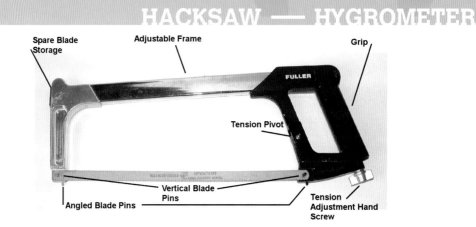

Spare Blade Storage

Adjustable Frame

Grip

FULLER

Tension Pivot

Vertical Blade Pins

Angled Blade Pins

Tension Adjustment Hand Screw

Hacksaw — A tool used for cutting metals. It is primarily a plumber's tool but certainly is an essential woodworker's tool as well. The hacksaw holds a fine-toothed, hardened steel blade under tension. Most hacksaw frames allow the user to install the blade for perpendicular cutting, and some have the option of setting the blade at a 45° angle for cutting in close quarters. Some frames are adjustable to accommodate both 10" and 12" long blades.

HACKSAW BLADES

Hacksaw Blades — a) Hacksaw blades are for use in a specially designed hacksaw frame (see below left) and are designed for cutting through metal, but they may also be used to cut plastics and even wood. These blades are generally available in 10" and 12" lengths and have tooth counts of 14, 18, 24 and 32 teeth per inch (tpi). The higher tpi blades are used for cutting sheet metal. Hacksaw blades are generally made from high speed steel (HSS), which is quite brittle but has a long life. Bi-metal blades are also available that have an M2 HSS strip welded to a more flexible blade. Silicon steel or a flexible HSS blade can also be used. These are less prone to breakage but do not last as long. b) The hacksaw blade is the basic tool of the incarcerated used to cut through the restraining bars in prison. The hacksaw blade is traditionally buried in a birthday cake and sent to the prisoner by friends or family. Fortunately, prison guards have been aware of this ploy for many years.

Bi-Metal M2 High Speed Steel

All Hard M2 High Speed Steel

Bi-Metal High Speed Steel

All Hard High Speed Steel

Flexible High Speed Steel

Flexible Silicon Steel

Half-Lap Joint — See Joints, Lap Joint.

Hammers — "When the only tool you own is a hammer, you tend to treat everything like a nail"
                                    — Anonymous.

I think it's safe to assume that one of the first tools that humans used was a hammer. Since those prehistoric days the lowly hammer has seen a multitude of changes, but two things have remained constant. The hammer is made of a head and a handle. Following is a just a small sampling of the hammer types and styles available today.

Ball Pein — (🇬🇧 Peen) Used primarily for metal work, the ball pein hammer is available in several weights.

Brick Layer's — This one has a square head and a chisel. The chisel is used to split bricks and the head is used for tapping the brick into position.

California Framing — A weighty hammer with a curved handle for additional leverage. This one has straight claws as is used for construction, not demolition. The face of the head is usually waffled for better nail contact.

Claw — Probably the most common form of hammer, this has a curved claw for removing nails. The claw hammer is available in various weights and handle types.

Dead Blow — This one-piece hammer is partially filled with lead shot. When striking, the lead shot prevents any bounce back.

Electrician's — This is similar to the claw hammer but with a straighter claw for removing staples and boxes.

Rawhide — This one is used for fine metal work where surface damage must be prevented.

Ripping — this is used more for demolition than construction and has nearly straight claws for prying.

Riveting — Used, as the name implies, for fastening rivets in leather or metal.

Rubber — Also called a mallet, the rubber hammer is used with force but prevents damage.

Sledge — This is the heaviest of the hammers and has a long handle to put heft behind the swing.

Soft Face — This hammer is used to help prevent damage or marring of surfaces.

Tack — Used mostly by upholsterers, the tack hammer has a small driving head and a magnetic starting head.

h

Hammer Drill — This is an electric or cordless power drill that is used for making holes in concrete and other hard surfaces. The drill usually has a two- or three-position switch that allows the user to choose between conventionally drilling into soft materials such as wood, using the tool as a screwdriver, or drilling into hardened cement or cinder block. It uses a special carbide-tipped drill bit. The drill rotates the bit while simultaneously vibrating (or hammering) the bit, much like a small scale pneumatic jack hammer.

Hand Block — (🏴󠁧󠁢󠁥󠁮󠁧󠁿 or Sanding Block) A resilient rubber or rubber-faced block that is used wrapped in sandpaper for flat surface hand sanding. These are either user-built or purchased. There are several manufacturers that produce these and they accept cut sheets of sandpaper. Some abrasive producers, like Sia, 3M and Norton, produce softer foam blocks that are pre-coated with abrasive. The softer foam blocks have the advantage of allowing the user to sand flat surfaces as well as curves.

FUN facts

HAMMERS

The hammer is probably one of the first tools used by humans, and to this day the hammer is still undergoing improvements. The original hammer was probably a handheld rock and then, like now, the user's thumbs were inadvertent targets.

Woodworkers of all disciplines have their favorite hammer and most will swear that it improves with age. I have met carpenters with hammers that are on their third or fourth hickory handle. The design of the hammer itself has improved as well. Most of the newer hammers contain shock blocks that prevent, or at least lessen, the shock of a hammer blow from resonating up the user's arm.

With the proliferation of compressed air-powered nailing tools, the common hammer is sadly being replaced on the job, but the hammer will always find a place on the woodworker's workbench.

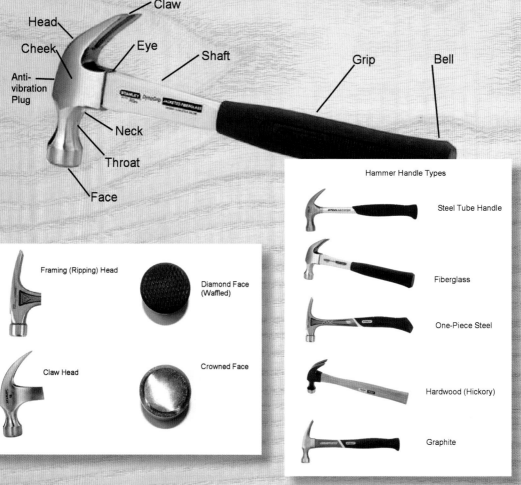

Claw

Head

Cheek

Eye

Shaft

Grip

Bell

Anti-vibration Plug

Neck

Throat

Face

Hammer Handle Types

Steel Tube Handle

Fiberglass

One-Piece Steel

Hardwood (Hickory)

Graphite

Framing (Ripping) Head

Diamond Face (Waffled)

Claw Head

Crowned Face

One company has pre-loaded sanding blocks with narrow sanding sheets in various grits. As one is worn out, the user simply pulls another out of the block.

Hand Hewn Timber — See Hewn Timbers.

Hand Plane — See Plane, Bench Plane.

Handrail — a) A safety feature usually found on stairways or walking ramps to assist the individual in ascending or descending. The handrail may be made from shaped wood or other materials. The hand rail is positioned between 34" and 38" vertically above the stair tread, ramp or floor. b) The upper horizontal portion of a railing.

Hand Sanding — Smoothing the surface of wood, or other material, with sandpaper grasped in the hand or in a hand block.

Hand Saw — See Saw, Hand.

Hand Tools — This term refers to almost any woodworking tool that is used manually, without motors of any kind.

Hardboard — A type of manufactured board, similar to particle board but more compressed, and with a much smoother face surface. Hardboard falls under the term *sheet goods* and is available in 4' x 8' sheets or larger. A common brand of hardboard is Masonite. A typical form of hardboard is pegboard, a perforated form of the material.

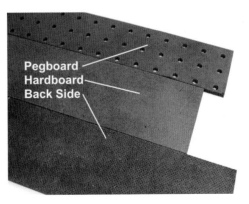

Pegboard
Hardboard
Back Side

Hardware — A general term used to describe material that is used to assemble woodworking projects. Hardware includes fasteners such as nails, screws, rivets and other forms like hinges, hasps, locks, handles and more.

Hardware Store — A term used before the advent of home improvement big box stores. The hardware store was a small neighbourhood business that had kegs filled with nails, bins filled with screws, sawdust on the floor and a weigh scale on the counter. The aroma that filled the store was a blend of putty, linseed oil and a hint of kerosene. The proprietor knew what you were building and always had free advice on how to do it.

Hardwood — Hardwood generally comes from broad leaf deciduous trees, but there are exceptions to this rule. These exceptions might include tropical angiosperm trees. Hardwood is generally denser than the softwood tree species. However, as in nature, nothing is written in stone. There are crossovers such as balsa wood, which is considered a hardwood.

 **Haunch** — (or relish or haunchion) In a mortise–and–tenon joint, the haunch is an extension or projection to a tenon that helps prevent twisting. The haunch also caps the end of any groove run through the end of the stile (a frequent occurance in power joinery).

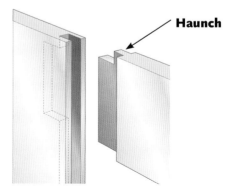

Haunch

Haunchion — See Haunch.

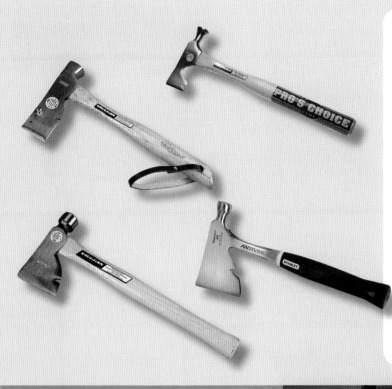

Hatchet — See also Axe. The term *hatchet* is from the French word *hache*, which means axe, and is more directly from the French *hachette* meaning small axe. The hatchet is smaller than an axe and generally weighs from three to five pounds. The hatchet also has a single blade and a hammer head. There are a number of hatchet styles designed for various and specific uses.

Head Stock — The portion of a lathe that turns the workpiece. The headstock may include a direct-drive motor or be powered through a series of drive belts. The workpiece is held in place with either a face plate or a spur.

Heartwood — This is the darker area of a section of a tree. The heartwood is generally considered to be dead but resistant to decay. As a tree grows, the inner portion of the sapwood begins to grow outward, becomes inactive and finally ceases to function, and the cells die off. Although the term would suggest that this area is vital to the life of the tree, the term *heartwood* only means that the wood forms the center of the tree.

Heat Gun — The heat gun is not unlike a lady's hair dryer in that it

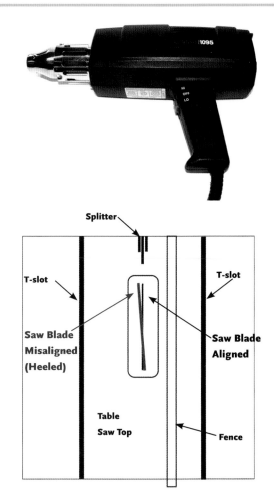

blows hot air. However, that's where it ends. The heat gun blows very hot air that may be used to hasten the curing of some epoxy adhesives, to bend plexiglass sheets, to tighten some heat shrink materials and more. Most heat guns are between 1,000 and 1,200 watts, and some have more than one heat setting.

Heeling — A potentially dangerous situation when the saw blade of a table saw is misaligned. Heeling is so called because the heel (the back part) of the spinning blade is not aligned with the T–slots and the saw fence. This misalignment causes the board that is being cut to get caught by the rear of the blade and will flip the board up or kick it back into the operator. Both the leading and trailing edges of the saw blade must be perfectly parallel with the T–slots and the rip fence.

Hepplewhite — See Georgian Furniture.

Herringbone — A method of applying bookmatched veneer and flooring in a mirror image with the grain patterns pointing upwards and downwards in a herringbone pattern.

Hewn Timbers — These are beams and other large timbers that have been cut from logs and shaped by an adze, draw knife or other handheld shaping tool. Hewn timbers are used in authentic timber construction.

Hex Bits — See also Screwdriver. Hex bits are screwdriver bits or tips that fit into a socket that fits into either a powered or manual screwdriver handle. The hex bits are available in various lengths and tip types, like

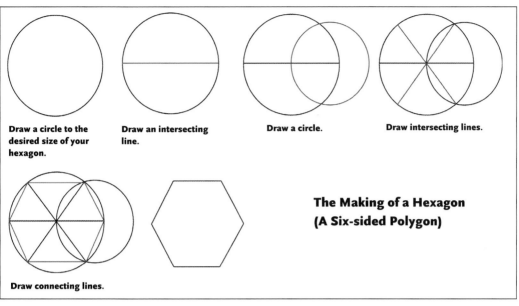

Draw a circle to the desired size of your hexagon.

Draw an intersecting line.

Draw a circle.

Draw intersecting lines.

Draw connecting lines.

**The Making of a Hexagon
(A Six-sided Polygon)**

flat, Phillips, Robertson (square), torx and more.

Hexagon — A six-sided polygon with 60° angles.

Hide Glue — This is a traditional furniture maker's glue that is long–lasting and very strong. It is available commercially in powder or flake form and is then mixed with water and heated. The glue is applied warm. Hide glue is also available in a liquid, pre-mixed form for more convenience and has similar characteristics as the traditional form. Hide glue is derived from collagen, a protein constituent of hide materials, tissues and bone.

Highboy — A tall chest of drawers in two levels, the upper being mounted on a lowboy. The New England styles were quite plain, but Thomas Affleck, a Philadelphia cabinetmaker (1740 – 1795), adapted many classical design features to his designs.

Hinges

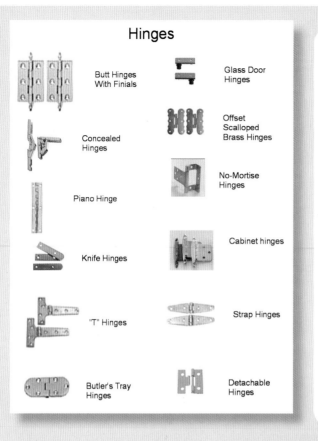

Butt Hinges With Finials

Concealed Hinges

Piano Hinge

Knife Hinges

"T" Hinges

Butler's Tray Hinges

Glass Door Hinges

Offset Scalloped Brass Hinges

No-Mortise Hinges

Cabinet hinges

Strap Hinges

Detachable Hinges

Hinge — Hinges are usually sold in pairs and are used to allow doors to open and close. The common butt hinge is a pivot consisting of a pin and two flaps. The pivot portion, where the pin is located, is called the knuckle. Butt hinges, and most other pin hinges, are measured by the height (when installed) and the overall width. For example, a 6"x6" hinge will have flaps that are 6" high and two flaps of 3" each. There are literally thousands of types of hinges for almost any type of door or lid.

Hold–Downs — (or Holdfasts) Hold–downs are a form of clamp used on a workbench. The hold–down is mounted onto a post that is inserted into a hole in a workbench and is designed to hold a workpiece firmly on the bench.

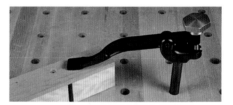

Hold-Down Foot — A combination blade guard and clamp installed on a scroll saw that maintains the workpiece flat on the saw table and prevents it from rising on the saw blade's upstroke.

Hole Saw — The hole saw is more like a large drill bit used for drilling large but relatively shallow holes. The hole saw is mounted in a mandrel, and the shaft of the mandrel is installed into the chuck of either a portable drill or a drill press. A pilot

bit keeps the hole saw running true. The sizes of a hole saw range from as small as ¾" up to 6".

Hollow Chisel — The hollow chisel forms the edge-cutting tool of an electric mortising machine. The chisel is square and hollow to accommodate a revolving auger or drill bit. The chisel has four very sharp edges that cut the sides that are drilled by the auger. The chisels have escapements on the sides to allow sawdust to escape. The hollow chisels are available in various sizes.

h

Hollow Ground — A knife, plane iron or chisel blade that has been ground with a concave bevel. This method of sharpening creates a thin and very sharp edge. Hollow grinding is achieved with a powered grinding wheel.

Honing — or Stropping. See also Sharpening. Honing is the last step in sharpening chisels, knives, plane irons and other flat blades. Sharpening shapes the edge but generally leaves a burr on it. The honing or stropping is done by hand with very fine (400 – 1200 grit) abrasives, rubbing compound, glass or a leather strop. The blade edge is rubbed to give it a finer edge at a slightly steeper angle.

Honing Oil — A natural, highly refined light oil that is added to oil stones and that facilitates faster and easier sharpening of blades.

Hook and Loop — An attachment system for abrasive discs with a backing of small fabric loops that attach themselves to a back-up pad with small hooks. This allows for a

quicker and more convenient way of attaching sanding discs to power sanders.

Hook of Teeth — or rake. This is the angle of attack that the tooth cuts into the material. If you place a straightedge though the center of a blade up to a tooth you will see this angle. Angles range from 20° to negative 7°. Solid wood is best cut with teeth with a positive hook, while melamine, laminates, aluminum and plastic should be cut with a negative hook. Also, sliding compound saws should be equipped with a negative tooth blade because the action of this saw is different from that of a table saw.

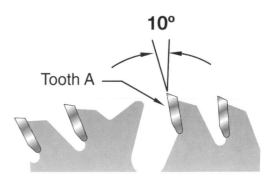

Horizontal — (hor-i-zaunt-ahl) See also Level. The true meaning of horizontal means level with the horizon, ninety-degrees to the vertical, true and flat. This line is horizontal if you are holding the page vertically.

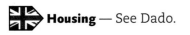

Hot Melt Glue — See also Glue Gun, Glue Sticks. The thermoplastic glue that is extruded from a glue gun.

Housing — See Dado.

HSS — This is the abbreviation for high speed steel, the material generally now used in the manufacture of woodworking saw blades, router bits and other machine-run cutting tools. Previously, carbon steel was used, but it would lose its temper due to excessive heat. HSS is an equally hard material, but it cuts faster (thus the name), stays cooler and is more resistant to high heat. High carbon steel is still the material of choice for chisels and plane irons.

Hydrogen Peroxide — A chemical used for bleaching wood. The pure peroxide is diluted with two-parts of water.

Hygrometer — See also Moisture Meter. A meter that measures the relative amount of moisture in the air or, if modified, the amount of moisture in wood.

h

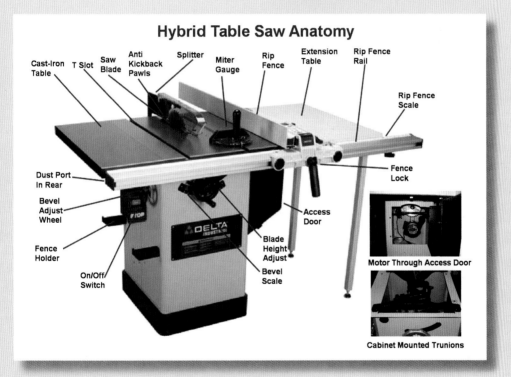

Hybrid Table Saw Anatomy

Cast-Iron Table — T Slot — Saw Blade — Anti Kickback Pawls — Splitter — Miter Gauge — Rip Fence — Extension Table — Rip Fence Rail

Rip Fence Scale

Dust Port In Rear

Bevel Adjust Wheel

Fence Holder

On/Off Switch

Access Door

Blade Height Adjust

Bevel Scale

Fence Lock

Motor Through Access Door

Cabinet Mounted Trunions

Hybrid — The term *hybrid* in woodworking refers to a type of table saw that is a combination of a cabinet saw and a contractor's saw. Typically the contractor's saw has a motor hanging out the back, a sheet steel open base and light-weight trunions mounted under the table. The hybrid looks more like a cabinet saw and has a fully enclosed cabinet. The trunions in most are mounted on the cabinet, which makes alignment easier. The motor is mounted inside the cabinet. The motor is a totally enclosed fan cooled (TEFC) type and sawdust is channelled to a standard dust port.

Idler Wheels

Idler Pulley

Idler — This is the non-powered wheel or roller on a belt sander that tracks and/or tensions the sanding belt. An idler pulley wheel may also be found on some multi-speed drill presses.

Imbrication — (im-brih-kay-shun) The term used to describe the carving of a wood surface, or the casting in metal, to represent fish scales. This form of decoration was used on chairs and tables in the early eighteenth century.

Inch — There are 12 of these in a foot and 36 of them in a yard. To see more, check out the Conversion Tables at the back of the book.

 **Incising** — (in-size-ing) The process of carving an object or pattern into a wood surface rather than making the pattern protrude with the background recessed. With incised carving only the outline of the design pattern is carved into the wood surface.

India® — A registered trademark by Norton for an aluminum oxide sharpening stone used to put a keen edge on blades.

i

Induction Motor — These electric motors are found in stationary tools such as table saws and drill presses. They are quiet and reliable but quite large, expensive and run at low speeds.

INFEED

Infeed — The area of a stationary power tool (usually a table such as the front surface of a thickness planer, jointer or table saw) where the workpiece is fed toward the cutting action.

Infeed Stand — An adjustable roller stand that, when positioned in front of your table saw or other stationary tool, helps to keep your longer work-pieces at the same level as the tool.

In the case of a thickness planer the infeed stand will help to prevent snipe. The stand is height–adjustable for use with most stationary power tools.

Inlays — See also Marquetry. Inlays are usually intricate borders made from thin veneers glued to a thin backing and then glued into a like-sized recess cut into the workpiece. Inlays are found on fine classical furniture and musical instruments.

Ionic — (eye-on-ick) The second order of Greek architecture.
The name derives from Ionia in Greece. Key: 1, entablature. 2, column. 3, cornice. 4, frieze. 5, architrave or epistyle. 6, capital (abacus and volutes). 7, shaft. 8, base. 9, stylobate. 10, stereobate.

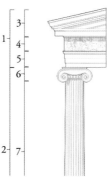

Intarsia — (in-tar-zia) The origin of intarsia dates back to Italy around the fourteenth century. Intarsia is an art form of carving where each individual carved piece is shaped to fit tightly into another. Different types of wood or other materials are used to add color to the finished form. Intarsia may be an abstract form, a landscape scene or even whimsical objects. The finished pattern is adhered to a solid background.

Iron — See also Bench Plane Anatomy. The iron is the cutting part of a bench plane, the blade.

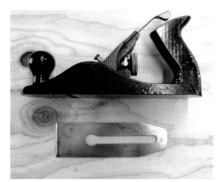

Jab Saw — See Keyhole Saw.

Jack Plane — See Planes.

FUN facts

Jacobean Furniture
Both King James I (1603 – 1625) and King Charles I (1625 – 1649) reigned through the era that produced a furniture style that would later be called Jacobean (jack-o-bee-an). This was another phase of Elizabethan style of the renaissance design. The Jacobean design heavily influenced the style of furniture produced by early American settlers in the northeastern U.S.

Jacobs Chuck — (jay-kubs) The brand (named for the inventor) of what is now a standard chuck used in corded or cordless drills, drill presses, lathe heads and tail stocks. The interior three jaws are centered and are opened and closed by rotating the outer collar. As the jaws close, they tighten on and hold the drill bit in place. The older models use a key to open or tighten the chuck, but now there are keyless chucks that are mostly found on portable drills.

Jamb — The vertical side member of a door frame. The residential doorjamb used to be a one-piece L-shaped structural member, but nowadays, the jamb is flat with a narrow, rectangular door stop. In cabinetry the jamb may still be the L type.

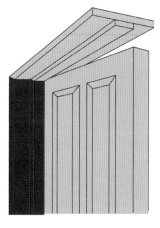

Japanese Nail Set — See also Nail Set. This is a multi-purpose tool for setting (sinking below the surface of the wood) the head of a nail. In addition to being a longer-than-usual (6") nail set, the short end can be used for setting nails in tight places. It can also be used as a small tack hammer or even as a small anvil.

Jig — a) A lively step dance such as that performed in Ireland, Newfoundland and/or Cape Breton Island, Nova Scotia.
b) A tool that is makes the woodworking procedure easier and quicker. For example, a dovetail jig allows you to cut dovetails with a router rather than with hand tools (a saw and chisel). Jigs may be home shop made like these angle-setting jigs.

Joiner — See Jointer.

Jigsaw Anatomy

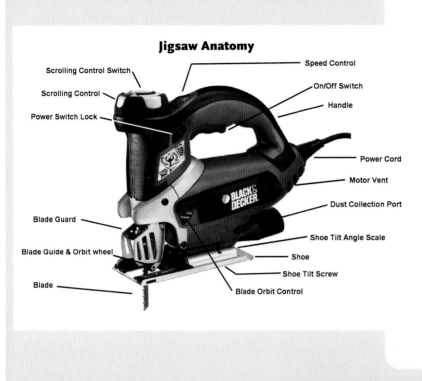

- Scrolling Control Switch
- Scrolling Control
- Power Switch Lock
- Blade Guard
- Blade Guide & Orbit wheel
- Blade
- Speed Control
- On/Off Switch
- Handle
- Power Cord
- Motor Vent
- Dust Collection Port
- Shoe Tilt Angle Scale
- Shoe
- Shoe Tilt Screw
- Blade Orbit Control

Jigsaw — The jigsaw is a tool used primarily to cut curved patterns in thin (1½") wood materials. The jigsaw may be a corded, electrically-powered tool or a battery-operated cordless tool. The jigsaw may also be used to cut metal and plastics using the appropriate removable blades. Some jigsaws are equipped with a free-turning scrolling feature that allows the user to cut tight curves with very narrow blades. See Blades, Jigsaw.

Joint — There are several definitions for joint. a) A residence for ne'er-do-wells. b) A knee like the artificial one that keeps me mobile. c) A sleazy bar. More importantly, and more relevant to this Woodworking Encyclopedia, it means the place at which two or more pieces of wood are joined.

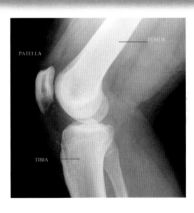

Jointer Knives — Jointer Knives are HSS (High Speed Steel), single– or double-edged blades that are 6" or longer to suit a particular make of jointer. The knives are usually about 1" – 1½" in width. Depending on the make of the jointer, the knives may be installed on the cutter head with a magnetic knife setting Jig that holds the knives parallel to the outfeed table. Some may have register notches that are automatically parallel.

Some Common Forms of Joinery

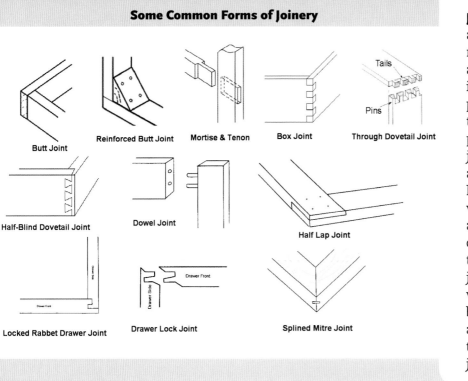

Butt Joint

Reinforced Butt Joint

Mortise & Tenon

Box Joint

Tails

Pins

Through Dovetail Joint

Half-Blind Dovetail Joint

Dowel Joint

Half Lap Joint

Locked Rabbet Drawer Joint

Drawer Lock Joint

Splined Mitre Joint

Joinery — The art (and it is most definitely an art) of joining two or more pieces of wood that may be permanently joined, removable and/or hinged. In woodworking there are hundreds of recognized types of wood joints, starting with the very basic butt joint and on through to a dovetail joint.

Jointer Plane — See Plane.

Joist — This is an architectural structural wood component that, when used in a residential (or commercial) building, goes from wall–to–wall to support a floor or ceiling. Joists, due to their limited strength, require additional support in longer spans. Joists are usually milled to 2" (nominal) thicknesses and may be 6", 8", 10" or 12" wide. Newer forms of joists utilize oriented strand board (OSB) bonded between a pair of 2x4's, called engineered I joists.

Joyned — Should you happen to be a really old or reincarnated archaic woodworker, then you certainly know that this is how they spelled *joined* in olde England.

Jointer Anatomy

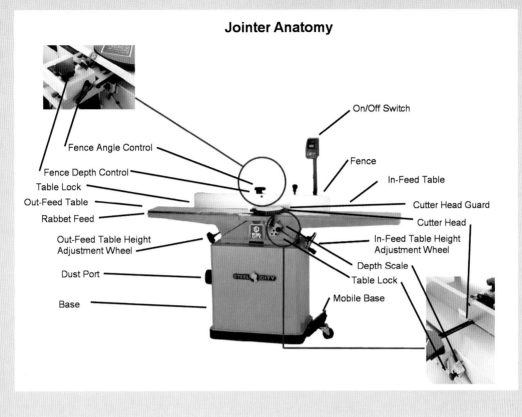

On/Off Switch

Fence Angle Control

Fence Depth Control

Table Lock

Out-Feed Table

Rabbet Feed

Out-Feed Table Height
Adjustment Wheel

Dust Port

Base

Fence

In-Feed Table

Cutter Head Guard

Cutter Head

In-Feed Table Height
Adjustment Wheel

Depth Scale

Table Lock

Mobile Base

Jointer — The jointer, as its name implies, is a tool that prepares workpieces for joining. The two surfaces to be joined should, in most instances, be perfectly flat. The jointer is an electric motor–driven rotating head that contains two or more sharp blades. These rotating blades shave the bottom surface of the workpiece to make it flat and even across its full length and width. The workpiece is fed on an infeed table that is fractionally lower than the outfeed table so that the workpiece remains parallel to the table surfaces due to the removal of wood. Another feature of a jointer is its ability to cut rabbets. See your jointer operation manual for instructions on how to perform this task.

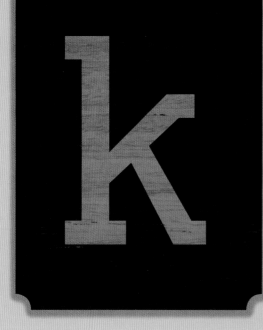

KD Furniture — The KD is an acronym and stands for knocked down. See also KD Furniture Hardware. This form of furniture is purchased and/or shipped unassembled. The advantage of making KD furniture is that it can be easily shipped in flat cartons. The purchaser assembles the furniture with the supplied tools and hardware. Probably the best known manufacturer of KD furniture is the Swedish company, Ikea. Usually only a screwdriver or Allen wrench are required to put the pieces together.

KD Hardware — Ikea, along with many other manufacturers, developed specific hardware components designed for KD (knocked down) furniture. These components are used to simplify the assembly (and disas-

sembly) of KD furniture, requiring no knowledge of furniture construction.

Kerf — It's very difficult to photograph a kerf as it is the space produced by the removal of the wood by any saw blade, powered or by hand.

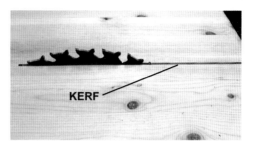

Kerfing — See also Bending, Steam Bending. This is the method of bending boards by crosscutting a series of cuts partway through a board. The kerfs or saw cuts are made across the grain of the board. The depth and spacing of the kerfing is determined by the radius of the desired bend, the wood thickness and the type of wood being used. Kerfing is most commonly performed by luthiers in guitar making.

Keyed Tenon — The keyed tenon is used primarily in the construction of tables to keep the table stretcher tight against the table legs.

Keyhole — a) In slapstick comedy of the 1930's and 1940's, the keyhole was used as a peephole to peek into the bedroom of a starlet. However, in woodworking the keyhole is used in furniture cabinetry restoration or duplication and is backed with a suitable lock. b) The keyhole, turned upside down, is used as a receptor for hooks or screws for mounting pictures and frames to walls. The keyhole is made today with a keyhole router bit.

Keyhole Router Bit — The keyhole router bit is used to make keyholes in cabinetry or to hang or secure workpieces or even tools. The router bit is shaped to penetrate the workpiece and then move laterally with a smaller diameter cutter.

k

Keyhole Saw — Also known as a 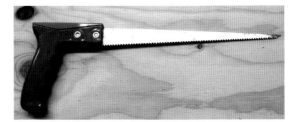 Pad Saw, Alligator Saw, Jab Saw or Drywall Saw. The keyhole saw has a fairly thick, stiff, 8" – 10" long blade and is tapered to a sharp point for ease of penetration into thin, relatively soft materials. There are two types of keyhole saw: one with a fixed blade and one with a folding or retractable blade. The keyhole saw is used in rough work and should not be used for delicate work, or to cut out an actual keyhole. The tool is misnamed. In olden days the cabinetmaker would use a drill to start and then cut the keyhole shape with a fret saw.

Kickback — An illegal form of remuneration (also known as payola), but in woodworking the term refers to a dangerous situation in which part or all of a workpiece is accidentally caught by a spinning blade or bit which violently kicks it back at the tool operator. Today, circular saw blades and router bits are made to prevent kickbacks from happening. When cutting on a table saw the riving knife or splitter (at right) also helps to prevent kickback. I have seen a kicked back board penetrate a double layer of drywall.

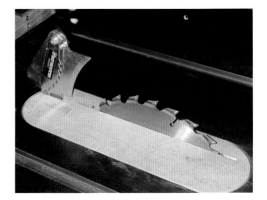

Kiln — An oven used to dry freshly cut or green lumber, either hardwood or softwood. The commercial kiln is a large enclosed structure that may contain many thousands of board feet. The heat evaporates the moisture in the fresh cut wood to bring the moisture content (MC), to an acceptable industry level.

Kiln Drying — When trees are milled into boards (lumber) the freshly cut material is extremely wet from the tree fluids (sap). The wet (green) boards have to dry at a controlled rate to prevent rapid shrinking and consequent warping. The boards are therefore placed in an oven (kiln) to quickly but controllably dry the wood to a workable moisture content, usually 14%. The boards are stickered to allow air circulation for even drying.

Knee Brace — (nee) a) Knee braces are used to ease the pain of injured knees. b) Or, in keeping with the theme of this tome, the knee brace is a diagonal support that reinforces a vertical post and a horizontal beam as found in post–and–beam home construction.

k

Knee Joint — (nee) I will refrain from using the human anatomy as an example, but in truth, the wood knee joint acts in a similar fashion. The knee joint is a modified mortise–and–tenon joint designed to move in a similar way to that of a hinge.

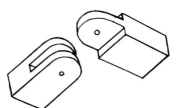

Knee Pads — (nee) These are used to help prevent the wear of knee joints. They are particularly useful when working on the lowermost parts of a cabinet. The knee pads are cushioned for comfort.

Knife — (nyfe) See also Carving Knives. Knives are the sharp blades used in jointers and thickness planers. These may be single– or double–edged and are generally made from high speed steel. However, more expensive knives are made from tungsten carbide or have carbide edges. These retain their keen edge for longer periods of use.

Knife Setting Jig — (nyfe) This jig is used to assist the woodworker in installing new or re-sharpened knives in jointers and planers. The knife setting jig (or tool) utilizes magnets to maintain the parallel position of jointer or thickness planer knives upon replacement installation. Most late model jointers and planers use indexed or slotted knives that are self-leveling.

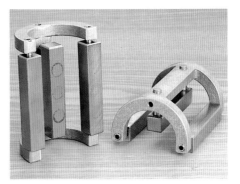

Knock Down Furniture — (nock) See KD Furniture.

Knot — (not) See also Sound Knot. This is a round or oval mark generally found in softwood. It is where a branch of the tree extended from the trunk. When the tree is milled into boards the branch is shown in this section. Live knots and are solid within the board and may be desirable in some cabinetry. Should the branch be cut off the tree long before the tree has been felled, it will produce a dead knot. This may show up as a loose knot and will fall out easily.

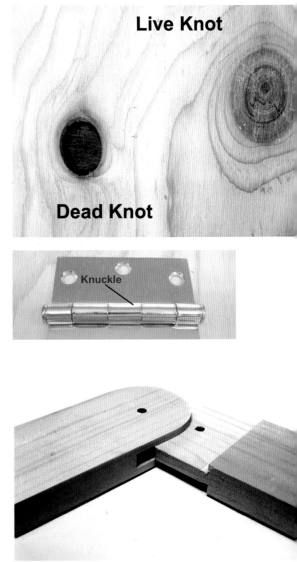

Live Knot

Dead Knot

Knuckle — (nuckle) The raised pivoting portion of a hinge through which the pin is inserted.

Knuckle

Knuckle Joint — (nuckle) A wooden variant of the joint shown above that may be partially made on most dovetail jigs. A single can also be created as shown at right. A knuckle joint has a hinge motion and is designed to be used as a cover or lid for what are known as hinged boxes.

1

Lac — (lahk) The lac is an insect found in Eastern Europe and Asia. The secretions of the lac are used to make traditional lacquer and shellac.

Lacewood — Also know as London Plane. When quartersawn, lacewood has very clear rays with a distinctive lace-like pattern. Lacewood is used in quality furniture as inlay.

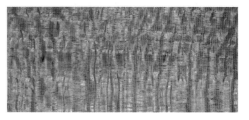

Lacquer — (lack-er) Today's lacquer is a commercial cellulose product that is generally a clear liquid that is sprayed on. Lacquer is a final finish in woodworking that is also referred to as a clear coat. It is applied in several built-up coats with fine sanding between each one, and is available in aerosol spray cans or as a brush-

on product. Lacquer is a fast–drying finish so several coats may be applied to your workpiece during a day's work. The fumes derived from spraying the product are highly toxic and proper precautions and safety measures should be adhered to.

 **Lacquer Thinner** — (lack-er) A solvent made to dissolve or thin lacquer. Lacquer thinner is also excellent in removing sticky-back labels from products like those UPC bar codes that they seem to stick on areas and cover up just where you want to read.

Lacquer Stick — See Burn-in Stick.

Ladder Back — This term refers to a style of chair back. The ladder-back chair was fashionable in the seventeenth century and may be found in some Sheraton furniture. The ladder–back chair style is still in use today. This style of chair has several, similar horizontal rails between the two back supports.

Laminate — (lam-in-aht) a) A term generally referring to plastic laminate, a hard plastic–coated material made in built-up layers. The most common names are Formica, Wilsonart and Pionite. Plastic laminates are used as durable countertops and are impervious to most liquid spills. Laminate, when heated, may be formed to include a back splash and a soft rounded leading edge. Laminate is available in thousands of patterns and textures and may replicate wood, stone, slate or marble.
b) Plywood is also a form of laminate in that it is made up of several layers of veneer. The grain of each layer is alternated in direction, therefore

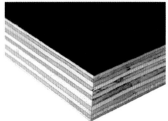

there are always an odd number of plies in a finished sheet of plywood.

Laminating — (lam-in-ait-ing) The process of layering thin wood to form various shapes. Thin veneer-like wood pieces are glued and clamped together in the desired final shape.

Laminate Trimmer — When installing plastic laminate on cabinet tops or countertops it is best to cut the laminate a little larger than the substrate. When the glue has set, a laminate trimmer is used to remove the overhang. A laminate trimmer is a small router-like power tool that is fitted with a special router bit that removes the excess and gives the edge a slight bevel.

Lap Joint — See also, Joints. The lap joint, sometimes referred to as a half-lap joint, is one of the weakest woodworking joints, but is stronger than a butt joint because there is more surface area to be glued and/or nailed.

Lapping — The process of making a steel surface perfectly flat, such as the back of a wood chisel or the sole of a hand plane. An abrasive is placed between the plane sole and a flat surface, such as a piece of plate glass. The abrasive might be 400-grit or higher, wet/dry sandpaper or even pumice powder used with honing oil. The idea is to start at lower abrasive numbers and work your way up until all high or low points have been eliminated. The process may be done by hand or with a machine. The chisel shown at right still has some low spots and needs further lapping.

1

Lapping Plate — A perfectly flat piece of material that may be made from plate glass or even cast iron. The pictured lapping plate is grooved to allow for the dispersion of the lapping abrasive and lubricant, such as honing oil. The surface of the tool to be lapped is held flat on the plate and moved in a figure eight motion.

Cast Iron Lapping Plate 5" x 10"

Lap Splice — The diagonal joint in a sanding belt where there is a diagonal overlap of the two belt ends. The diagonal lap is more efficient and stronger than the old way of having a right angle splice. The diagonal lap splice is a smoother joint that does not bump on the drive or idler wheels.

Laser Level — (lay-zer) Laser is an acronym for *light amplification by stimulated emission of radiation*. In layman's terms, the laser is a narrow beam of light that doesn't refract the way a common light bulb does. As a result, the laser beam always points in a straight line. The laser level emits an orange beam from gimbals and, when aimed at a particular target, projects a perfectly level line. Laser levels are used to install false ceilings or to assure that the installation of chair rails are parallel to the floor.

Latewood — A cross section of a tree shows the annual rings and if you look closely at these rings you will notice one portion is lighter than the other. The darker portion, the late wood, is produced in the summer, the lighter portion is early wood and is produced in the spring.

Latch — A latch is used to secure a cabinet door in the closed position. When released it allows the door to open. The latch may be a mechanical fastening or a magnetic device.

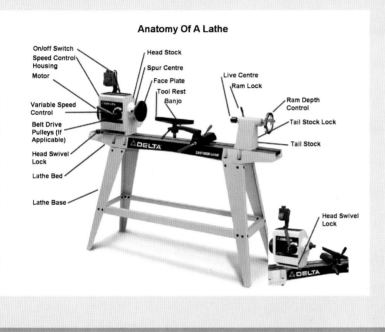

Anatomy Of A Lathe

On/off Switch
Speed Control Housing
Motor
Head Stock
Spur Centre
Live Centre
Ram Lock
Face Plate
Tool Rest
Banjo
Ram Depth Control
Variable Speed Control
Belt Drive Pulleys (If Applicable)
Tail Stock Lock
Head Swivel Lock
Tail Stock
Lathe Bed
Lathe Base
Head Swivel Lock

Lathe — (laythe) The lathe is an electric motor-powered tool that enables the user to turn a variety of wood species into bowls and spindles. The more adept turners can turn oval-shaped products and can hollow out decorative objects.

Lathe Chuck — (laythe-chuk) A self-centering chuck designed to hold wood members (bowl blanks, spindles, etc.) perfectly centered in the head stock of a wood lathe. The lathe chuck is threaded and screws into the lathe, and a special T–wrench opens or closes the jaws to fit the workpiece. There are several types of lathe chucks, but the one pictured is the most common one.

Lattice — (lah-tiss) A wood material in a crosshatch pattern comprised of a series of 1½" wide x ³⁄₁₆" thick slats stapled diagonally to form a (uusally) 4' x 8' sheet.

Lead Bearings — Wheels with encased ball bearings that control the depth of cut on router bits. The lead bearings may be in various positions on the shaft (shank) of the router bit. The bearings may be of different diameters and may be changeable to give the bits more or less depth.

Lead Bearings

On The Level

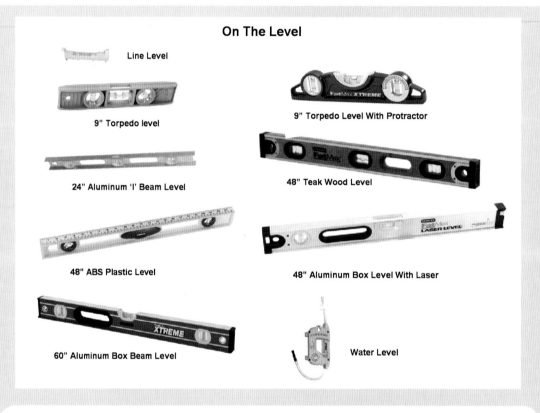

Line Level

9" Torpedo level

9" Torpedo Level With Protractor

24" Aluminum 'I' Beam Level

48" Teak Wood Level

48" ABS Plastic Level

48" Aluminum Box Level With Laser

60" Aluminum Box Beam Level

Water Level

Level — See also Laser Level. a) Level or parallel to the horizon. b) There are several tools available to ensure that you are on the level, or at least your workpieces are. The most common is the spirit level, so called because the tool contains a glass (or plastic) vial partially containing an oily liquid. I say partially because there is an air bubble in the liquid that tells the user when the tool is level. The spirit level is a perfectly straight bar-type tool that comes in many lengths and styles. The level may be made from wood, aluminum, plastic or other materials. The level may contain several vials positioned horizontally, vertically and diagonally. Some vials may be rotated like a protractor, and a scale tells the user the exact angle chosen. There are water levels that are used for longer measurements in construction and landscaping.

Lid Stays

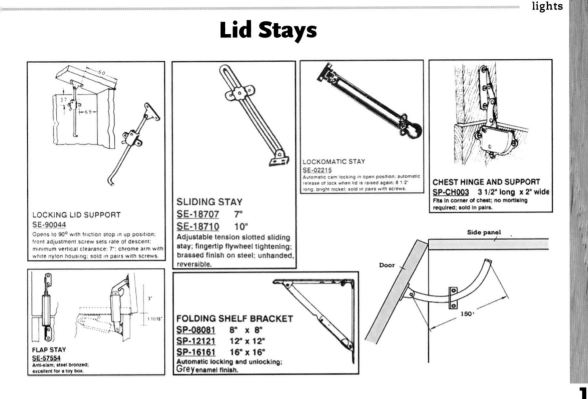

LOCKING LID SUPPORT
SE-90044
Opens to 90° with friction stop in up position; front adjustment screw sets rate of descent; minimum vertical clearance: 7"; chrome arm with white nylon housing; sold in pairs with screws.

SLIDING STAY
SE-18707 7"
SE-18710 10"
Adjustable tension slotted sliding stay; fingertip flywheel tightening; brassed finish on steel; unhanded, reversible.

LOCKOMATIC STAY
SE-02215
Automatic cam locking in open position; automatic release of lock when lid is raised again; 8 1/2" long; bright nickel; sold in pairs with screws.

CHEST HINGE AND SUPPORT
SP-CH003 3 1/2" long x 2" wide
Fits in corner of chest; no mortising required; sold in pairs.

FLAP STAY
SE-57554
Anti-slam; steel bronzed; excellent for a toy box.

FOLDING SHELF BRACKET
SP-08081 8" x 8"
SP-12121 12" x 12"
SP-16161 16" x 16"
Automatic locking and unlocking; Grey enamel finish.

Side panel

Door

150°

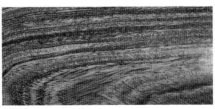

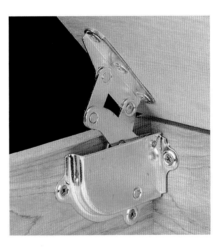

Lid Stay — An essential hardware component in cabinetry used to safely hold cabinet lids in the open position. Some utilize springs or air compression to assist the opening, while others are basic slides with detents to keep the lids open.

Lignum Vitae — (lig-num vee-tay) This is the heaviest of all wood species and is sometimes referred to as iron wood. Lignum vitae weighs between 70 and 80 pounds per cubic foot and will not float in water. The wood is used for propeller shaft bearings in ships due to its natural lubricating effect. Lignum vitae is believed to have medicinal qualities as well.

Lights— Panes of glass in a cabinet door separated by mullions (dividers).

Limed Oak — Liming is particularly suitable to open-grained wood species such as oak. Liming leaves a white finish in the openings of the grain. The top surface can either be left in its natural color or it can be stained a darker color for contrast. Today liming is accomplished with commercial liming products or by wiping the wood surface with white paint and then wiping off the top surface. Traditional liming is accomplished through the use of slaked lime in water. This process is rarely used today.

Link Belts — Link belts are a relatively new innovation that replaces the conventional V– belt on a table saw, drill press, jointer and other machinery that use drive pulleys. Some advantages of link belts, or twist belts as they are sometimes called, are greatly reduced vibration, easy sizing by adding or removing links and extended life. They are made from polyurethane polymers and polyester fabric.

Linseed Oil — or Flaxseed Oil. Linseed oil is derived from dried flaxseed and is obtained by pressing the seeds. Linseed oil has traditionally been used as a binder in the manufacturing of paint. Linseed oil is used as a wood finish, but it is different than most as it soaks into the pores of the wood. Linseed oil is not as hard as clear polyurethane finishes, but it is easier to repair. Caution should be used when working with linseed oil as the rags used may spontaneously combust. Hang used rags outdoors on a clothes line until perfectly dry.

Boiled — Boiling linseed oil causes it to dry faster and makes it will polymerize and oxidize which makes it thicker. Boiled linseed oil, due to additives, is inedible.

Raw — Raw linseed oil takes considerably longer to dry than boiled linseed oil does. The raw oil is used not only as a paint binder but also in sealants, linoleum, caulking compounds, textiles, leather treating and many, many more.

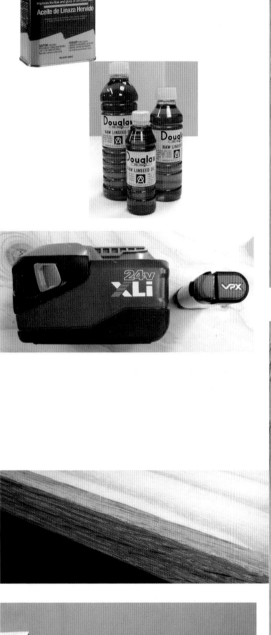

Li-ion — This is the abbreviation for Lithium-ion, a material used to make re-chargeable batteries for cordless power tools. Li-ion has the following superior qualities to previous re-chargeable batteries: Each cell contains higher voltage, the cells are lighter in weight, they have a steady discharge rate, and they do not self-discharge. An 18volt Lithium-ion battery pack is about half the size of NiCad or Ni-MH battery packs of the same voltage.

1

Lipping — Lipping a is term used in the U.K. for adding a solid wood edging to a cabinet, counter edge or shelving edge. The wood used in lipping is generally of a more attractive and expensive species.

Live Center — For many years the tail stock of a lathe was simply a steel cone-shaped point to hold the workpiece for spindle turning. This cone had to be constantly lubricated to prevent it from burning. This was soon replaced with a ball–bearing–equipped tail stock that allowed the spindle to turn freely without friction.

Live Knot — See Knot, Sound Knot.

Log — The section of a tree that can be cut and used for making veneer or milled into usable boards. Logs are chosen for the estimated number of quality boards they can produce.

Lost Head Nail — A British term for a finishing nail or a brad nail.

Low Angle Plane — A hand plane with its iron set at 12° and used primarily for planing end grain.

Lumber — (Timber) Lumber is wood that has been milled into dimensional sizes. In the U.K. the term *timber* refers to the wood still standing as trees or the milled dimension sizes. The trees are rough-cut to nominal dimensional sizes and then milled (planed) to actual sizes. The charts at right explain the board sizes you can expect to buy at your home improvement center. Lumber is divided into three categories. Boards: 1" – 1½" thick x 2" wide or more. Dimension Lumber: 2" – 4" thick x 2" wide and more. Timbers: 5" and thicker x 5" wide and more. Lumber Abbreviations – The following lumber abbreviations apply to Britain, Canada and the United States, but some may be country–specific.

Luthier — (looth-year) A woodworker who specializes in the making of fine wooden stringed instruments like violins and guitars. Most luthiers are well versed in the art of French polishing as most instruments, by tradition, require this type of finish.

Softwood Dimensional Lumber Sizes

Nominal	Actual	Nominal	Actual
1 x 2	¾" x 1½" (19 x 38mm)	1 x 10	¾" x 9¼" (19 x 235mm)
2 x 2	1½" x 1½" (38 x 38mm)	2 x 10	1½" x 9¼" (38 x 235mm)
1 x 3	¾" x 2½" (19 x 64mm)	1 x 12	¾" x 11¼" (19 x 286mm)
2 x 3	1½" x 2½" (38 x 64mm)	2 x 12	1½" x 11¼" (38 x 286mm)
1 x 4	¾" x 3½" (19 x 89mm)	3 x 4	2½" x 3½" (64 x 89mm)
2 x 4	1½" x 3½" (38 x 89mm)	2 x 14	1½" x 13¼" (38 x 337mm)
1 x 6	¾" x 5½" (19 x 140mm)	4 x 4	3½" x 3½" (89 x 89mm)
2 x 6	1½" x 5½" (38 x 140mm)	4 x 6	3½" x 5½" (89 x 1140mm)
1 x 8	¾" x 7¼" (19 x 184mm)	6 x 6	5½" x 5½" (140 x 140mm)
2 x 8	1½" x 7¼" (38 x 184mm)	8 x 8	7¼" x 7¼" (184 x 184mm)

Examples of Dimensional Lumber Sizes (Softwood & Hardwood)

Inch name	Sawed	Swedish	Australian
2 x 4	50 x 100 mm	45 x 95 mm	45 x 90 mm
1 x 3	25 x 75 mm	22 x 70 mm	19 x 70 mm
3 x 3	75 x 75 mm	70 x 70 mm	70 x 70 mm
2 x 7	50 x 175 mm	45 x 170 mm	Not Used
2 x 3	50 x 75 mm	45 x 70 mm	45 x 70 mm
1 x 4	25 x 100 mm	22 x 95 mm	19 x 90 mm
1 x 5	50 x 125 mm	22 x 120 mm	19 x 120 mm
2 x 5	50 x 125mm	45 x 120 mm	45 x 120 mm

Hardwood Dimensional Lumber Sizes

Nominal	Surfaced 1 side (S1S)	Surfaced 2 sides (S2S)
⅜"	¼"	³⁄₁₆"
½"	⅜"	⁵⁄₁₆"
⅝"	½"	⁷⁄₁₆"
¾"	⅝"	⁹⁄₁₆"
1" (⁴⁄₄)	⅞"	¹³⁄₁₆"
1¼" (⁵⁄₄)	1⅛"	1¹⁄₁₆"
1½" (⁶⁄₄)	1⅜"	1⁵⁄₁₆"
2" (⁸⁄₄)	1¹³⁄₁₆"	1¾"
3" (¹²⁄₄)	2¹³⁄₁₆"	2¾"
4" (¹⁶⁄₄)	3¹³⁄₁₆"	

Lumber Abbreviations

a.d. — Air Dried
bd. — Board
hdwd. — Hardwood
k.d. — Kiln Dried
m.c. — Moisture Content
p.a.r. — Planed All Round
p.e. — Planed Edge
p.t & g. — Planed, Tounged and Grooved
S1E — Surfaced One Edge
S2E — Surfaced Two Edges

S1S —Surfaced One Side
S2S — Surfaced Two Sides
S1S1E — Surfaced One Side and One Edge
S1S2E — Surfaced One Side and Two Edges
S2S1E — Surfaced Two Sides and One Edge
s.e. — Square Edged
t&g — Tongued and Grooved
t.g.b. — Tounged, Grooved and Beaded
t.g.v. — Tounged, Grooved and V-Jointed
u.s. — Unsorted

1

m

Magnets — Devices that attract materials made of iron. Magnets are used in woodworking as magnetic door latches (⚑ catches) in cabinetry (as shown) and are also used to hold tools and on fixtures mounted to machinery (see featherboards).

Major Axis — The longer of the two axes used in laying out an ellipse.

Mallet — See also Hammer. A wooden hammer-like tool used primarily to strike the ends of chisels. Mallets are traditionally made from hardwood (to not damage the material or tool being struck) and may be round or rectangular in shape. The round mallet is used in woodcarving and is made to strike at various angles. Rubber and plastic are two common materials used to make the heads.

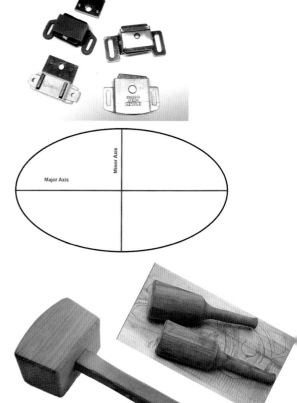

Major Axis

Minor Axis

Mandrel — (man-drill) or Arbor. A mandrel is the part of a table saw that holds the saw blade. In a lathe it is the hollow shaft in the head stock that is driven by the motor. The mandrel on an angle grinder is the component that holds the grinding wheel.

Mantle — (man-tul) A shelf, usually made of wood, over a fireplace or as part of a fireplace surround. Mantles may also be made from slate, marble and other materials. Pictured is a painted wooden mantle.

Marine Glue — Marine glue is a two-part form of adhesive that may be used below the waterline for an extensive period of time.

Marking Knife — See Striking Knife.

m

Marking Gauge — The marking gauge is used to scribe a straight line on a workpiece parallel to a straight edge. The tool consists of a stem or bar on which there is a sliding stock or register. The register locks into position through the use of a thumbscrew. The bar has a scribing pin on the end which marks the line. There are inexpensive, basic plastic types, but there are also elaborate gauges that are made from exotic wood species or even brass. Some use a sharp wheel at the top of the bar to do the scribing. Others have two or more scribing pins that are used to mark mortise spacings while another has a sharp knife that is used to cut veneer or other thin wood.

Marquetry — The decorative inlaying of veneer into a shallow recess cut into a workpiece. This could be a tabletop or apron. Thomas Chippendale was noted for his furniture designs that included marquetry.

Masonite — A trade name for an oil-tempered, pressed hardboard sold in 4' x 8' or larger sheets and usually ¼" or ³⁄₁₆" thick. Masonite is usually used for cabinet back panels but is also be used for interior doors, left flat, wood grain embossed or shaped like raised panels. In 1925 George Mason was running a steam press making low density fiberboard acoustic ceiling tiles. On one lunch break he forgot to take the product out of the press, so the pressure increased and the heat built up. When he returned the tile was brown and very dense. His employer allowed George to patent the process, and the Masonite was born.

Matte Finish — A desirable finish on some workpieces. The matte finish has no sheen to it and does not reflect light.

MDF (Medium Density Fiberboard) — Invented in the 1960s, MDF is made from wood fibers rather than wood chips. The fibers, along with a binding agent (adhesive), are tightly compressed and cut into sheets, the most common size being 4' x 8' with thicknesses as low as ⅛". MDF is quickly replacing other core or substrate materials in the making of commercial furniture due to its consistent and precise dimensions. The material is stable and will accept oil or water-based paints and finishes. MDF may be cut and shaped with conventional woodworking tools,

but they must be sharp. When cut or shaped with a router it generates a lot of fine dust, so the woodworker should wear a mask and have a good dust collection system.

Measure — What most experienced woodworkers do twice so that they only have to cut once.

Medullary Rays — (mehd-you-larry) Lines or striations that appear in quarter-sawn oak and some other wood species. They radiate from the pith of the tree and are a feature in Stickley style furniture.

Metal Detector — This is not for your security but for your tools. Scanning your workpieces with a metal detector can save you hundreds of dollars if you are using recovered wood from some unknown project. A simple nail can cause permanent damage to your thickness planer or jointer or even your saw blades if they happen to strike an embedded nail or screw.

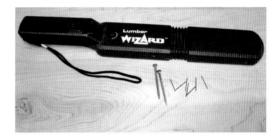

m

Meter — Metre. There are 100 centimeters in one of these, but for more details see our Conversion Chart at the back of the book.

Methyl Alcohol — (Industrial Alcohol) Also know as wood alcohol, methanol. This is used in lacquer thinners, paint removers and wood stains. Methyl alcohol is toxic and can be absorbed through the skin.

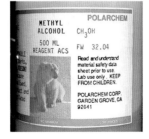

Metric — For more information, see the metric Conversion Chart at end of book.

Mill — In woodworking terms the mill is the place where logs are turned into boards for us to use in our trade or hobby. In the process the tree is limbed and then hewed and transported as a log to the mill. The mill de-barks the log and then squares it. The log is moved lengthwise through the saw (a large circular blade or a bandsaw blade), which slices the log into boards. The thickness of the boards is determined by the market demands on the mill. The boards then go to an edger that trims, squares, and cleans the edges of any remaining bark residue. The boards are then stickered and stacked to be placed into a kiln for drying.

Millimeter — (🇬🇧 millimetre) – To get all the details on the metric system see our Conversion Chart at the back of the book.

Milling — The process of cutting and shaping wood from the cut log to the finished product. Once the logs are cut into boards and dried, the milling process may continue to process the boards into mouldings and other shapes.

Millwork — Wood products that have been made for the building industry and that have been smoothly finished. These include mouldings, door and window frames, cabinetry and other specialty wood products.

Mineral Spirits — (🇬🇧 White Spirit) Mineral Spirits is a petroleumbased solvent that replaces turpentine. Mineral spirits can be used as a cleaner of and a thinner for oil-based paints and wood stains.

Mission Furniture —Gustav Stickley (1858 – 1942) believed that wooden furniture should be simple in style and utility. He started *The Craftsman* periodical to promote this idea and his furniture. His furniture became known as Mission Furniture and was handmade from primarily quarter-sawn white oak.

Miter — (⊞ Mitre) A type of head covering in some religious orders, but in woodworking the miter refers to a type of saw cut or joint.

Miter And Spline Joint — (⊞ Mitre) See also, Joints. The miter joint is in itself a fairly strong joint but the addition of a spline, a narrow, short strip of wood, will do much to add additional strength. The spline may be in a contrasting wood species.

Miter Box — (⊞ Mitre) The miter box is the predecessor of the powered miter saw. This is probably the first jig used by woodworkers for hundreds of years. The miter box is used to make 90° corners in frames and cabinetry. They are cut with a back saw. Although usually made from a hardwood species like oak, some are made from plastic like this one from Stanley.

Miter Gauge — (⊞ Mitre) The miter gauge is an essential accessory found with most table saws. The miter gauge slides in a T–track on the saw table and allows the user to crosscut workpieces from 30° to 90° both left and right of the saw blade. The user locks in the desired angle with the workpiece held firmly to the face of the gauge and then slides it through the rotating saw blade.

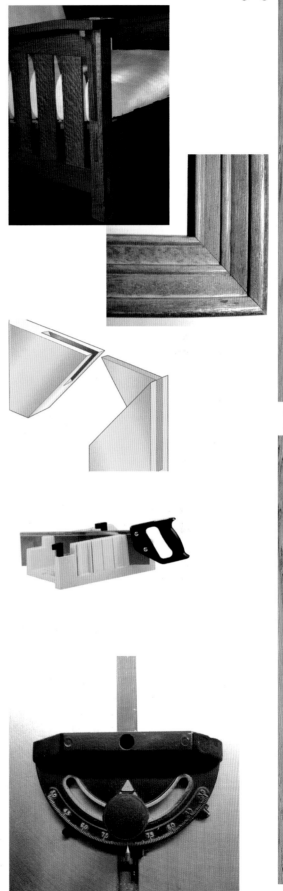

m

Sliding Compound Miter Saw Anatomy

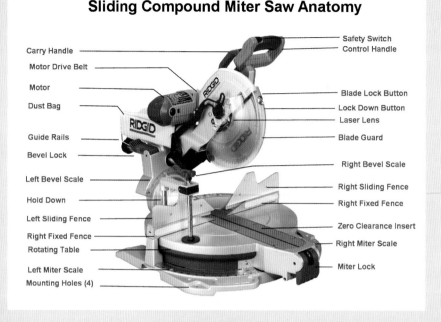

Carry Handle
Motor Drive Belt
Motor
Dust Bag
Guide Rails
Bevel Lock
Left Bevel Scale
Hold Down
Left Sliding Fence
Right Fixed Fence
Rotating Table
Left Miter Scale
Mounting Holes (4)

Safety Switch
Control Handle
Blade Lock Button
Lock Down Button
Laser Lens
Blade Guard
Right Bevel Scale
Right Sliding Fence
Right Fixed Fence
Zero Clearance Insert
Right Miter Scale
Miter Lock

Miter Saw — (🇬🇧 Mitre) Also known as a Compound Miter Saw, Sliding Compound Miter Saw. This is an electrically powered tool that is designed to cut miters and compound miters like those found at the corner joints of crown moldings.

Moisture Content — Expressed as %MC, it is the relative amount of moisture (water, sap) found in freshly cut or dried wood. Air drying or kiln drying the wood reduces the moisture content and shrinks the wood accordingly. The amount of shrinkage is dependent upon the species. Workable moisture content in hardwoods is 6% - 10%.

Moisture Meter — A hygrometer-type tool that measures the moisture content in wood. A reference book is usually included with the meter that lists various wood species and their density. This is an essential tool for the woodworker as it will tell him/her if the wood is properly seasoned.

Morse Taper — The definition of a morse taper would usually be found in a metalworks dictionary, but there are several cases in woodworking where the morse taper is used. For example the hollow mandrel of the lathe headstock or the quill of a drill press. The morse taper is a steel rod with a very slight taper to it. In both of the above cases, accessories (such as a drill chuck) have similar tapered openings and are press fitted to the quill. There are various degrees of morse tapers and each is numbered. The male and female tapers must match.

Molding — See Moulding.

Mortise — See also Joints. The mortise is the female half of a mortise–and–tenon joint. The mortise is made either through the use of a chisel or through the use of a dedicated mortising machine. See Mortiser.

Mortiser — The mortiser is a dedicated machine or a drill press attachment that produces mortises for mortise–and–tenon joints. The tool utilizes a hollow chisel in which there is a drill bit. As the mortiser is lowered into the work piece, the drill makes a round hole while the chisel squares off the hole. The mortiser may utilize a number of different sizes of chisel and matching drill bits.

Mortise–and–Tenon Joint — See also Beadlock, Joints. The mortise–and–tenon joint is one of the most secure joints in woodworking. It is made with a mortiser and a tenoning jig, or it is hand cut with a wood chisel. There are several types of mortise–and–tenon joints, but all are based on the same theme of the tenon fitting into the mortise opening. A little imagination helps to make your own style. Shown is a wedged, through mortise–and–tenon joint.

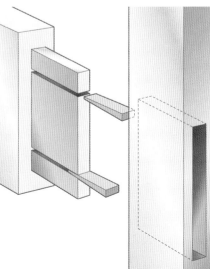

m

FUN facts

The Dremel Motor Tool

Over 100 years ago a penniless Austrian immigrant sailed to the United States with a head full of innovative ideas and an intuitively adept mechanical aptitude. Throughout this immigrant's life he was awarded an impressive 55 patents for his inventions. In 1936 he founded a manufacturing company in Racine, Wisconsin. The name of this immigrant? Albert J. Dremel, and he founded the Dremel Manufacturing Company.

The first product out of that plant was an innovative razor blade sharpener. The tool became so popular that the razor blade manufacturers were forced to cut their prices by half. This then forced Dremel to come up with his best ever invention, the high–speed rotary tool that he dubbed the Dremel Moto-Tool. The Moto-Tool was and still is a compact, lightweight and incredibly versatile tool that was an almost instant success. Woodworkers, craftspeople and hobbyists alike embraced the Moto-Tool as their 'electric Swiss Arm Knife'. The Moto-Tool was later adapted for surgeons and dentists.

Among Dremel's other inventions were an electric shoe polisher, a fish scaler, a chicken egg laying counter, electric screwdrivers, electric sanders, scroll saws and the original walk-behind electric rotary lawn mower.

Not only was Dremel an innovative designer, but he was also an innovative employer. In 1948 Dremel became famous for giving his employees a 30% year-end profit sharing bonus. He was also an advocate of the employers' responsibility to provide a safe and comfortable work place.

Over the years, Albert Dremel started a tradition of producing ingenious tools that met their customers' evolving needs.

Albert J. Dremel passed away on July 18, 1968.

Motor — The electric motor is the basic tool in almost all woodworking shops as it converts electricity into motion or mechanical energy. There are two types of electric motors that concern the woodworker: the universal motor as found in portable tools such as the drill/driver or circular saw, and the induction motor as is typically found in stationary tools like a table saw. Without getting into the nitty-gritty, the universal motor can put out very high RPMs (revolutions per minute) and has replaceable brushes. The Dremel tool may turn at speeds of 30,000 RPMs. The induction motor usually turns at a constant rate (1,750 or 3,400 RPMs) driving a series of pulleys and belt to vary the speed.

Moto-Tool — Motor-Tool. The rotary tool is also referred to as a Dremel tool because of the inventor's name, Albert J. Dremel. See side bar page 164. The rotary tool has been copied by many manufacturers, but the Dremel is still the favored tool. There are hundreds of accessories and attachments available for the tool that will sand, buff, grind, sharpen, cut, shape, carve and drill.

m

Moulding — (Molding) Moulding is used as a decorative addition to furniture and interior woodworking. Mouldings are found in a great number of shapes and styles and are used as decorative transitions from one surface to another. A ¼ –round moulding, for example, will soften the transition between a sharp horizontal surface to a vertical surface. A crown moulding softens the transition between the vertical wall and the ceiling.

Mullion — An upright divider between lights (panes of glass) in a door or divisions in a panel.

Mullion Door — See Sash Door.

MultiMaster® — See also Detail Sander. The MultiMaster is a tool manufactured by Fein (pronounced fine) in Germany. The tool started out as a detail sander but has evolved into an almost universal tool. The drive of the tool oscillates in an elliptical motion at a high rate of speed, but a variable speed tool is available. The tool can cut wood, remove grout and caulking, scrape and sand.

n

Nail — See also Brads, Finishing Nails. In this entry we deal with common nails. The poor lowly common nail, always getting hammered on the head. Unlike the brad and the finishing nail, the common nail has a very prominent large, flat head for striking. There are many stories about the nail, but we here in Canada have a strange one. Several decades ago our government decided that we should convert from the English measure to the metric system. Well, it seems that we half-switched. Only in Canada can you go into a home improvement warehouse and buy a kilogram of 2" nails. Hmmm!
In Canada and the United Kingdom we still use the inch when referring to the

Common Nails

Inch Size	Penny Size	Quantity/Lb.	Quantity/Kg.
1"	2d	850	1,874
1¼"	3d	540	1,093
1½"	4d	290	587
1¾"	5d	250	506
2"	6d	165	334
2¼"	7d	150	304
2½"	8d	100	203
2¾"	9d	90	182
3"	10d	65	132
3¼"	12d	60	122
3½"	16d	45	91
4"	20d	30	61
4½"	30d	20	41
5"	40d	17	34
5½"	50d	13	26
6"	60d	10	20

length of a nail, and yet our closest neighbour, the U.S. uses the old penny (d) system. To try to simplify the confusion between our nations you will find a simple chart above. It also shows roughly how many of each size there are to a pound or a kilogram. Nails smaller than 1" are referred to by their fraction name, and neither brads nor box nails are referred to by the penny system.

Nail Driver — See Brad Nailer.

Nail Plate Connector — Or Gang Nail. The nail plate connector is used in the prefabrication of roof trusses and similar construction components. This is a piece of galvanized metal that has many sharp prongs punched in it. The nail plate connector is then pressed into joining pieces to connect them.

Nail Puller — This is a tool used primarily in the construction and destruction industry. The tool has moving claws that dig into a board and clamp onto the head of the nail. The nail is then levered out.

Nail Guns

21ga. Pinner

18ga. Brad Nailer

1/4" Crown Stapler

16ga. Finish Nailer

Flooring Nailer

Coil Roofing Nailer

Palm Nailer

Framing Nailer

Cordless (Battery) Finish Nailer

Cordless (Battery) Framing Nailer

Cordless (Gas) Framing Nailer

Nail Gun — The nail gun is a replacement for a hammer. The nail gun fires nails of various sizes and gauges into the workpiece using compressed air as the power source. There are also nail guns that are powered by rechargeable batteries, compressed gas cylinders and through the use of .22 caliber cartridges. These are mainly used to drive hardened nails into concrete and sheet steel.

Nail Punch — See Nail Set.

Nail Set — A small steel tool that is used to set or recess the heads of finishing nails or brads. The head of the nail set is tapped with a hammer to do the recessing. This is done to leave an opening in which to apply filler that will hide the nail.

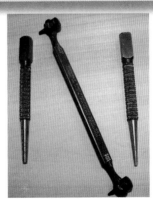

Natural Seasoning — See Air Drying.

Naptha — A highly flammable petroleum distillate used for thinning lacquer and other finishing liquids.

Naval Jelly — Certainly nothing to put on your toast aboard ship. In

fact, you can't even put it on wood. However, if any of your woodworking tools get rusty, or if you have some rusted antique hardware to restore, then Naval Jelly is what you should use. This is a trusted recipe used for years, but it is very caustic. You simply brush it on the rusted area of steel or cast iron, let it set a while and then flush it off with water. Apply a clear finish to protect the surface.

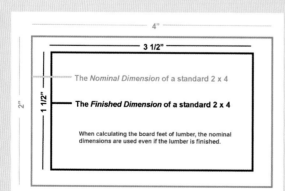

Newel — Or Newel Post. The main or starter post of a staircase that carries the handrail.

NiCad — This stands for Nickel Cadmium, a chemistry used to make rechargeable batteries to power cordless woodworking tools.

Ni-MH — Nickel–Metal Hydride is a chemistry for making re-chargeable batteries used in cordless woodworking power tools. Ni-MH batteries offer twice the power of the conventional NiCad battery packs but have fewer recharge cycles in their lifetime.

4"

3 1/2"

The *Nominal Dimension* of a standard 2 x 4

2"

1 1/2"

The *Finished Dimension* of a standard 2 x 4

When calculating the board feet of lumber, the nominal dimensions are used even if the lumber is finished.

Nominal Size — The actual rough unfinished size of dressed lumber. For example, a 2" x 4" is actually 1½" x 3½", but when calculating board feet the nominal size is used.

Nosing — The rounded front edge of a stair tread, shelf or even countertop. The nosing on a shelf edge may be formed by the woodworker using a route and the appropriate router bit. Stair treads are premade and are sold in various depths and lengths.

Nut

Nut — the other half of a bolt. A nut and a bolt together form a fastener.

Nut, Acorn — Or Cap Nut. The acorn or cap nut is a decorative but utilitarian nut. They are usually found finished in chrome, stainless steel or brass.

n

Octagon — (okt-a-gone) See also Polygon. An eight-sided polygon figure with sides of equal length. The angles are 135° with miters set at 67½°.

Offset Saw — See also Backsaw. An offset saw is a variety of backsaw but with a bend in the wood or plastic–covered steel shank handle. The saw may be used vertically as a dovetail saw but may work better as an undercut saw. This is an ideal tool for cutting the lower part of a door casing or moulding when installing new flooring so that the flooring material fits under it. The same tool may be used as a flush-cut saw for cutting off dowel ends.

Ogee — (oh-jee) As a moulding, the ogee has a flat back and a serpentine face and is used as a finishing touch in cabinetry or as a crown moulding between the walls and ceilings.

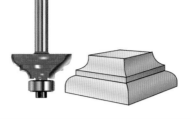

Oils, Finishing — See also Danish Oil, Linseed Oil, Tung Oil. These are products that are used as a final clear coat on wood. These may include raw or boiled linseed oil or tung oil. After the final sanding and the removal of any sanding residue with a tack cloth, the oil product is applied and wiped thoroughly into the grain of the wood, allowed to dry and then reapplied. This may be done several times to achieve the desired smooth finish. Wet-sanding may be done between applications. Caution: oil-soaked rags may spontaneously combust. Allow cloths to dry by hanging outdoors on a clothes line.

Oil, Honing — A highly refined lubricant used specifically to lubricate sharpening oil stones. The purpose of the oil is to suspend particulates removed from edged tools when sharpening or honing and to reduce friction, thus keeping the edge cool.

Oil Stain — See also Wood Stain. Oil stain is similar in makeup to paint in that it is comprised of three components: a pigment, a binder and a solvent. The pigment is the most predominant one. Oil stain is designed to add transparent color to wood surfaces while leaving the grain of the wood visible. It is not a finishing product, but is rather designed to be applied before the application of a clear finishing material. Oil stains are made to enhance the natural color of the wood species or to totally change the wood to have the color appearance of another species. An example of this is using a walnut stain on pine or spruce.

Old Growth — This term refers to the trees in undisturbed forests around the world. We think of old growth as primarily those gigantic mono-liths found in the western United States, the redwood trees. The term also refers to the trees found in South American rain forests and rain forests throughout the world that are being tragically infringed upon and even destroyed. There is no reason for us woodworkers to use old growth, domestic or exotic spe-cies, when a great number of these species are available from controlled and managed wood lots and planta-tions.

One-Two-Three Blocks — Measur-ing tools used for setting saw blade heights, drill press depths and table saw fences. Each block is precisely 1" x 2" x 3", so a complete set provides a variety of measurements.

Open Assembly Time — See Assembly Time.

Open Coat — This is a classification of abrasives (sandpaper) in which only 40 – 70% of the backing is covered with abrasive grains. Open

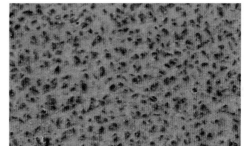

coat sandpaper is mostly used in power sanding such as with a belt sander or orbital sander. The open coat deters the buildup of sawdust on the sandpaper that reduces its efficiency.

Open Grained — This term refers to wood species that have prominent pores showing on the finished (cut) surfaces. These species include ash, beech, butternut, chestnut, elm, hickory, mahogany, oak and walnut just to name a few. The woodworker may find these open pores undesirable and may choose to use a wood filler product on them to even out the final finish.

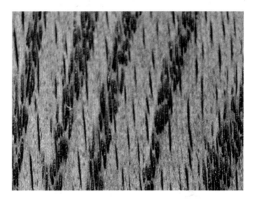

Open Wrench — A wrench with both ends open as opposed to a box wrench with both ends closed. There are also combination wrenches with one closed and one open end.

Open Time — Open time is the amount of time the woodworker has available to join and clamp workpieces together after applying the glue to the surfaces.

O

Orange Peel — A pocked or pebbled finish. This undesirable effect occurs when spray-painting lacquer or other finishes, as a result of using lower air pressure than required or the incorrect air/lacquer mix.

Orbital Sander — See also Palm Sander, Random Orbital Sander. A palm-type electrically–powered sander whose sanding pad rotates in a circular motion. This tool is referred to as a half-sheet sander and is used mostly as a finishing tool for flat surfaces. It is not designed to remove large quantities of material.

Oriented Strand Board (OSB)

(🇬🇧 Sterling Board) — This is a panel product used as a sheathing or underlay material that is vaguely similar to plywood. The "plies" in OSB are, in fact, uniform wood shavings laid out with the grains going in one direction in the first layer. Additional layers are added with the grains going in opposing directions. These shavings are highly compressed in a resinous bonding material. They are then cut into sheets, like plywood in various thicknesses. Oriented Strand Board is made from fast-growing, small diameter round logs and is an improved, superior product based on the old waferboard.

Oscillating Spindle Sander

— This sanding tool uses a vertical spindle that holds a rubber drum. An abrasive (sandpaper) tube fits on the drum, and a bolt tightened on the spindle compresses the drum to secure the sandpaper tube. The spindle rotates, and oscillates on the vertical plane. The purpose of the oscillating is to help eliminate sanding marks on the workpiece.

Outfeed

— See also Outfeed Table. The part of a woodworking tool where the workpiece exits from the saw blade or cutters. On tools such as a table saw or thickness planer, an outfeed table usually stabilizes the piece and keeps it level with the tool table.

Outfeed Table

— See also Outfeed. The outfeed table stabilizes the workpiece as it exits a woodworking machine. The outfeed table helps to keep long workpieces level with the tool to prevent snipe when using a

thickness planer. Outfeed tables may be simple flat table extensions or supports with rollers to allow freer movement of the workpiece.

Out Of Plumb — An expression used to denote that a frame or other workpiece is not truly vertical and may cause the piece to be Out Of Square.

Out Of Square — An expression used to denote that a cabinet carcase or other structure is not built with 90° angles.

Out Of Truth — This is a British term meaning that the carcase or frame of a cabinet or structure is Out Of Square.

Oval Nail — See Finishing Nail

Oven Dried — See Kiln Dried.

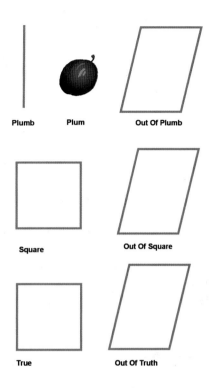

Plumb   Plum   Out Of Plumb

Square   Out Of Square

True   Out Of Truth

O

Ovollo — A classic moulding shape formed with a router bit installed in a router. The router bit may make a variety of shapes depending on the woodworker and the configuration of the bit.

Overarm Guard — This is an upgrade or aftermarket item available for table saws. An overarm guard is a blade guard that is suspended above the table saw blade. It is mounted on a pivot to lift out of the way of some saw operations, making it easier to use than standard blade guards. Overarm guards should still be used with a splitter mechansim for maximum safety.

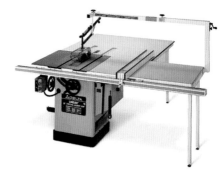

Oxalic Acid — Although Oxalic acid is not poisonous, it is caustic. Protective gloves and goggles should be worn when using it. Oxalic acid may be used to bleach both soft and hardwoods and is also excellent for removing water spots from wood. Use a pasty mix of oxalic acid powder and water to cover the water spot or slather it on a board to bleach it. The longer it is left on, the more it will bleach. When done, wash the surface with water and wipe it dry. Apply household ammonia to the surface to neutralize it.

Pad Sander — See also Finishing Sander. This term usually refers to an electric sanding machine with a square or rectangular flat pad. The sandpaper is attached to the pad with spring clips. The sanding pad rotates at high speed and in very small circles.

 **Pad Saw** — See Keyhole Saw.

Paint — Any liquid that may be spread by brush, pad or sprayer onto a substrate and that converts to a thin opaque film. The most common types of paint are oil-based, alkyd-based, latex-based and water-based. The first two require a solvent, such as mineral spirits to thin or to clean up. The latter two are cleaned up with water. Very few of today's paints contain VOCs (Volatile Organic Compounds), and are instead considered to be "green".

p

Paint Scraper — A tool with a handle and a blade attached. The blade may be triangular with three edges and the corners for use, or it may be U-shaped with dual edges. The tool is pressed to the surface and pulled towards the user while it scrapes the paint or other material from the surface.

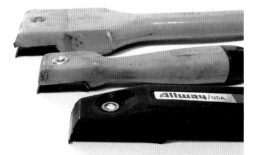

Paint Remover — See Stripper.

Panel Saw — A large fixture designed to cut sheet materials such as plywood and other paneling. The plywood is placed on edge near the base of the tool. The saw (usually a circular saw) is attached to a set of rails that allow it to travel vertically or horizontally. A measuring scale allows the user to cut the panel in precise pieces.

Paring — Reducing, as in woodcarving, through the use of a paring chisel.

Paring Chisel — A lighter chisel used without striking. The blade is beveled and somewhat longer than a standard wood chisel. Some paring chisels have bent blades for better maneuverability.

Parquetry — Similar to marquetry but more rectangular and repetitive in pattern. Parquetry uses veneers or wood solids. A typical parquetry pattern is similar to a chess board where veneers are precision–cut and fitted tightly together.

Particle Board — (⇄ Chipboard) See also Flakeboard. A generic name for sheet materials made from wood shavings, sawdust and/or wood particles. These materials are compressed with an adhesive binder and formed into sheets of varied thicknesses. Particle board is used in the construction and cabinet making industries. For cabinet making the particle board is faced (both sides) with a wood or plastic (Melamine) veneer for both appearance and strength.

Parting Tool — A type of chisel used in wood lathe turning to remove a turned bowl from the faceplate on the headstock of the lathe. The end of the tool is triangular in shape and kept sharp for clean cutting.

Paste Wax — see Bees Wax, Carnuba Wax, Wax.

Peavey — A peavey is a long hardwood pole with a sharp steel point and a pivoting hook attached to it. The peavey is used as a lever for rolling or positioning logs, either in the woods or at a saw mill. It is a basic necessity for any lumberjack. The peavey was invented in 1858 by Joseph Peavey, who was a blacksmith in Maine. The peavey is an improvement over the cant hook because of the addition of a sharp spike on its end. Yes, there is another Peavey, but that's a guitar amplifier and not very useful for rolling logs.

p

PEG — Polyethylene Glycol (PEG) is used to stabilize green wood for turning by replacing the water molecules in the wood cells to prevent further shrinkage as the wood dries. The workpiece has to be soaked in the PEG solution for a period of time before it can be turned. After turning, the piece must be sealed with a clear coat finish.

Pegs — Pegs are turned from hardwood and used in some forms of Shaker furniture. Pegs are used to hold cups in some cabinets or as coat hooks. The shape is unique to Shaker furniture.

Pegboard — See also Hardboard, Masonite.

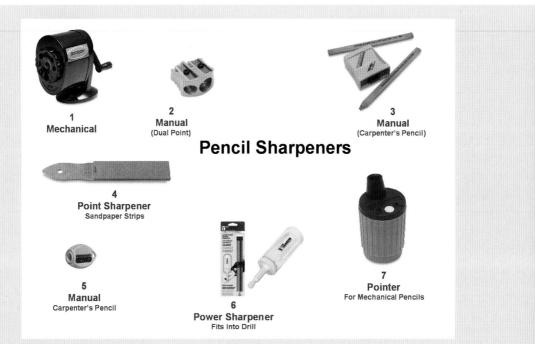

Pencil Sharpeners

1
Mechanical

2
Manual
(Dual Point)

3
Manual
(Carpenter's Pencil)

4
Point Sharpener
Sandpaper Strips

5
Manual
Carpenter's Pencil

6
Power Sharpener
Fits Into Drill

7
Pointer
For Mechanical Pencils

Pencil Sharpener — Every woodworker has a pencil in his/her shop apron or lying on the workbench. There are a number of pencil types that we use, but the best are those that can be sharpened to a sharp point. There are a variety of pencil sharpeners available that can keep that lead point sharp. (1). This sharpener will put a point on a variety of round pancils. (2). A handheld round dual pencil sharpener. (3). A manual carpenter's pencil sharpener. (4). These tear-off sandpaper strips will put a new point on your pencils. (5). Another type of manual carpenter's pencil sharpener. (6). This carpenter's pencil sharpener takes the effort out of sharpening. Simply chuck it into your portable drill. (7). The pointer is mounted on your bench and, with a couple of turns, puts a fresh point on your mechanical pencil.

Pencils, Shop — Two of the best pencil types for the woodshop are the rectangular carpenter's pencil and

the draftsman's mechanical pencil. The former is an excellent tool for drawing general woodworking lines and marks. The lead is rather broad so even with a sharp point, it is not the best for fine woodworking. The draftsman's mechanical pencil is the better option for precision marking as the point is easily restored with a bench– mounted pointer. A recent innovation is a carpenter's pencil that is made from solid graphite (no wood) that will mark on most surfaces.

p

Penny System — See also Nails. A system for defining the sizes of nails. Although originating in England, the system is no longer used there. There are many theories as to the origin of the term penny and the symbol d. One thought is that the term was started in ancient Rome, where the d was an abbreviation for the denarius, a Roman equivalent to a British penny. That same d in England was the abbreviation for *pound* in weight. The theory goes that 1,000 ten–penny nails weighed ten pounds hence the 10d symbol for 3" long nails.

Pickling — See Bleaching.

Pilot Bearing — A roller bearing fitted to the shaft of a router bit. The purpose of the pilot bearing is to follow an edge or template so that the router bit will shape the workpiece accordingly. Some router bits facilitate a variety of sizes that allow the router bit to cut at different depths.

Pilot Bit — A drill bit, usually of a small diameter, that fits into the center of a larger bit, such as a hole saw. The pilot bit starts the hole and proceeds to keep the larger drill bit aligned with the center. The pilot drill bit precedes the larger bit.

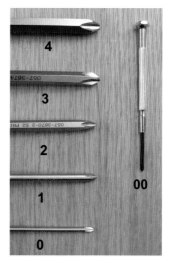

Pinch Dogs — A form of clamp. When they are hammered into the ends of two joining pieces, the angles on the pins draw the pieces together. Pinch dogs may be used in edge gluing as well as miter joining.

Pinch Sticks — See Bar Gauge.

Pinner, Pneumatic — See Nailer.

Phillips Screwdriver — The Phillips screwdriver is made specifically to drive Phillips screws. There are five generally–used sizes: No. 0, 1, 2, 3 and 4. However, other job-specific sizes may be found. Finer sizes are used by jewellers and computer technicians like the 00 size shown here.

Pier — See Column.

Pilaster — (pill-ass-ter –or- pye-last-ter) A pilaster is a flattened, non-structural fluted column used as an architectural feature usually found as accents on cabinet ends or surrounding doors and windows.

The Time: 1933
The Place: Oregon, U.S.A.
The Person: J.P. Thompson
The Event: The invention of a new screw

A new screw and screwdriver design was invented by J.P. Thompson, who passed on the invention to (or sold it to) Henry F. Phillips. They were immediately patented and thus the Phillips screw was born. By 1936 Phillips had formed the Phillips Screw Company and had four patents for the new screw. The original cruciform design came to a sharp point both on the screw recess and the screwdriver. The modified and much improved design had a shallower recess and a rounded bottom. The unique design of the Phillips screw allowed more torque to be applied to tighten the screw, but if over-tightened the screwdriver would cam out. This would prove to be a beneficial asset to Phillips and a boon to the automobile industry. Phillips was not able to manufacture the new screws himself and so approached the American Screw Company to produce them. They reluctantly did so and in 1938 they convinced General Motors to use the new screws on the '38 Cadillac models. The Phillips screws had a self-centering feature to them and this proved advantageous to the automobile industry's automated assembly lines.

By 1940 the U.S. government was building an enormous amount of military vehicles, like the Jeep, and sales of the Phillips screw skyrocketed.

Henry F. Phillips died in 1958 at the age of 68.

The Phillips Screw Company still exists and is based in Wakefield, Massachusetts.

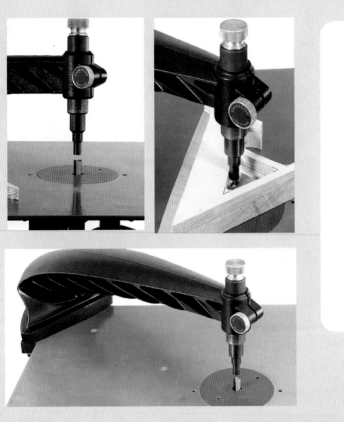

Pin Router — The pin router is more of an attachment, rather than its original dedicated machine. The pin allows the user to follow a pattern. The pattern is attached to the workpiece and then traced with the overhead pin. A router below the table, fitted with the desired bit, duplicates that pattern on the workpiece.

Pipe Clamps — Attachments that fit onto standard black iron plumbing pipe to convert the pipe into woodworking clamps. The advantage of pipe clamps is that they can be as long as you want them to be. If you buy the pipe and have it threaded you can purchase a threaded coupling to extend the length as well. The pipe clamp mechanisms slide onto the pipe, and grippers prevent them from sliding when the screw is tightened. The black pipe may mar or leave a stain on your workpiece if it makes contact. Foam pipe insulation used between the pipe and the work can prevent this from occurring.

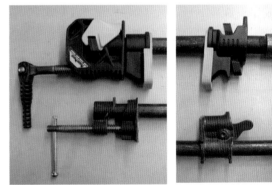

Pipe Wrench — A tool only sometimes used in woodworking, but if you have any plumbing in your shop you'll be glad you have one or two of these on hand. The pipe wrench has very aggressive jaws in a loose fitting adjustment. The fitting is loose to allow the jaws to tighten as pressure is applied to undo the threaded plumbing fittings. You may, in fact, need a pipe wrench to tighten a coupling when extending the pipe clamps in the preceding listing.

Pith — The center or core of the tree in around which the annual rings grow each year. Many woodworkers find this area less stable and, therefore, cut around it or discard it altogether.

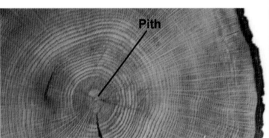

Pith

Planer — See also Thickness Planer. An electrically– or battery–powered hand plane. The motor in the tool turns a rotary cutting head at a high rate of speed. There are usually two very sharp–edged knives installed in the cutter head. The tool is used in the same way a hand plane is used. The front surface of the planer is adjusted up or down to determine the amount of wood material to be removed. Most planers come equipped with a dust collection bag or attachment as well as a fence to help maintain a square edge on the workpiece.

p

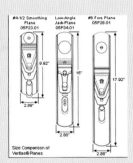

#4-1/2 Smoothing Plane 05P23.01 — Low-Angle Jack-Plane 05P34.01 — #6 Fore Plane 05P28.01

9.92"   15"   17.92"

2.89"   2.80"   2.88"

Size Comparison of Veritas® Planes

Plane — The plane is probably one of the most important hand tools in a woodworker's inventory. Traditional woodworkers will use the hand plane for just about every thicknessing, leveling, smoothing, routing and joining operation that power tools can perform.

The author wishes to thank Lee Valley and Veritas Tools for their assistance in supplying the following illustrations and information.

Apron Plane — A small, low angle block plane. It has a 12° bed angle that excels at working end grain. The apron plane is so called because of its size and weight (14 oz). It fits nicely in the pocket of a shop apron. The apron plane is 5½" long and 1¾" wide.

Bench Plane — The frog on the bench plane extends all the way to the sole for total iron support and to prevent any chance of chatter. The mouth of the bench plane can be adjusted down to a narrow slit for fine shavings or opened up for larger cuts. The bench plane is 12" long.

Block Plane — An essential tool for the woodworker. The block plane is a compact tool at 6⅜" long and only 2" wide. The 20° bed angle and the 25° blade bevel make this an all–purpose plane.

Bullnose Plane — This is actually two planes in one. Use it as a bull-nose, or remove the toe piece to use it as a chisel. The toe has a set screw that is used as a stop to set the mouth opening. The mouth narrows for fine shavings, and the tool has a low 15° bed angle.

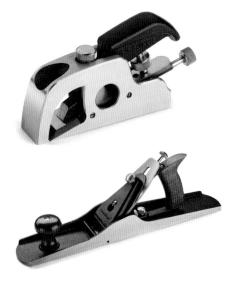

Fore Plane — An excellent tool for flattening large surfaces. The blade iron is fully supported by the frog that extends to the sole. It has an adjustable mouth opening and the sole is 18" long.

Jack Plane (Low Angle) — The perfect plane for shooting miters, working end grain and initial smoothing. This tool has a 12° bed

angle and, combined with the 25°
blade bevel, minimizes fiber tearing. The jack plane is 15" long and
2¾" wide.

Jointer Plane — The jointer plane
can do almost as much as the
electrically–powered stationary
jointer. This 22" long plane has a
12° bed angle that, combined with
the 25° blade iron bevel, reduces
fiber tearout. The throat is adjustable, and an optional fence ensures perfect joining.

Router Plane — This tool is perfect
for cutting dadoes, either with
or against the grain. A fine screw
controls the depth of cut, and the
tool is usually supplied with three
blades. The router plane will cut
to a depth of 1".

Scraping Plane — For smoothing
highly figured wood species like
burls and birdseye maple, the
scraping plane is the tool to reach
for. It has a large sole, 3½" wide
by 9½" long. The adjustable frog
allows for blade angles of 0° to 25°
for precise control.

Scrub Plane — The scrub plane
is the tool to use for major stock
removal and for flattening rough
stock. This is a 10¾" long single
iron tool with no cap iron or chip
breaker.

Smooth Plane — The smooth plane
is the essential general purpose
hand plane for the woodworker.
This plane is perfect for smoothing, finishing, trimming and many
odd jobs at the workbench. The
frog on this model extends to the

p

sole to lessen chatter and the mouth is adjustable. The sole is 9½" long.

Smooth Plane (Low Angle) — An excellent plane for smoothing surfaces and end grain work. The bed angle is 12° and the blade bevel is 25° and this means minimal fiber tearout. The sole on this one is 10½" long and 2½" wide. This model has a unique stop screw in the throat adjusts to the mouth opening. Loosening the front ball adjusts the mouth opening.

Smoother Plane — This is a low angle smoother plane that is 10" long and 3⅛" wide. An excellent plane for finishing up with difficult grain patterns. The 12° bed angle and the 38° blade angle yields a 50° cutting angle known as a York pitch. This smoother plane has an adjustable mouth with a unique stop screw for repeat settings.

Smoothing Plane — once the surface has been worked on then this smoothing plane will finish it up nicely. Blade chatter is reduced due to the frog extending right down to the sole. This 10" long x 2⅞" wide plane has an adjustable mouth.

Plane Iron — The plane iron is just another term for the blade in a hand plane. The plane iron has a sharp edge and is honed to a specific angle depending on the type of plane that it is made for.

Plane Sawn —See Flat Sawn.

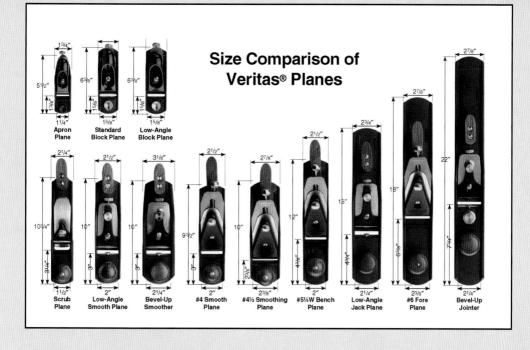

Size Comparison of Veritas® Planes

Apron Plane · Standard Block Plane · Low-Angle Block Plane · Scrub Plane · Low-Angle Smooth Plane · Bevel-Up Smoother · #4 Smooth Plane · #4½ Smoothing Plane · #5¼W Bench Plane · Low-Angle Jack Plane · #6 Fore Plane · Bevel-Up Jointer

Plasterboard — Also called Drywall, Gyproc, Gypsum Board, this is a mixture of gypsum plaster and other chemicals that is pressed into sheet form in various thicknesses widths and lengths. The gypsum is sandwiched between layers of special flame retardant paper and the sheets are used as a replacement for plaster.

Plates — See also Biscuits. Oval-shaped biscuits used to reinforce glue joints.

Plate Jointer — See also Biscuit Joiner. The tool used to create slots into which the plates are fitted.

Pliers — Pliers are tools used for grasping, and come in a variety of shapes and styles from needlenose (for tight work) to slip joint (offering wider opening jaws).

p

Plug — A plug in woodworking is not at all like one found in a sink. A woodworking plug is a small dowel that fits into a drilled hole. A plug is often used to facilitate a fastening screw. The plug is usually made of the same wood species as the workpiece and is glued in place and then cut flush with the surface.

Plug Cutter — A tool used to make the abovementioned plugs. The shank of the plug cutter is installed in a drill press and the depth is set so as not to go all the way through the wood. After several plugs are drilled, the piece of wood is turned on edge and put through the bandsaw. As the wood is cut the plugs drop out and are ready to be used. Plug cutters are available in a variety of diameters and lengths.

Plumb — A term that refers to the vertical trueness of a structural member. Plumb is mostly used in construction but may be used in woodworking as well. Being *plumb* is precisely 90° from horizontal.

Plumb Bob — Or Plummet. The plumb bob doesn't bob at all, in fact it should stay pretty steady. The plumb bob is a pointed, usually brass, weight that is hung on a string. The string is tied inside the tool, knotted and fed out of the center of the top. When hung by the string and steadied the plumb bob will hang truly vertical. The point directs the user where to make the mark. Originally plumb bobs were made of lead thus the Latin name origin *plumbum*. In days of yore a plumb bob would be hung from a scaffold and point to a datum mark , a vertical reference mark. As the building was built the plumb bob string would be raised. In many older churches a brass datum mark can still be seen directly below the spire.

Plummet — See Plumb Bob.

Plunge Router — A relatively new development in the design of routers. Traditionally, when the woodworker is working in the center of the workpiece, the router would be tilted into the workpiece while running. The tool manufacturers designed a safer way of doing this by making a spring-loaded base for the tool. The tool starts in the up position, is placed over the workpiece and then turned on. The user presses down on the tool until the proper depth of cut is attained and then locks the router in that position. Normal routing is then performed. The router's depth of cut can be set through a turret that sets progressive depths.

Plywood — See sidebar on page 194. A large sheet of wood made up of a series of wood veneers glued and pressed together with alternating grain direction. There are always an odd number of plies with the outer plies running the length of the sheet.

Plywood Plies — The quality of a sheet of plywood is usually dependent on the number of plies within it. In any thickness, the more plies the stronger the sheet and the less apt it is to shrink, twist or warp. The individual plies in a sheet of plywood are usually made from faster growing wood species such as aspen or even alder. The better quality plywood (especially that made for the furniture making industry) is devoid

7-Ply Oak Plywood

p

193

FUN facts

Plywood

Although the origin of plywood is attributed to the Egyptians, modern plywood invention is credited to the son of the inventor of T.N.T., Immanuel Nobel in the mid 1800's. The Egyptians lacked ample supplies of large trees and found that by gluing thin slices of wood together they could make a wide variety of furniture.

Plywood is made from thin sheets of wood peeled from logs. The sheets, called plies, are laid one on top of the other. The grain directions of each ply are at right angles to the previous one. The grain on the bottom and top sheets is oriented in the same direction, usually the length of the finished sheet. There are always an odd number of plies that make up a sheet. The plies are glued and pressed together under great pressure. Plywood sheets are cut into a number of standard sizes the most common being 4' x 8'.

Plywood, in this writer's opinion, is probably the greatest single invention for woodworkers. Plywood has given us a whole new dimension to work with.

Michael Thonet, a German cabinet maker, patented his bentwood solid wood furniture designs that went on to influence other designers. They, however, used plywood to extend the scope of their designs. One example, created more than a half-century later, is the side chair designed by Charles and Ray Eames, shown above.

World War II saw plywood designs extend into new realms due to shortages in various essential metals. An excellent example of this is the famed Royal Air Force Mosquito Dive Bomber that was built almost entirely of plywood.

Plywood has its place indoors, outdoors and even underwater as marine plywood. It makes an excellent substrate and the top surface may can be a very expensive hardwood species or even a less expensive plastic laminate. It is important when using plywood as a substrate that a backing sheet be used to balance the internal stresses of the wood plies.

of voids. When purchasing plywood check the edges for voids or spaces. If there are spaces along the edges you can be pretty sure that there are large ones in deeper and they will show up when you are cutting the plywood to size.

Pocket Hole Joint — A wood joint that has been put together and secured with special pocket hole screws. The pockets are drilled using a special stepped drill bit fitted into a pocket hole jig.

Pocket Hole Jig — A tool that facilitates the making of pocket holes for joinery. The Kreg jig, shown here, is set at a specific (15°) angle so that the specially made stepped drill bit makes a hole in which to fit the screw. The jig clamps the workpiece into position for accurate drilling. A drill stop prevents the drill bit from drilling too far.

Pocket Hole Screws — Since the advent and recent popularity of pocket hole joinery, a variety of wood screws have been tried. Mass makers of pocket hole jigs use step drill bits that will facilitate a special pan head screw with very aggressive threads. These specialized screws are thought to be a more secure fastener.

Points — See TPI.

Polishing — See also French Polishing. The term used in woodworking is usually the final step in wood finishing. After several coats of your finishing material you may opt to give the workpiece a final polishing with bees wax or some other buffing compound to provide a high gloss finish.

Polyethelene Glycol — See, PEG.

p

Polygon — (polly-gone) A geometric term denoting closed plane figures having three or more straight sides and has nothing whatever to do with the fact that the parrot has left its cage.

1. Triangle (equilateral)
2. Triangle
3. Square
4. Pentagon
5. Hexagon
6. Septagon
7. Octagon
8. Nonagon
9. Decagon
10. Dodecagon

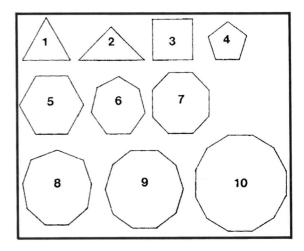

Polyurethane — (polly-yura-thane) A polymer with a vast number of densities depending on its total chemistry makeup. In this instance, we are discussing the clear liquid wood finish similar to varnish. Polyurethane liquid is a clear top-coat finish that is extremely durable. It offers the same benefits as varnish but is more durable, and will not turn milky if water is spilled on it. It sands well between coats and is available in a flat, semi-gloss and high gloss finish. Unlike varnish, polyurethane will not yellow over time and will get harder as it cures. Polyurethane is available as a solvent– or water–based product and is also available as a finish for exterior use. Polyurethane can be applied as a brush-on finish or in aerosol spray containers. Varathane is a trade name for polyurethane.

Polyurethane Glue — (polly-yura-thane) This glue is an excellent wood glue product with a high shear strength. Many are able to be used in wet conditions such as in the build-

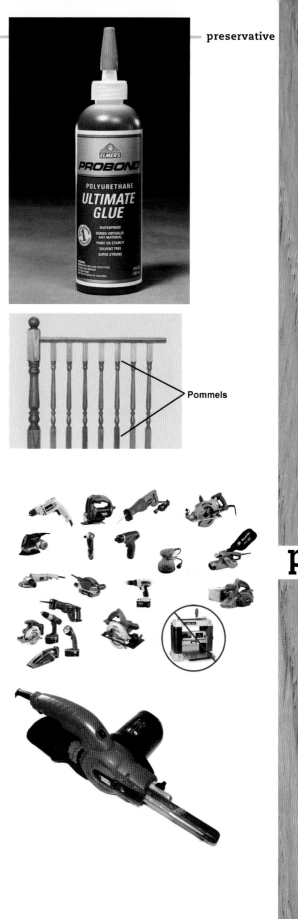

ing of outdoor furniture. Some claim to be waterproof and can be used below the waterline. Polyurethane wood glue is excellent at filling slight gaps in the joining pieces. Poly glue uses moisture in the work-pieces or from the surrounding air as a catalyst. It is best to mist a little water on one of the surfaces. As the glue dries it will foam up and the foam may seep out of the joint. When dry, this seepage can be sim-ply scraped off without damage to the surface.

Pommel — A term used in spindle turning. The pommel is the shoulder of the square end of the spindle.

Pommels

Portable Tools — This refers to any woodworking power tool that can be easily carried around the shop by hand. This generally refers to drills, sanders and some saws. On occasion, manufacturers have been guilty of exaggerating the meaning of *portable* to encompass any tool with a handle on it. An example of this might be a 90-pound thickness planer. In this writer's opinion the term *portable* should be restricted to tools that can be toted with one hand.

Powerfile — A versatile power tool that consists of a narrow belt sander used for sharpening, filing and sanding. The tool is also used for sculpting, rust removal and removing bolt heads and is ideal for working in tight spaces.

Preservative — See also Pressure-Treated Lumber, ACQ, PTL. A chemi-cal applied to lumber through a pressure process that will prevent rotting and damage caused by wood eating insects.

Pressure Sensitive Adhesive — Some abrasives, such as sandpaper discs, have backs that are coated with pressure sensitive adhesive (or PSA) which adheres the disc to the backing pad on a sanding tool (such as a random orbit sander). The sanding discs have a peel-off protective backing that must be removed before using. Some woodworkers dislike these as they are not generally re-useable. Once removed, the protective backing can seldom be re-applied on the disc and any sawdust adhering to the PSA may render the disc unusable. Peeling off the back for those with short finger nails has been a problem, Norton now has a tab to help with revomal.

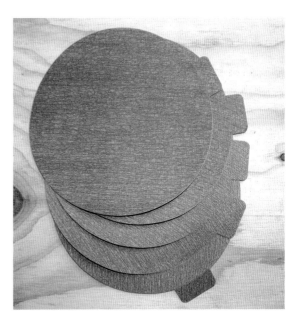

Pressure Treated Lumber — See also ACQ, PTL. Lumber used exclusively for exterior purposes that has been infused under pressure with a preservative chemical (usually ACQ) to retard rot and insect damage. Pressure treated lumber can be harmful to the environment and dangerous to handle.

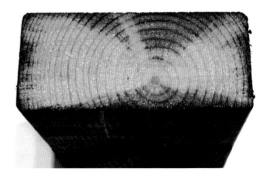

Profile Gauge — A marking tool (usually 6" in length) composed of a series of stiff wires lined up and protruding from both sides of a central sleeve. The wires move but with a little resistance. If you press one side against a profile, that shape will be mirrored on the other. You can then trace that shape for matching and duplicating.

Profile Sander — See also Detail Sander. A powered sander that has a variety of interchangeable hard–rubber shapes. These shapes are covered with a strip of adhesive-backed sandpaper. The woodworker chooses

the profile that best matches the workpiece detail. The tool operates in a back–and–forth motion, usually with the option of variable speeds. Many profile sanders offer blank hard-rubber shapes for custom profiles.

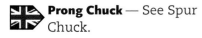 **Prong Chuck** — See Spur Chuck.

Protractor — A tool that gives you a whole new angle on woodworking. The tool is either a circular or semi-circular piece of clear or coloured plastic that is printed or engraved with lines of degrees. It is used to either mark an angle or to determine an angle that is already laid out.

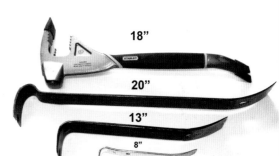

Pry Bar — See also Wonderbar. This is a tool that all woodworkers will be happy they have at some point in their woodworking life. The pry bar can fix a multitude of mistakes. The pry bar is based on Archimedes theory stating that "Equal weights at equal distances are in equilibrium, and equal weights at unequal distances are not in equilibrium but incline towards the weight which is at the greater distance." Two of the most recent and better improvements of the pry bar are the Stanley Wonder Bar and the Stanley FuBar.

18"
20"
13"
8"
6"

PSA — See Pressure Sensitive Adhesive.

P System — See Sandpaper.

Pumice — See also Abrasives. Pumice powder is an abrasive used for fine finishing. Derived from lava rock, pumice powder is quite light and porous. In fact, pumice stone will float on water. Pumice powder is

usually used with boiled linseed oil and rubbed into the finish. Using No. 2 provides a satin sheen and if it is followed up with No. 4, a semi-gloss finish will be attained.

Punches — Punches are made from hardened steel and are used for making holes of various sizes and shapes in a variety of materials. One use for punches in woodworking is to create punched tin panels for cabinet doors. The punch head is struck with a hammer with just enough force to fully penetrate the workpiece or to just make an impression.

Purfling — A decorative inlaid strip that has traditionally outlined the perimeter of a violin or other stringed instrument body. There are many fine and intricate patterns available either made by the luthier or another source. The purfling is usually a sandwich of an exotic wood species such as ebony on the top and bottom with abalone in the middle. Abalone is used today as a replacement for the more traditional (though much less humane) ivory.

Push Drill — See Yankee Screwdriver.

Push Pads — (Or Push Blocks) These are usually rubber–faced tools with a hand grip that are designed to allow you to safely push a workpiece through the spinning knives of a jointer.

Push Stick — The push stick is a safety item designed to keep all five digits on the woodworker's hand. After many decades and hundreds of surveys the results are finally in.

Woodworkers work better and more accurately with all fingers fixed firmly to their hands. The push stick may be a factory made or a shop-made tool but in any case it will allow you to safely push a workpiece through a spinning table saw blade.

PVA — See also Glue, White Glue. These initials refer to Polyvinyl Acetate, a type of woodworking glue also known as white glue.

Pyrography — See Wood Burning.

p

Quarter Cut — One way in which boards are cut from a log. The log is sawn lengthwise into quarters and then those quarters are sawn. This produces boards with a straight grain and pronounced medullary rays such as those found in quarter cut oak. Quarter cut boards are less prone to warping and twisting and are more shrink resistant. Quarter cut oak boards and veneer are much desired in producing Stickley style furniture.

Quarter Measure — Lumber thickness is often referred to as 4/4 and pronounced as four quarter. Other thicknesses are called five-quarter (5/4), six quarter (6/4) and eight quarter (8/4). These measurements are the thickness of the lumber when it comes from the mill or

FUN facts

Queen Anne Furniture

By the end of Queen Anne's reign (1702-1714), the Baroque styles of furniture design had reached their peak. During her reign, furniture designers and cabinetmakers rose in importance. The Queen Anne style was finely decorated and elegantly proportioned. Very little in the way of clustering scrolls and heraldic motifs were apparent on Queen Anne furniture. Walnut was the wood species of choice.

when it is first sawn. It refers to the rough size of the board. The thicknesses increase by ¼" increments, so a 1¼" thick board is a five quarter board. An 8/4 board is 2" thick. When dressed, the 4/4 board, in fact, measures ¾".

Quarter Sawn — See Quarter Cut.

q

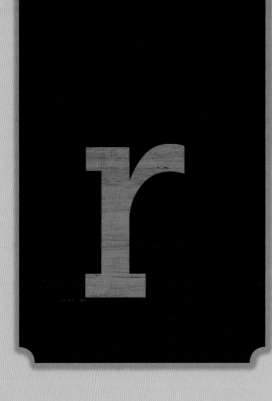

Rabbet — See also Rebate. A recess along the edge of a piece of wood, set in from two faces of the wood. Most commonly used in joinery to house another piece of wood.

RADIAL DRILL PRESS ANATOMY

Radial–Arm Drill Press – A versatile tool with a deeper–than–average throat (the distance from the center of the chuck to the support post). The radial–arm drill press may be a stationary floor tool or a shorter bench tool. The horizontal post allows the tool to greatly extend as well as swing and tilt. That, along with the tilting table, provides extended bevel drilling.

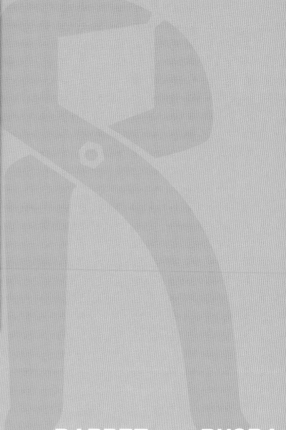

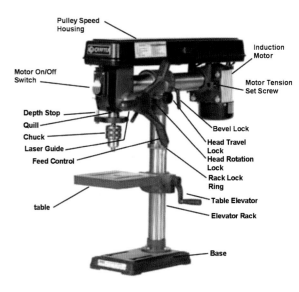

Pulley Speed Housing

Induction Motor

Motor On/Off Switch

Motor Tension Set Screw

Depth Stop
Quill
Chuck
Laser Guide
Feed Control

Bevel Lock

Head Travel Lock
Head Rotation Lock
Rack Lock Ring

table

Table Elevator

Elevator Rack

Base

Radial–Arm Saw — The radial–arm saw used to be called the all–in–one tool, but over the years safety issues have caused it to wane in popular-

RADIAL ARM SAW ANATOMY

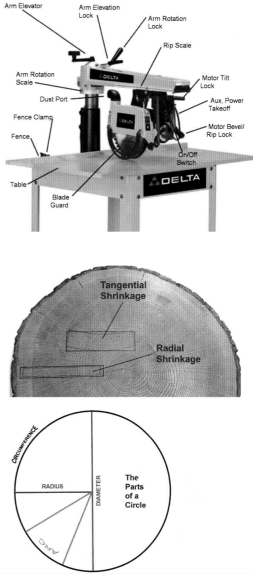

ity. The tool consists of a circular saw blade and motor mounted on an overhead arm. The motor/saw blade unit slides forward on the arm for crosscutting or laterally for ripping. The radial–arm saw has been virtually replaced by the sliding compound miter saw for cross-cutting operations, it has many more functions, including: ripping, bevel cutting, mitering, creating dadoes and even shaping.

Radial Shrinkage — See also Shrinkage, Tangential Shrinkage. Radial shrinkage of wood occurs as the natural moisture evaporates when the tree has been cut into boards. The way these boards dry depends upon the way they were cut from the tree. In the case of radial shrinkage, the boards have been quarter cut.

Radius — This takes me back to high school when I was certain that pies were round. The teacher, however, tried to convince me that pies are square. The radius is half the diameter, or the measurement from the center of a circle to the outer edge.

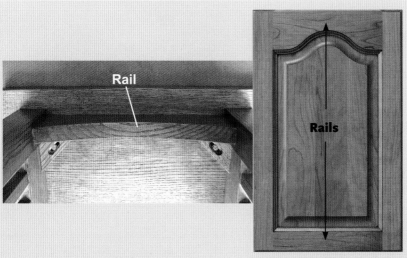

Rail — a) A vertical board that runs the length of the underside of a table. b) The horizontal top and bottom part of a raised panel cabinet door.

Railing — See also Handrail. The railing is a safety feature that surrounds the open area of a staircase or balcony. The railing usually consists of newel posts, balusters and a handrail. The railing may be made of several materials, not the least of which is wood.

Raised Grain — A rough, fuzzy condition on the surface of a board caused by the initial application of a water-based or oil-based wood stain. The moisture in these products raises the wood fibers above the surface of the board. A light sanding of the surfaces will generally remove them.

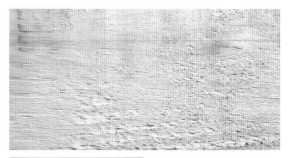

Raised Panel — This appears on doors (cabinet, interior or exterior) made of wood. The edges of the center panel are tapered to fit into dadoes which are cut into the frame pieces (called rails and stiles). The raised panel floats in the frame to allow for expansion and contraction of the panel. The style is sometimes referred to as Colonial.

Random Orbital Sander — A small electric or pneumatic hand sander used for finish sanding. A circular disc either holds the sandpaper in place with a hook and loop fastener or is smooth to facilitate (PSA) adhesive-backed sanding discs. The sander rotates the disc in a random concentric motion to alleviate swirls in the finished wood. These sanders are generally available in 5" or 6" diameter sizes and are meant for sanding flat surfaces.

Rasp — See also Sureform. A rasp is either a voice like Jimmy Durante or very coarse file tools. I'll pick

the latter. Rasps are used for shaping wood in the same way files are used, except that rasps remove more material. There are many different types of rasps with different degrees of coarseness.

Ray — a) Ray cells carry the nutrients to the tree and "radiate" outwards from the pith to the bark. These rays can be prominent in quarter sawn wood such as oak. b) A ribbon–like figure caused by the strands of cells which, extend across the grain in quarter sawn lumber.

Rebate — See Rabbet.

Rechargeable Batteries — See Batteries.

Reciprocating Saw — A versatile electrically– or battery–powered tool that is used in both construction and destruction. The reciprocating saw may be used to cut wood, plastic pipe, copper pipe, steel rebar, drywall and many other materials. The reciprocal saw can accept standard blades that vary in length from 4" to 12". The motor drives the saw blade in a back–and–forth motion and may have a ¾" – 1¼" stroke. Some manufacturers have added an orbital stroke for more aggressive cutting.

r

Relief Carving — An ornamental form of carving in which the carver cuts into the workpiece, removing the wood that surrounds the pattern. High relief occurs if, for example, you are carving a ball and more than half the circumference is showing. Low relief is much shallower. J. C. Caron from Nova Scotia carved this fine example.

FUN facts

Regency Furniture

The late eighteenth and early ninteenth centuries saw the introduction of Regency/Georgian styles of furniture in which and the biggest change was the choice of wood being used. Mahogany was the cabinetmakers' wood of choice. More intricate carvings were prevalent. The important designer of the era was William Kent, and his styles were Italian-influenced. Later in the Regency period, Thomas Chippendale became the renowned designer more noted for the smooth flowing cabriole leg.

Relish — See Haunch.

Re-Sawing — Re-sawing is what the woodworker does if he/she wants to turn a two-inch thick board into two one-inch thick boards. More commonly, re-sawing is the safest way to create thin (¼") material for bent laminations, intarsia or other woodworking processes requiring thinner material. Re-sawing is usually done on a bandsaw fitted with a special re-sawing fence that helps prevent the bandsaw blade from wandering. The re-saw fence can be purchased commercially or it can be shop-built by the woodworker.

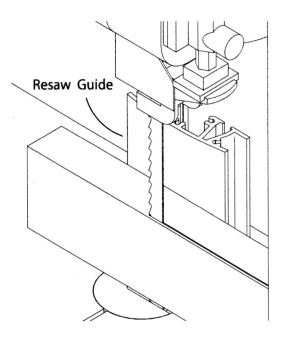

Resaw Guide

Respirator — See also Dust Mask. A sophisticated form of dust mask. The respirator generally has provision for installing a variety of filter types that may protect the user from inhaling dust as well as some toxic vapours and smoke. In order to be effective, the respirator must fit tightly around the nose and mouth. Some respirators are in the form of a full face mask with a filtered air supply.

 **Reveal** — A decorative cut made in furniture to (a) give the appearance of a floating top or base and/or (b) to make a thick top appear thinner. A reveal may be purposely placed in a workpiece to improve the appearance of a joint or seam.

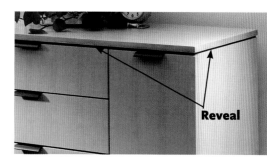

Reveal

FUN facts

Restoration Furniture
The Restoration period, also known as the Carolean (after King Charles II) in England, brought the English furniture tradition back in line with the European design movement. This occurred in the late fifteenth century during the realm of Charles II. This was the beginning of the British Baroque Period and thus ended the Puritan furniture design styles. Charles II spent many years in exile in France and Holland which made him appreciate, admire and promote their designs.

Rifflers — See also Files, Rasps. Rifflers are small shaping files used in woodcarving or any other type of woodworking. Rifflers may be used to remove small defects like burrs in metal as well.

 **Ring Saw** — See Hole Saw.

Rip Cut — See also Ripping. Sawing wood in the direction of the grain of the board.

Rip Fence — See Fence.

Ripping — The act of sawing a board on a table saw, bandsaw, circular saw or hand saw in the direction of the grain. Ripping may be done to plywood as well if the cutting is done with the grain on the top ply. Ripping may also be done to other sheet materials if the cut is made in the direction of the longest dimension.

Ripsaw — See also Saw, Hand. This term usually refers to a hand saw with teeth designed to give smooth cuts in wood when cut in the direction of the grain. The teeth of the rip saw have a zero rake, and there is only a slight set to them.

Riser — a) The area on a staircase that is between the treads. A riser is generally between 7" and 8" high, but most importantly, all risers in a staircase must be equal in height. b) A cast-iron block (usually sold as an accessory) that fits in the frame of (generally) a 14" cast iron bandsaw. The riser increases the height capacity of the tool, usually from 6" to 12", and is more suitable for re-sawing. A longer blade is required when a riser is used.

Rise

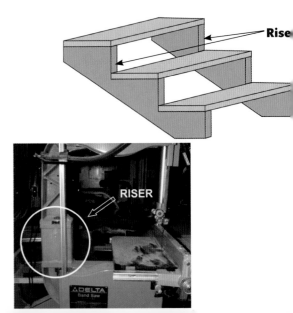

RISER

Rivet — A fastening device usually used to fasten metal components together. Rivets may be used to fasten other materials as well. The rivet consists of the head, the shaft and the bucktail, or plain end. The rivet is inserted into a pre-drilled hole equal to the diameter of the shaft. It is then hammered to re-shape the bucktail to a larger diameter, thus holding the parts together. The most common rivet used today is called a pop rivet. This is an aluminum hollow rivet with a nail going through the center. A special tool pulls the nail through and pops it off.

FUN facts

P.L. ROBERTSON
In 1908, P. L. Robertson began to manufacture a square recess impression in the head of a screw in Milton, Ontario, Canada. At that time, it was a revolutionary change in the fastener industry. Although Americans, in general, were reluctant to adopt the new screw, Robertson convinced the Ford Motor Company to use the screw in manufacturing the Model T. Ford realized the enormous savings the screw would provide because it would not 'cam out'. Ford

and other automobile makers wanted some control over the manufacturing process, but Robertson staunchly refused. Although the Robertson screw was widely accepted in both Canada and Britain, the Americans were slow to use them. The first patent for the Robertson screw and screwdriver was issued in 1909, and the last patent expired 55 years later in 1964. P.L. Robertson screws and screwdrivers carry his name to this day. Now, square drive screws and screwdrivers are in wide use, and they are still made in Milton, Ontario.

It is important to note that the Robertson screw recess is tapered inward and that design helps to secure the screw to the driver. Most copycat manufacturers have neglected to add this important feature.

Riving Knife — See also Splitter. The riving knife is a curved piece of sheet steel that trails behind the blade on a table saw. The riving knife mimics the height and angle of the saw blade and its purpose is to prevent kickback. The riving knife is (should be) the same thickness as the blade that is installed in the table saw, and it prevents the kerf of the workpiece from closing up.

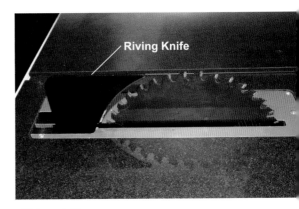

Riving Knife

Robertson Screw — Or Square Drive Screw. The Robertson screw is an invention of P. L. Robertson and has a square recess in the screw head. The recess is tapered downward, and a matching screwdriver helps to keep the screw snug on the screwdriver for one-handed screwing. There are four recess sizes. See page 211 for more.

Robertson Screwdriver — The Robertson screwdriver has a square tapered tip designed to fit snugly into the corresponding Robertson screw. There are four commonly used tip sizes: 0, 1, 2 and 3. They are color coded for easy recognition: yellow – 0, green – 1, red – 2 and black – 3.

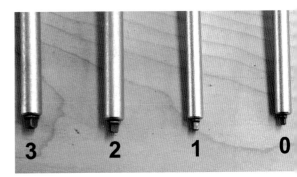

3   2   1   0

Rotary Cutter — See Rotary Tool.

Rotary Cut Veneer — Imagine tearing sheets off a paper towel roll. This is the basic concept of rotary cut wood veneer. First, the tree is de-barked and then put on a lathe to make it perfectly round. The log is then put in a hot bath and soaked. After a predetermined amount of time the log is then put on a special lathe-type machine that has a very sharp knife. The log is turned and the knife peels it into thin, long veneer sheets.

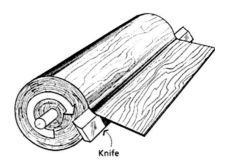

Knife

Rotary Tool — Or Rotary Cutter, Roto-Zip. Roto-Zip is a brand name of the originator of the rotary tool. It was developed primarily for the construction industry and is a hand-held, electrically–powered cutting tool. Designed primarily to cut openings in plaster board to provide for electrical outlets. The tool uses specially made drill-type bits that cut material like a jigsaw blade, but it rotates like a drill. The rotary tool has been adapted into woodworking as a plunge cutter used to make various openings, including mortises. The rotary tool has a variety of cutting bits and accessories available to cut or carve many materials.

Rottenstone — Also known as Tripoli. A finely ground stone product used in furniture finishing. After the woodworker has gone through the sandpaper numbers, the next step is to use pumice powder. Rottenstone would be the next and probably final step and provides a glass-like final finish to your workpiece. Rottenstone, like pumice, is mixed with boiled linseed oil and rubbed in with a soft balled–up cloth.

Roto-Zip — See Rotary Tool.

Round-Over — The softening of a sharp cabinet or table edge by the use of a shaped radius. A round-over is usually created with with a round-over router bit fitted with a pilot bearing. The bits are available in a variety of radii sizes to accomodate a small jewelry box, or the edge of a conference table.

Router — (rout-er) The router is an essential power tool in any well equipped woodshop. The router

r

can be used for shaping mould-ings or making raised panel cabinet doors or even jointing. Most routers are variable speed tools. They may have fixed bases or plunge bases, and some are sold with both. Rout-ers are generally able to use ½" and ¼" shank router bits for versatility. Smaller routers, called laminate trimmers, are single purpose de-signed but may be used as a router as well. The router may be used freehand as a portable power tool to trim and shape edges, or it may be used under a router table for more versatility.

Router Bit — A router bit is the heart of the router and its *raison d'étre*. The router bit is a shaped cutter usually with two cutting surfaces made from tungsten carbide. There are hundreds of shapes produced by various manufacturers for a mul-titude of purposes. Router bits are bonded to steel shanks, which may be ¼" or ½" in diameter.

Router Bushing — (See also Guide Bushing) The router bushing fits on the router base and is used to guide the router bit through the edges of a template. The router bit is installed through the bushing and into the router collet. The router bushings are available in a variety of sizes, are usually sold as a set and are made of brass, steel or aluminum.

Router Plane — A hand plane used to make dadoes. The plane uses a narrow center-mounted blade to cut a groove or dado in wood. The plane uses blades of various widths and has an adjustable depth control.

Router Table — The use of a router table is a way to turn your portable router into a stationary or benchtop tool. The router is mounted upside down under the tabletop. The table itself may be on a short base for use on a work bench or it may be on a table that the woodworker uses while standing. The router table is usually equipped with a fence for routing in a straight line and a T-slot to use with a miter gauge. The fence of the miter table is split to compensate for surface removal on the workpiece. The router table may also be used as a shaper and a jointer.

RPM — The abbreviation for revolutions per minute. This term is used in reference to the speed of electrical power tools that turn, such as drills, lathes, drill presses and the motors that power them. In many cases the motor has a fixed rate of RPMs speed while the working part of the tool is higher or lower due to the adjustment of pulleys.

Rubber Cement — The name seems to indicate that this glue is used to cement rubber parts, but in fact it is used primarily on paper and cardboard. Rubber cement is also used in woodworking to temporarily glue templates to a workpiece. The templates may easily be removed, and the cement residue may simply be rubbed off. It is made from latex polymers mixed with acetone and/or heptane.

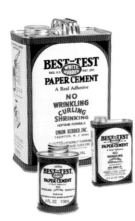

r

Rubber Mallet — A hammer-like tool that is used to prevent damage to surrounding areas. The hard rubber head is securely fastened to a hickory (or other hardwood) handle. The rubber mallet is not designed for driving rubber nails or any other type of nail. The tool may be used with wood chisels or to "persuade" the fit of wood components.

Rubbing — A method of achieving a final finish on wood such as in French Polishing. The workpiece is rubbed with a pad, oil and a fine abrasive to attain a high gloss finish.

Rubbing Alcohol — See Alcohol, Denatured.

Rule Joint — A joinery method used in drop leaf tables where the table-top has a convex profile and the leaf has a concave cut. The two pieces are joined by a special hinge. The joint is formed with a router and two special router bits.

Rule Joint Hinge — A special hinge with unequal leaf lengths. The hinges are recessed into the underside of the tabletop and the table leaf.

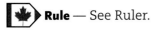 **Rule** — See Ruler.

Ruler — A tool for measuring dimensions. It may be made of wood, plastic or steel. Rulers are very straight and are divided into inches and their fractions or into centimeters and millimeters. Rulers are generally available in lengths of 6" and more. A three-foot ruler is called a yardstick.

Rungs — The horizontal members of a chair stretching between the

RUNGS

legs. The rungs help strengthen the position of the legs, especially when they are splayed. There are generally four rungs or more on a chair. While they seem like a good foot rest, rungs are also hard to replace when broken.

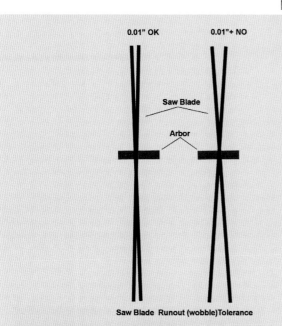

0.01" OK   0.01"+ NO

Saw Blade

Arbor

Saw Blade Runout (wobble)Tolerance

Runout — The term *runout* in woodworking refers to trueness of a circular saw blade. *Wobble* might be a synonym. If the body of a saw blade is not perfectly flat and the saw arbour is not turning true, you will get runout. Some runout is acceptable so long as it is below 0.01".

Rust — An undesirable condition that happens to steel and cast iron when left out in the rain or in damp shops. Rust is the formation of iron oxides caused by mixing iron with oxygen. Rust can be very damaging to your tools, so they should be protected from elements that may cause rusting. The use of paste wax on cast iron surfaces will help prevent rust, as will products like Rust-Chek.

r

Ryoba — (ree-oh-bah) - A japanese saw that cuts on the pull stroke as opposed to the push. This allows for a thinner blade that cuts more efficiently, is easier to control and leaves a narrower kerf.

Saddle Square — A layout tool to mark your workpiece for cutting tenons and other projects. The saddle square sits on one edge of the workpiece and is perfectly square.

Sander, Belt — See Belt Sander.

Sander, Drum — See Drum Sander, Surface Sander.

Sander, Finishing — See Finishing Sander.

Sander, Oscillating Spindle — See Oscillating Spindle Sander.

Sander, Random Orbit — See Random Orbit Sander.

Sander, Surface — See Surface Sander.

Sanding Block — See Hand Block.

Sanding Discs — Sanding discs that fit on random orbit sanders are used in great quantity by woodworkers. There are two popular sizes (5" and 6"), and they are available in both hook and loop or pressure sensitive adhesive (PSA) backs. They are made without perforations or with six or eight holes to facilitate the sander's dust collection openings. Sanding discs are available in grits from P40 on up to P6,000 or more, and in various grit types.

Sanding Drum — See also Drum Sander. A sanding drum is either solid rubber or air–filled. A cardboard or paper tube of varying sizes are meant to fit on it. The tube fits loosely at first, but then a threaded shaft running through the middle gets compressed by tightening a nut on the top. The pneumatic drum is filled with air to secure the sanding tube. The tubes are available in a multitude of sizes and grit numbers.

Sanding Sponges — There are two types of sanding sponges. First there are rubber-like blocks that have an abrasive coating on four sides. Usually there are two grit sizes on each sanding sponge: fine/medium and medium/coarse. These are meant for flat sanding. The other type of sanding sponge is made from less dense material and in a more specific abrasive grain size meant for sanding soft corners and round objects. They are especially efficient for sanding wood turnings.

S

Sanding Tubes — See also Sanding Drum. The sanding tube is a hollow

(Definition continues on page 222)

Sandpaper — What would a woodworker do without sandpaper, the essential wood-workers tool? Where did this essential tool originate, and how did it evolve?

First and foremost, sandpaper is not paper coated with sand. The origin of the term seems to be unknown.

It can be assumed that artisan peoples of all ages wanted to smooth out the roughness of their crafts, even in ancient times. It seems, though, that the first–ever recorded use of a sandpaper-like product appeared in the 1200s in China. Apparently, some smart Chinese people used crushed seashells, seeds and, yes, sand and bonded them to parchment using pine tar or other gummy natural resin. Later, sharkskin was used as a smoothing agent. Sandpaper was for some time called *glass paper* because some used glass particles as the abrasive.

Written information indicates that Elizabethan (sixteenth century) and Queen Anne (early eighteenth century) furniture styles were smoothed using of metal scrapers and other smoothing tools.

John Oakey of Wellington Mills, England, first developed a process for manufacturing glass paper in 1833. Oakey developed new adhesive techniques and processes that allowed glass paper to be mass produced.

In the United States it was Isaac Fischer, Jr. of Springfield, Vermont who patented a process for making sandpaper on June 14, 1834.

Sandpaper has developed greatly over the centuries and will continue to do so, but the early forms of sandpaper came in but two colors: black or beige. In recent years, however, manufacturers (and there are now many) have distinguished their individual products by using dyes in blue, brown, yellow, orange and even lilac. Now, only the natural abrasive materials, like garnet and emery, show their true colors.

Over the years manufacturers of sandpaper have researched many materials that last a considerably longer time and still remain sharp and abrasive. Some of these are:

Aluminum Oxide – This is the general sanding choice for most materials. Aluminum oxide is an excellent product for power sanding and hand sanding alike. Aluminum oxide works well on wood and metal and although not as sharp as other materials, it does last longer.

Aluminum Zirconia – This is an alloy of aluminum oxide and zirconium oxide. It is both sharp and durable but not as long–lived as ceramic. Aluminum zirconia is used mostly on sanding belts and discs for power sanding. In the lower grit numbers it is excellent for heavy stock removal. Aluminum zirconia is known for its self-renewal. As the parts of the grit break off they leave sharp edges that continue being effective.

Ceramic – Ceramic is the most expensive of the abrasive materials, but it is also the most effective. Ceramic is sometimes bonded with aluminum oxide, and it remains sharper longer. Ceramic is used effectively for power sanding.

Chomium Oxide – This is used only in the very fine or high P numbers for final finishing.

Silicon Carbide – This material is extremely sharp and hard and will even cut glass. The downside is that it wears out quickly. It is best used for between–coat sanding. The higher P numbers are used for wet sanding a final coat.

Sandpaper Types

There are two natural materials that are used as abrasives.

Emery – This is an excellent material for smoothing metal for painting and usually has a cloth backing. Emery is much too soft for continuous wood sanding.

Garnet – After glass, garnet soon became the standard abrasive for sanding wood, but compared to today's synthetics, garnet dulled quite quickly and, therefore, became ineffective.

S

cardboard tube with sanding grit on the outside face. The sanding tube is designed to fit on sanding drums that are compressed to keep the tubes in place while sanding. The sanding tubes are made in a variety of diameters and lengths as well as a variety of grit sizes.

Sandpaper — See Grit and page 220.

Sapwood— The part of the tree that is closest to the bark. Wood in a tree is first formed as sapwood and its purpose is to feed water from the tree roots to the leaves. As the tree grows, the heartwood becomes larger and new sapwood forms.

Sash Cramp — See Clamps, Bar.

Sash Door — (Or mullion door) The sash door is a bookcase door that is divided into rectangular glass panes divided by mullions. Or, the door may be glazed with one piece of glass with false mullions.

Saw Bench — See Saw, Table.

Saw Blades — This entry refers to Circular Saw blades. See chart on page 223.

Sawdust — The part of your workpiece that gets left on the shop floor, in your dust collection system or, in the case of a saw mill, in large piles outside. See toxic types in sidebar on page 264.

Sawdusters – A nickname for woodworkers.

Sawhorse — Although four-legged, this is not the equine type that you can make bets on. However, you can

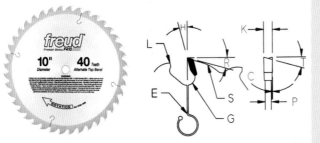

Anti-Kickback Limitor - (L) The projection at the back of the shoulder to limit the tooth bite.
ATB - (T) Alternate Top Bevel, where the teeth alternate their angle.
Bore - The arbor hole diameter.
Expansion Slots - (E) These cuts are laser made to control the blade expansion due to heat and centrifugal force.
Gullet - (G) - The cut-out area in front of each tooth for chip removal.
Hook Angle - (H) The angle of the face of the tooth run from the center of the bore.
Kerf - (K) The width of the cut that the blade makes.
Plate - (P) The thickness of the saw body.
Radial Side Clearance - (C) Clearance angle on the side of the tooth.
Relief Angle - (R) The angle at the top of the tooth.
Shoulder - (S) The blade body directly behind the tooth.
Triple Chip Grind - One flat top tooth followed by a trapezoidal tooth that is slightly higher to eliminate chipping in laminates and particle board.
Top Bevel Angle - (T) The angle at the top of the tooth.

- There are also specialty circular saw blades designed for cutting plastics, laminates and non-ferrous metals. These are ATB (alternate top bevel) where alternate teeth are bevelled. They are as follows: one beveled left, one flat topped and then one beveled right.

- A great majority of circular saw blades manufactured today are made with tungsten carbide tipped teeth. These teeth are brazed to the blade.

- Many circular saw blades are made with narrow kerfs. These provide smoother cuts, less wastage and are easier on saw motors.

- Manufacturers now use lasers to cut expansion lines in the body of the saw blades. These allow the saw blades to run cooler and help prevent blade distortion due to heat buildup.

Circular Saw Blades can be put into three categories: crosscutting, ripping and general purpose. The pitch or hook and the bevel angle of the teeth vary depending on the usage.

Crosscutting: A fine crosscutting circular saw blade should provide a fine, smooth cut on wood, plywood, particle board and soft plastics. These blades are found in compound miter saws and radial–arm saws. The blade hook is 10°, the bevel angle is 10° and they generally have a high tooth count.

Ripping: This is a blade that is generally used for rough ripping to dimension both soft and hardwood. There are blades available (called jointer blades) that leave a perfectly smooth and square edge. These blades have a 20° hook and a 10° bevel.

General Purpose: These blades are also known as combination blades and give a fair finish in both a crosscut and ripping situation. The hook is 10°, and the bevel is 10° as well.

bet that you will find at least one of these (but usually a pair) in most woodshops. These are usually shop-made, but there are now a number of companies that make a folding version that is easy to store when not in use. Having sawhorses is like having an extra workbench that is particularly handy when working with sheet goods.

Sawing — The act of cutting wood, whether by hand or through the use of a power saw.

Sawing Horse — See Sawhorse.

Saw, Hand — See also saws by specific types. Some sort of hand saw is responsible for all (well almost all) man/woman–made construction in the world. The saw is a tool with a handle and a (usually) steel blade that has one edge notched with sharp teeth. These teeth have a "set" to them in that they are alternately (sometimes) bent out to the left and the right. These teeth have a sharp edge to them for cutting wood. A rip saw has a straight front edge (zero rake) and is designed to give a smooth cut. The crosscut saw has teeth that are angled back (negative rake) and have a beveled edge.

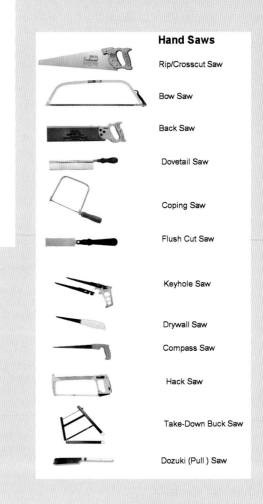

Hand Saws

Rip/Crosscut Saw

Bow Saw

Back Saw

Dovetail Saw

Coping Saw

Flush Cut Saw

Keyhole Saw

Drywall Saw

Compass Saw

Hack Saw

Take-Down Buck Saw

Dozuki (Pull) Saw

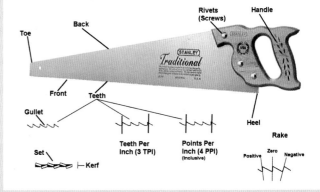

SawStop — A brand name for a unique table saw with a safety feature that senses when your finger or hand gets dangerously close to

Table Saw Anatomy

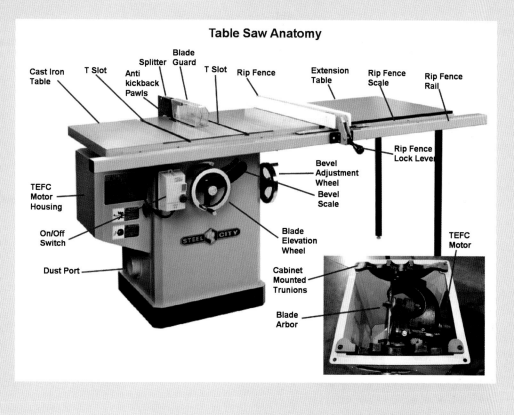

Cast Iron Table — T Slot — Splitter — Blade Guard — Anti kickback Pawls — T Slot — Rip Fence — Extension Table — Rip Fence Scale — Rip Fence Rail — Rip Fence Lock Lever — Bevel Adjustment Wheel — Bevel Scale — TEFC Motor Housing — On/Off Switch — Dust Port — Blade Elevation Wheel — TEFC Motor — Cabinet Mounted Trunions — Blade Arbor — STEEL CITY

Saw, Table — See also Contractor's Saw. The table saw is an essential tool in a well equipped woodworking shop. There are two basic types of table saw; the cabinet saw and the contractor's saw. The cabinet saw has a fully enclosed base or cabinet and is usually a higher powered tool. The cabinet saw is a heavy tool, and therefore, is not easily moved. The trunions of the saw are heavy and are mounted to the cabinet for generally easier alignment. The motor is mounted within the cabinet. The cabinet saw is usually a large tool with long extension tables and, conversely, a long rip fence rail.

The contractor's saw is a lighter table saw meant primarily for moving from job site to job site. The motor is usually smaller with less horse power and is mounted outboard of the tool stand. The trunions are mounted to the underside of the table, and the table is generally smaller. The extension wings are open grid due to weight considerations, and the fence rails are relatively short.

These are the two basic types, but there is one more that is a hybrid of the two of them. Because of the popularity (and lower cost) of the contractor's saw among home woodworkers, manufacturers developed a hybrid that has the features of both types: a full cabinet with an interior mounted motor (although less powerful) and cabinet mounted trunions.

the spinning saw blade. When this occurs, the saw blade stops immediately, so the worst that can happen is a small scratch on your finger. The sensor drives a plastic cartridge against the teeth of the saw blade to instantly stop it and simultaneously stops the saw motor. When this happens the blade is rendered useless and must be replaced, and the Saw-Stop mechanism cartridge must be replaced as well. This is a small price to pay for saving a thumb, finger or an entire hand. When demonstrating the tool the manufacturers use a hot dog in place of a finger, and there is barely a nick on it.

Scale — The scale we are referring to here is the scale used in architectural or designer drawings. The designer must scale down his/her designs/drawings for ease of handling. Woodworking drawings may be scaled to ½" = 1' or smaller. For some specific details the drawings may be in full scale (actual size).

Scarf Joints

Scarf Joint — (skarf) The scarf joint is a modified lap joint used to lengthen boards. There are a number of ways to further strengthen the joint such as cross splines.

Strengthened with cross-splines.

SCFM — Standard Cubic Feet per Minute. The amount of air produced by an air compressor.

Scissors — Scissors are not normally considered woodworking tools but they sure will help you open the packages they come in. The so–called blister packages usually require a good pair of scissors to cut through, and some might even require a stick of two of dynamite. Also good for cutting out patterns.

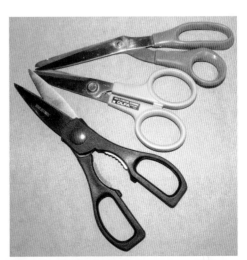

Scoring Blade — A very fine saw blade that cuts a fine line on a panel or other workpiece just ahead of the actual saw blade. The scoring blade counter rotates that of the actual saw blade. This is done to prevent tearout or break-off in plywood and laminates. The scoring blade is a material and work saver for production cabinet makers. An after-market scoring blade attachment is available that has a 6" primary blade and a 2" scoring blade and will install in most table saws.

Scraper — There are two types of scrapers, one for finishing and one for undoing. The finishing scraper (cabinet scraper), is a rectangular or shaped fine steel blade that is honed to a square edge and used to remove small amounts of wood from a shape or surface. The scraper blade may be used alone or in a spoke shave handle. The scraper can replace the function of a belt sander in finishing a project. It's the perfect tool for removing glue squeeze-out. The undoing scraper is used in the removing finishes, such as paint, and is a more crude type of scraper. It usually has a U-shaped dual–edge–steel blade that fits on a handle and may be re-sharpened. The user of both types should be careful to keep the blade flat against the surface to prevent gouging.

Scratch Awl — See Awl.

Screw Cup — See also Washer, Cup. A fancy washer that accentuates the use of a screw instead of hiding it. The screw cup is a dished out washer that is made for the heads of either a round–head or an oval–head screw to fit into.

S

WOOD SCREWS

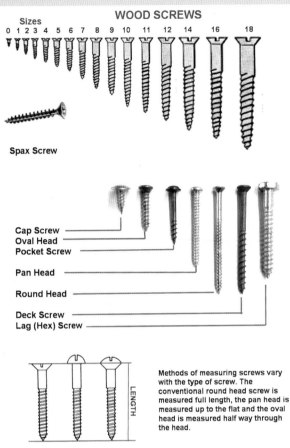

Sizes
0 1 2 3 4 5 6 7 8 9 10 11 12 14 16 18

Spax Screw

Cap Screw
Oval Head
Pocket Screw

Pan Head

Round Head

Deck Screw
Lag (Hex) Screw

LENGTH

Methods of measuring screws vary with the type of screw. The conventional round head screw is measured full length, the pan head is measured up to the flat and the oval head is measured half way through the head.

Screw — A steel, brass or other metal shaft with a helical thread and a head. The head has a provision for turning the screw with a driving tool. The screw was invented by Archimedes (287 – 212 B.C.) in Greece.

Screw Extractor — A tool designed to remove screws or bolts that have broken heads. The screw extractor has a tip with reverse threads and a square head to fit a socket wrench or screw gun. The user inserts the extractor and then turns the bit in reverse. As the extractor begins to bite into the broken screw, it turns the screw and draws it out. There are various sizes to fit a variety of screws.

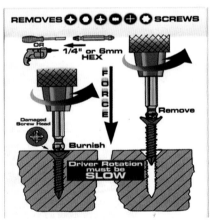

Screwdriver Bits — A recent innovation for screwdrivers, bits are hexagonal in shape and fit into (usually) magnetic holders that fit into cordless or manual screwdrivers. They are more convenient in that they are disposable and not expensive to replace.

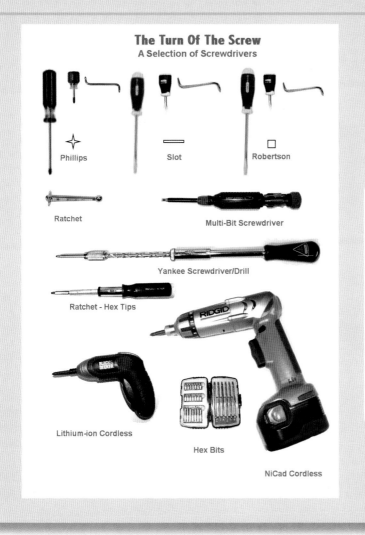

The Turn Of The Screw
A Selection of Screwdrivers

Phillips

Slot

Robertson

Ratchet

Multi-Bit Screwdriver

Yankee Screwdriver/Drill

Ratchet - Hex Tips

Lithium-ion Cordless

Hex Bits

NiCad Cordless

Screwdriver — The screwdriver is one of those essential tools for the woodworker. There are a multitude of screwdriver types and sizes, but the types that should most concern the woodworker are the flat head, the Phillips head and the square (Robertson) drive.

Screw Gauge — This tool is an aid to woodworkers in sorting the plethora of loose screws usually found in most woodshops. The gauge helps the woodworker identify the number gauge and size of the loose screws. Many gauges will indentify the proper pilot drill bit to use with each screw size.

Screw Nail — See Spiral Nail.

Scribe — The scribe is a compass-like tool with two arms on a pivot. One arm contains a point and the other a pencil. The purpose is to use one edge to trace a contour while the pencil traces it on a workpiece for later coping.

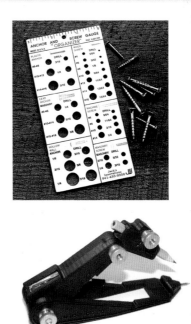

S

Scroll Saw Anatomy

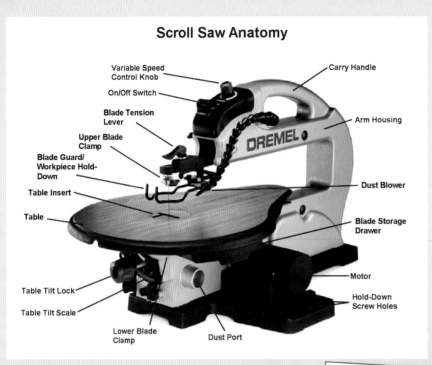

Variable Speed Control Knob

On/Off Switch

Blade Tension Lever

Upper Blade Clamp

Blade Guard/ Workpiece Hold-Down

Table Insert

Table

Table Tilt Lock

Table Tilt Scale

Lower Blade Clamp

Dust Port

Carry Handle

Arm Housing

DREMEL

Dust Blower

Blade Storage Drawer

Motor

Hold-Down Screw Holes

Scroll Saw — The scroll saw is the perfect tool for doing fretwork, intarsia and many other fine wood-working forms due to the fine-ness of the scroll saw blades and their ability to cut extremely tight corners and curves. The piece (pictured below) by Dave Tarr of Nova Scotia won a Canadian National competition.

Scroll Saw Blades — Blades for a scroll saw are very fine and of two types: pinned and pinless. The pinned type has a small diameter short pin intersecting the blade at the top and bottom. Its purpose is for positioning the blade in the saw. The pinless blades are held in position with clamp-like holders in the upper and lower arms of the saw. The blades vary in width, thickness and tooth count. There are bi-directional toothed blades for cutting on both the down and up strokes, twist blades for reverse cutting and skip-tooth blades for more aggressive cutting.

Scrub Plane — See Plane.

Sculpting — See Wood Carving.

Sealant — See Caulk.

Sealer — Lacquer sealer or sanding sealer should be used prior to using a brush-on clear lacquer. This acts as a primer that seals the wood to make subsequent finishing coats go on smoothly. The sealer should be lightly sanded prior to applying the next finishing coat. Sealer can also be used prior to staining to keep the stain from penetrating unevenly into very porous wood species. The sealer is applied with a brush, allowed to dry (in about 2 hours) and then sanded.

 Seasoning — See Air Drying, Kiln Drying

Secretary — See Bureau.

Select Lumber — Select lumber (wood) is the top grade and is clear and free of knots.

 Self-Centering Chuck — See Lathe Chuck.

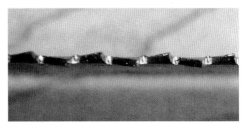

Set — This term refers to the set of the teeth on a saw blade, or the angle at which the blade is bent outwards from the blade of the saw. The set may vary depending on the purpose of the blade. Almost all saw blades have a set to them as it is this set that, with the sharpness and hook of the blade, makes the cut.

S

Settle — A hall bench with arms and a back. The settle has a lift-up seat with a storage bin below. The bin is used for storing gloves and scarves, and the seat is used for sitting while putting on and removing boots and overshoes.

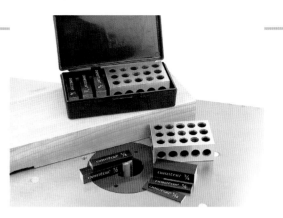

Setup Blocks — Setup blocks are usually a tool for the machinist, but woodworkers can use them as well. Similar in style to one-two-three blocks, these setup blocks are precision–made from aluminum. The larger block is exactly 1" x 2" x 3".

Shaker Furniture — Mother Ann Lee, the Matriarch of the United Society of Believers in Christ's Second Appearing, more popularly known as the Shakers, came to the United States in 1774. She arrived from Manchester, England. Members of the Shaker sect, upon settling in New England, began making their own furniture. They made furniture primarily for themselves but soon began producing products for sale as well. Their particular style of furniture was quite plain, but their innovative joinery, quality and functionality made it stand out among the rest. The Shakers were noted for their tables and chairs as well as their cabinetry.

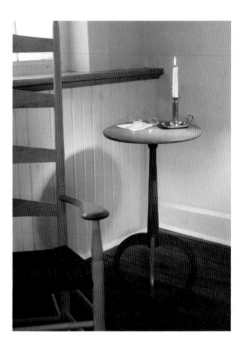

Shakes — Shakes or shingles are usually made from cedar (typically, western red cedar). Shakes differ from shingles in that they are split, not sawn. Shakes are usually longer than shingles and may be as long as 24" or more. Even 48" shakes are not uncommon. Wood shingles and shakes are made from logs that have been salvaged from logging operations. Shakes are a long–standing traditional roofing and siding material.

Shaper — The shaper is similar to a large router, but it is designed to produce large quantities of mouldings. The shaper is a stationary machine generally meant for com-

Staying Sharp

Sharpening can be a tedious chore at best but with the right tools the work can be made much easier. oil, water and diamond stones sharpen blades equally as well and slip stones are shaped to fit specific blades. The wet or dry sharpening machines can put a mirror shine and a razor edge on your tools in less time.

Triple Oil Stone

Dual Waterstones

Slip Stones

Dual Diamond & Quad Diamond

Work Sharp Dry Sharpening

Delta Wet Wheel

Sharpening — This is the part of the woodworking process that most woodworkers shy away from. Keeping your bladed tools sharp, however, makes woodworking easier and more precise. In today's world sharpening tools has become less tedious, more accurate and less time consuming.

Sharpening Materials
Oil stones are Crystolon or India stones that are used with a light honing oil. The purpose of the oil is to allow fragments of both the steel blade and the stone to be suspended and to prevent them from being embedded into the stone

Coarse Crystolon — A fast cutting man-made sharpening stone for quick edge sharpening. It is best for really dull and nicked blades.

Medium Crystolon — Use this to smooth the edge after the coarse Crystolon.

Fine Crystolon — The final honing after the coarse and medium Crystolon stones.

Coarse India — A medium cutting rate, man-made stone for sharpening dull blades.

Medium India — A follow up to the coarse India.

Fine India — The finishing touch after the medium India.

Soft Arkansas — A natural stone that gives a low metal removal rate but an extra fine finish. Use the Arkansas after medium stones.

Hard Translucent Arkansas — Very low removal rate but provides an ultra fine mirror-like finish.

mercial woodworking shops, but there are some smaller units available. The shaper has a motor–driven vertical spindle on which a large cutter is attached. The shaper has a fence which is adjusted forward or backward to comply with the type of moulding being shaped. The shaper is designed to shape larger profiles than a router is capable of doing.

Shavings — See Wood Shavings.

Shears — See Snips.

Shear Strength — Shear strength refers to the strength of glue and other adhesives. The glue manufacturers do not refer to the strength of glue by breaking or snapping a board at the glue joint but rather by trying to separate the pieces by sliding them apart laterally.

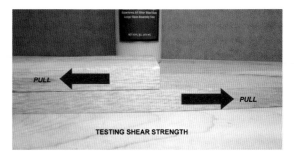

TESTING SHEAR STRENGTH

Sheet Goods — This is a term referring generally to all building materials available in sheet form. These materials include plywood, particle board, flakeboard, waferboard, oriented strand board, tentest, hardboard, masonite, pegboard, plasterboard and panelling.

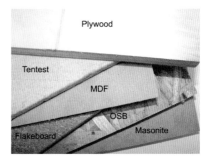

Shelf — A horizontal board found in bookcases and other cabinets used to store or display books and knick-knacks or even tools in a woodshop. The shelf need not be enclosed but may be attached to a wall or other vertical members through the use of brackets or other means of support.

Shelf Life — This is the useful life of such products as adhesives and finishing products. The woodworker should check the "best before" date on any product before using it. Some products have date codes on them, but if you go to the manufacturers' Web site your may find the coding breakdown.

Shelf Supports — See also Brackets. Shelf supports come in a great variety of types that may fit into holes drilled into cabinet sides or into rails that are screwed into the sides. They may also be angle or L brackets screwed to walls or other areas used to mount shelves.

Shellac — (shell-ack) Shellac is a resin excreted from the lac beetle. The lac is collected, crushed, washed and dried. After processing, it is drawn into sheets of finished shellac. These sheets are broken down into flakes and mixed with denatured alcohol in various proportions, called cuts, to make either a spit coat or a finish coat. Shellac is probably the finish of choice for a majority of fine woodworkers. Shellac is an all-purpose finish; as a wash it is an excellent sealer and may be used as a wood conditioner as well. Shellac has been the traditional wood finish for centuries but not just for woodworkers. The next time you take a pill look closely at that glossy finish. And take a close look at some of those candies you eat. Yup, they may be coated with shellac. And, when you next hear that familiar "ding-dong" at your door? Yes, Avon uses shellac as well. The drug, cosmetic and confectionary industries are the biggest consumers of shellac.

Shellac Stick — See Burn-In Stick.

Shims — See also Wedges. Thin wedge-shaped pieces of wood or other material used to adjust the level, or plumb of some wood members. They are most commonly used on door jambs or sills.

S

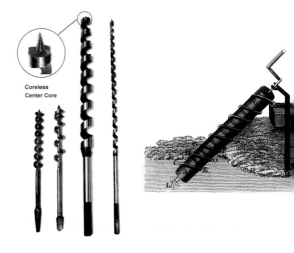

Coreless
Center Core

Ships Auger — The ships auger is the closest woodworking tool to Archimedes' original invention, the water lift. However, the ships auger is made to drill deep holes in wood. A normal twist drill has difficulty drilling deep holes in wood because it cannot evacuate the chips and tends to burn. The large open space in the ships auger allows for the speedy evacuation of wood chips. Ships augers may be as short as a few inches or as long as 2 feet or more. Some have a solid center while others are open twists.

Shooting Board — See also Bench Hook. The shooting board is a shop-made workbench accessory for use with a hand plane and/or a back (tenon) saw and is not unlike a bench hook.

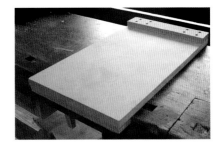

Shop Vacuum — An industrial portable vacuum cleaner used to suck up sawdust and other shop residue as well as water. It is also called a wet/dry vacuum. The shop vacuum can double as a dust collector by hooking the hose up to the various sawdust–making woodworking tools in the shop. The shop vacuum is fairly noisy, so if it is being used on a regular basis it's best to buy a longer hose and isolate the machine. Shop vacuums are usually measured by the tank capacity in gallons or liters.

Shoulder — The shoulder is one of two parts of a tenon in a mortise–and–tenon joint. The shoulder is the broad part at the end of the tenon that butts against the joining workpiece.

Tenon Shoulder

Shrinkage — Refers to the shrinkage of wood from when it was cut

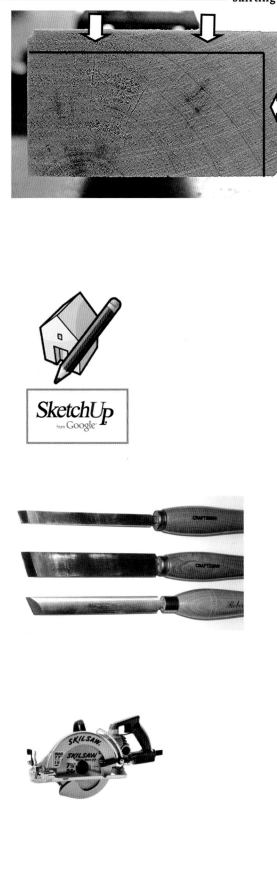

and green to the kiln-dried ready to use 2x4. The shrinkage is due to the evaporation of the moisture in the wood. Even though wood has reached its equilibrium it will continue to contract and expand somewhat due to its environment.

Silicon Carbide — See Sandpaper.

Site Saw — See Saws, Contractor's, Table.

SketchUUp — SketchUp® is a type of CAD (Computer Assisted Design) program that is extremely easy to learn and use, with basic components available free on the Internet (sketchup.google.com). The SketchUp program is a great tool to help woodworkers draw scale furniture plans along with all necessary dimensions. Once the basic plan is done, SketchUp allows you to rotate it and see it in many views.

Skew — A type of chisel used in lathe turning. The skew has a flat blade that is skewed or angled at the end. The blade end is sharpened to a V edge, is best used as a shaving tool on the lathe, and requires a high angle of attack.

Skew Nailing — See Toe Nailing.

Skilsaw —See also Circular Saw. Although the name skilsaw has become a generic term for any portable circular saw, the name actually belongs to Skil tools, one of the earliest makers of the portable circular saw.

Skirting — See Baseboard.

S

Sliding Bevel — A tool with a stock and a blade. The blade pivots and slides and adjusts to almost any angle. The sliding bevel is used to duplicate angles, and the thumbscrew tightens the blade. When closed, the blade fits safely into a slot on the stock.

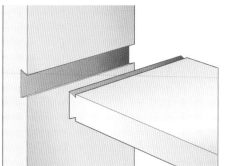

Sliding Carriage — See Sliding Table.

Sliding Dovetail Joint — The sliding dovetail joint is used for drawer slides, or to attach table aprons to table legs, and is particularly useful for installing shelves to cabinet sides.

Sliding Square — This square is a compact tool meant for fine work, like laying out for hand cut dovetails. There are a number of different brands. The one pictured is from C.H. Hanson.

Sliding Table — A table saw extension table mounted on rails and usually equipped with a miter gauge. The sliding table and miter gauge combination makes the crosscutting process easier and more accurate. Some table saws, like a couple of Ryobi models and some more expensive Grizzly tools, have these as standard equipment.

Slip Joint Pliers — Slip joint pliers are pliers that have an expandable throat. Most have two positions to make the jaws wider, but some are multi–positioned for extremely wide jaws. In woodworking use care with this tool as the jaws are grooved and will easily damage the wood surface. Slip joint pliers may be used as a temporary form of clamp by wrapping an elastic band around the jaws.

Slotted Screwdriver — See Screwdriver.

Sloyd — (Slöjd) Sloyd was a term used for woodworking classes in grade school or high school. It specifically referred to the making of wooden crafts. It was thought that sloyd was formative and that woodworking helped to build a child's character. Sloyd was developed in Finland as a system designed to progressively build the skills of the young students.

Smooth Plane — See Plane.

Smoother Plane — See Plane.

Smoothing Plane — See Plane.

Snap Line — See Chalk Line.

Snipe — (snype) a) Snipe most often occurs at the beginning or end of a board that has been put through a thickness planer or a jointer. The snipe is a gouge or a deep cut in a board due to the lack of downward pressure applied to the board as it enters or exits the machines. In most cases, snipe may be eliminated with the use of a head lock, or a longer outfeed table in the case of a thickness planer. With a jointer, care should be taken to assure that proper downward pressure is applied and that the tables are properly set. b) This has absolutely nothing to do with woodworking, but it is a beautiful bird and, coincidentally, is called a wood snipe. It is native to the Himalayas.

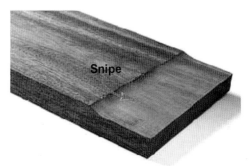

Snipe

Snips — These are also referred to as *tin snips* and are meant for cutting thin sheet metal, like copper and tin.

S

Snips are made in several configurations for making straight cuts, left hand turns, right hand turns and combinations. While not a common woodworking tool, they are frequently useful for removing packing bands from lumber and machinery.

Socket Wrench — Although the socket wrench is certainly not a woodworking tool, you will find it most helpful when assembling newly–purchased woodworking tools. The socket wrench is available in ¼", ¾" and ½" sizes. The sizes refer to th8 shank size of the tool which plugs into the socket. The tool has a ratchet drive that allows the user to use the tool's leverage to tighten or loosen nuts and bolts.

Softwood — This is the term given to the wood derived from conifer trees, which are trees that have needles. These include (but are not restricted to) cedar, cypress, Douglas fir, fir, hemlock, larch, pine, redwood and yew. There are exceptions to the rule however. For example, balsa wood is very soft but is technically a hardwood. Douglas fir, a softwood, is much harder than some hardwood species. Softwood is the wood most used by humankind and is the material of choice in residential construction.

Soldering Iron — (saw-der-ing) The soldering iron, like most tools, has undergone a vast amount of change over the decades. It is now a self-igniting tool that is powered by a butane cartridge and will heat up to or exceeding 1,000° Fahrenheit. The soldering iron is also supplemented by a soldering gun which is electrically–powered and, like the iron, has a variety of tips available.

Sole — See also Hand Plane, Circular Saw. The sole is the bottom face of a hand plane, circular saw or portable plane. In each case, it is preferable if the sole is flat to get the best performance from the tool.

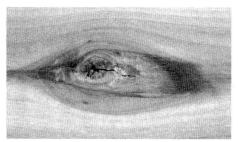

Sore Thumb — The part of the human anatomy that is most often struck by a hammer when missing the intended target. Extreme care should be taken of this digit as it is one of the most useful body extremities.

Soss Hinge — (sauce) See also Hinge. A concealed hinge that is set into the frame of the cabinet and the edge of the door. The soss hinges may be small enough to hinge a jewelry box or large enough to hinge full–sized oak entry doors. The round ones in the illustration are also called barrel hinges.

Sound Knot — A knot in either hard or softwood that is tight and will not move. The knot is found more in softwood lumber than in hardwood boards. The sound knot is acceptable in some grades of lumber but not in "clear" grades.

S

Spade Bit — See also Drill Bits. A flat–bladed drill bit with sharpened leading edges and a point for starting the drill. The spade bit is made in sizes from ¼" to 1½", cuts a fairly rough hole, is slow–cutting and is not suited to fine woodworking. The spade bit is best used in rough construction drilling of 2x4s to pass wiring and plumbing through.

Spalting — A dark brown to black vein irregularly running through wood. This is caused by rotting and,

if left alone, will continue through the entire piece of wood. Spalting is a desired appearance by some wood turners. (Bowl courtesy of Don Moore).

Spanner — See Wrenches, Spanner.

Spax Screws — See also Torx Screws. Wood screws with a very aggressive thread that does nor require pre-drilling, even in oak and other hard-wood species. The spax screw has a bugle–shaped head and is fitted to be turned with a torx screwdriver.

Speed Square — A durable triangu-lar square used as a protractor and for scribing lines at 45° and 90°. The speed square can be used to verify saw cutting angles and can act as an accurate guide for a circular saw. The prime purpose of the speed square, however, is to layout angles for hips, valleys and rafters in resi-dential construction.

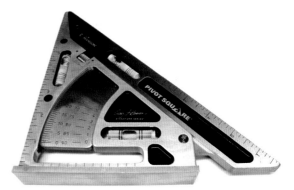

Specific Gravity — In woodworking, this is the density of wood divided by the density of the water in it. I'm no scientist, but what it means to me and other woodworkers is the dry weight of the wood after it has been kiln dried.

Spikes — Spikes are nails that are over 6" in length or, in the case of the U.S, way of measuring, any nail over 60d.

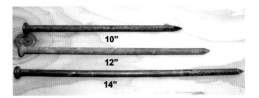

Spindle Moulder — See Shaper.

Spindle Sander — See also Oscillat-ing Spindle Sander. For many years the spindle sander was just that. A large machine with a spindle on it

that simply rotated. Today, however, the spindle sander not only turns but also oscillates up and down to help prevent sanding marks. The spindle sander has a shaft that accepts a number of sizes of rubber drums, and sandpaper sleeves fit on the drums. The tool is an excellent one for sanding contours, and the one pictured at right is portable rather than mounted on a workbench or table.

Spiral Nail — (Or ardox nail and screw nail.) The spiral nail, as its name implies, is a conventional nail with a twist, literally. The shank of the spiral nail is square and, when hot, has been twisted several times. The purpose of the spiral is to provide a firmer grip in the joining workpieces. Spiral nails are made in a variety of lengths.

Spirit Level — See Level.

Spirits — See Mineral Spirits

Spit Coat — A sealer used on unfinished wood to balance the absorption of stains or clear finishes. The spit coat is made from two parts denatured alcohol and one part orange shellac.

Splay — The outward angle of some types of chair or table legs.

Splat — The wider upright found in the middle of the back spindles of some types of chairs. The splat is a more decorative piece for the back support of a chair.

Splitter — The splitter is a rectangular steel blade that sits behind the

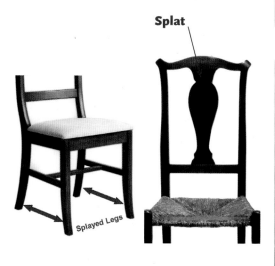

Splat

Splayed Legs

S

saw blade as part of a safety guard on a table saw. The splitter prevents wood that is being sawn to bind up or twist onto the spinning saw blade, thus helping to prevent kickback.

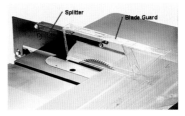

Spokeshave — The spokeshave is a type of plane in that it shaves wood, but the spokeshave is used primarily in shaping spindles and, perhaps, chair legs. The spokeshave is a steel, wood or brass tool that has a sharp blade mounted between two handles. The blade is set at an angle that allows it to scrape or shave the workpiece. The spokeshave works as it is drawn towards the woodworker. The exposure of the blade is adjustable, and it may be straight or curved.

Spreader — A hybrid bar clamp. Most manufacturers of bar clamps have modified their products to allow the tail end of the clamp to be reversed so that the tool can be used to spread the legs of chairs when repairing them. Longer spreaders may be used to support upper cabinets during installation.

Spur Chuck — The spur chuck is used in the head stock end of a lathe to hold one end of a workpiece for turning. It is usually used in spindle turning. The center point of the chuck corresponds with and penetrates the center of the piece. The spurs dig in and grasp the piece, preventing it from slipping when the workpiece is being turned.

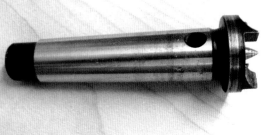

Square — See also Combination Square.
    Carpenter's — Also known as builder's square, framing square,

steel square. The carpenter's square is a large square that looks simple to use but, in fact, used to be a very complex tool. Older (before the computer) squares had many scales and formulas etched into the blade that gave the user methods to calculate hip, valley and rafter angles and measurements. Today, though, the steel square is still used for things other than just determining if a workpiece is square or plumb. The square is always made the same way by manufacturers, the blade is 24" long x 2" wide. The tail is 16" long x 1½" wide.

Try — A small square used to measure and to "try" the work-piece to make certain that it is square. The try square consists of two parts: the blade (usually tempered steel) and the stock or handle. The blade is firmly fixed to the handle to ensure its squareness. Some try squares are made from exotic wood stocks and brass inserts and rivets.

Square-Drive Screw — See Robertson Screw.

Square-Drive Screwdriver — See Robertson Screwdriver.

Square Nail — The square nail is reminiscent of the olden days of woodworking when nails were individually made. The square nail was made in many sizes just like today, but now they are used primarily in traditional boat building. A hole is drilled into the hull plank, and the nail is driven in so that the corners cut into the hole. The points of the nails are then hammered over to secure the nail.

S

Squeeze-Out — Squeeze-out is a normal occurrence in the process of gluing two or more boards together. Even if spread sparingly (but don't starve the joint), the glue will seep out of the joints. Squeeze-out should be cleaned up with water or an appropriate solvent as quickly as possible so that the glue does not permanently stain the workpiece.

Squeeze-out

Stain – See Wood Stains.

Staple — The staple is, in fact, a staple in woodworking. The staple is a length of stiff wire bent into an inverted U. The legs of the U are cut on sharp angles to facilitate their penetration into wood. Woodworking staples are driven by a pneumatic stapler and are usually called *narrow crown staples*. The stapler drives these ¼" crown staples of varying lengths, and the staples are generally used to fasten thin backs to cabinets or to fasten upholstery.

Staple Gun — a) A pneumatic tool that shoots staples one at a time or sequentially, depending on the staple gun setting. The staple gun may shoot staples of various lengths and widths. b) A spring-loaded tool that shoots staples of a finer gauge, like those used to fasten paper together. This stapler, however, does not close the staples once fired. This staple gun is used for fastening carpet underlay and the like. c) Also known as a *staple hammer*, this tool is hammered onto the workpiece and, as contact is made, a staple is ejected with force to drive the staple home. This, like the stapler, fires fine gauge staples.

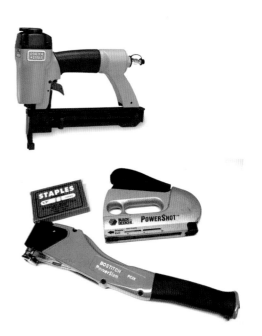

Starved Joint — A weak wood joint where insufficient glue has been used to properly adhere the two or more pieces of wood.

Stationary Tools — The heavy tools in your shop, the ones that you may have to put on a mobile base to move. These include such tools as a bandsaw, table saw, thickness planer, jointer, drill press and sanding center.

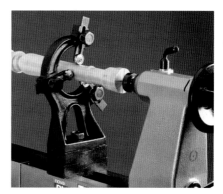

Steady Rest — A stabilizing tool that fits on the bed of a lathe and is designed to prevent long turning workpieces from wobbling or even breaking while you are turning. The steady rest pictured here has three adjustable bearing wheels to keep the turning steady.

Steel Wool — See also Abrasives. Steel wool is not just a finishing material: the coarser grades can be used to assist in stripping off old finishes as well. There are eight grades of steel wool, number 4 being the coarsest and the grade numbers decrease down to 0000 for the finest. The 00, 000 and the 0000 are often used in rubbing in tung oil and linseed oil with excellent results.

S

Steel Wool Grades

Grade	Woodworking	Metalworking	Stain/Paint
0000	Final Finishing with tung or linseed oils.	Cleaning precision tools.	
000	Scuff between coats to remove surface flaws.	Remove rust spots from chrome.	Remove paint drips or spatters.
00	Remove old finish with remover.	Restore aluminum, copper, brass, etc.	Remove burns from wood, change high gloss to semi-gloss.
0			Remove final paint residue.
1	Smooth raised grain.	Remove rust from iron, prep copper pipes for soldering,	De-gloss paint for new coatings.
2		Etch porcelain and metal.	Remove paint from tight spaces.
3	Remove old finishes with strippers.		
4			Remove tough finishes with strippers.

Never use steel wool as a between–coats abrasive when using water-based finishes, like stains and some polyurethanes. The small threads can break off and will leave rust spots on your finish.

Steam Bending — Sometimes a straight piece of wood just won't do. It has to be bent like the backs of some chairs. Bending dry wood will snap it, so it must be steamed first. There are many ways to steam wood. The Internet is full of ideas on how to steam and how to set up molds. Basically, it requries building an enclosed long box into which you channel the steam. Your workpiece is then placed in it and once the piece is hot and pliable, the wood is set into a mold or pattern and keep it clamped there until dry. The best wood species for bending are oak, hickory, elm, walnut, ash, cherry and maple. Some bend easier than others.

Steers Bit — See Drill Bits, Expansive Bit.

Sticks — See Stickers.

Stickley Furniture — See Mission Furniture.

Stile — See also Raised Panel Doors. The stile is part of a cabinet door (generally, the vertical side members of a panelled door, as in a raised panel door).

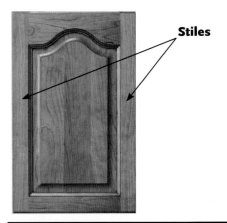

Stiles

Stickers — Stickers aren't sticky. In fact, the name is kind of a misnomer. Stickers are spacers used to make air spaces between newly–milled boards that are stacked for either air or kiln drying. Stickers are

usually thin (1½" thick x 2" wide) pieces of wood and are spaced about two feet apart along each layer of boards.

Stop — A jig that allows the woodworker to make consistently long cuts or to drill consistently deep holes. Most drill presses have a built-in depth stop and some compound miter saws have stops built into them to make repetitive cuts in boards. The stop can be shop-made by using a piece of scrap wood clamped to a saw fence.

Stop, Bench — See Bench Dogs.

Straightedge — (strayt-ehj) A tool for drawing or for cutting straight lines. The straightedge is usually thin and flat and may be made of steel, aluminum, wood or plastic. It may be as short as 12" or as long as is practical for the woodworker to handle. Usually, though, a straightedge is 48" long. The straightedge is also used to true up and align outfeed and infeed tables for tools.

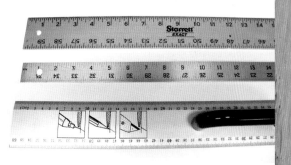

Straight Grain — The term *straight grain* may refer to the grain characteristics of a specific species of wood, or it may refer to the way the wood is milled. For example, quarter cut oak (like most other species) produces a straight wood grain figure. Walnut is one of these, as are red gum, zebra wood, teak and others.

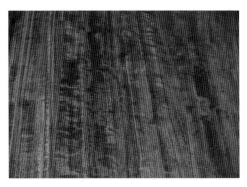

S

Stretcher — A horizontal structural member that is used to brace the legs on wood tables. The stretcher ensures that the legs remain plumb and true. The picture is of a stretcher on a pine trestle table. (Note the keyed tenon connection.)

Striking Knife — An old but trusted tool used to mark a line. The striking knife is kept very sharp and flat on one side. The purpose of using a striking knife is that it marks a very clear line and is not subject to erasures like a pencil is. The striking knife also cuts the top of the wood grain and, therefore, helps prevent tear-out.

Stringer — One of three parts of a staircase. The stringer is the long wooden member that goes from one level to the next. The stringer is usually a 2x10 or a 2x12 with notches cut out of it for the stair treads. The third part of the staircase is the riser, and that is the vertical cut of the notch on the stringer.

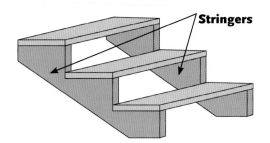

Stringers

Strip Hinge — See Piano Hinge.

Stripper — One type of stripper has nothing to do with woodworking, but perhaps a little levity is in order. However, a stripper is a liquid chemical used to remove paint, varnish and/or stain from a workpiece that you want to refinish. Care must be taken in handling some strippers as they may contain chemicals that can burn skin. Most contain methanol, toluene and acetone. There are safer strippers available that may or may not be as effective.

Stroke Sander — A large woodworking tool that uses a long horizontal sanding belt. Typically, the stroke sander has a sliding (in and out) table on which to place your workpiece. The belt rotates at right angles to the table. A pad is lowered onto the back (inside) of the belt so that

it makes contact with the work-piece. The pad may be moved to the left and right while the workpiece moves in and out for total surface coverage. The stroke sander is made for commercial woodworking shops.

Strop — (strop) A thick, tanned leather strap or pad used to remove the burr from a newly sharpened blade. A stropping compound is added to the leather as lubrication. The blade is then rubbed on the flat strop to form an ever–so–slightly more acute angle than the original blade edge.

Stud Finder — A tool used to locate wall studs and floor joists. There are several types of stud finders. The earliest of them uses a magnet on a pivot. As you move the tool along a wall or floor, the magnet swings as soon as a nail or screw head is detected. This gives you an approximate location of the stud. The more accurate stud finders made today use a form of radar that can actually detect both edges of the stud or joist and then indicate their exact center. These also detect live electrical wires and plumbing pipes that are in close relation to the wall or floor. They can usually penetrate ¾" or more.

Sureform — See also Rasp. Sureform is a Stanley Tools trade name for a series of stainless steel rasps. The stainless steel is quite thin and has directional teeth punched into it. Sureforms come in a number of shapes and are used for shaping wood. Handles are available for the flat blades as well. A similar product is called a Microplane® and works in much the same way. They also double as a good kitchen grater!

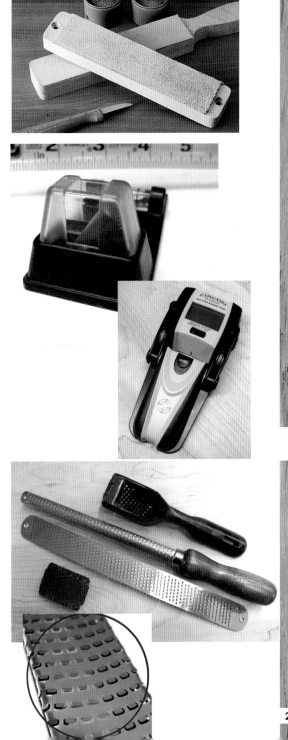

S

SURFACE SANDER ANATOMY

Dust Port

Drum Access Cover

Sanding Drum

Elevation Scale

Conveyer Belt

On/Off Switch

Elevation Control

Conveyer Belt Tracking Control

Induction Motor

Conveyer Speed Control

Conveyer Motor

Tool Stand

Surface Sander — The surface sander is a variation of a drum sander. It is a steel drum with sandpaper spiralled around it, and it spins to sand large surfaces. The sanding drum is lowered onto the workpiece by an elevation handle. A conveyer belt feeds the workpiece through the opening. The open ended surface sanders are able to sand wide workpieces by sanding half of it at a time. For example, a $^{16}/_{32}$" surface sander can surface sand a workpiece up to 32" wide. There are similar sanders with closed ends, but they are made in specific widths.

Surface Measure — To measure the surface area of a workpiece you measure the length and multiply it by the width. L x W = area.

Surfaced Timbers — See also Dressed Lumber. Wood that has been put through a thickness planer to smooth the surfaces and removes the rough fibers.

Surfacing — See also Thickness Planer. Surfacing is the planing of a board, either with a thickness planer or with a hand plane, to remove coarse wood fibers from both faces and both edges of the

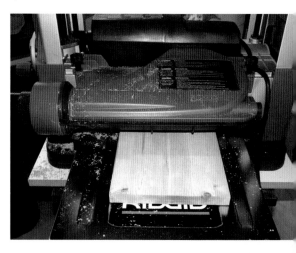

board. Using a thickness planer also allows the woodworker to adjust the final thickness of the board.

Swaged Hinge — (sway-jed) Swaging is the slight offset in the hinge leaves which permits them to close to a parallel position as the door closes. A hinge can by swaged on only one leaf, to leave an gap of approximatley ¹⁄₁₆" (top illustration), or both leaves of the hinge can be swaged, to allow a gap of ¹⁄₃₂" or less. Hinges can be purchase swaged by the manufacturer, or the woodworker can swage the hinge in the shop carefully using a hammer and an anvil.

Half Swage

Full Swage

Swan Neck Chisel — See Chisel, Cranked.

Swirl — See Crotch.

Syringe — This is not the same type of syringe that we feared as kids. This is a syringe that is used to inject glue into tight spaces. The syringe is a tube with a small spout attached (not a sharp one). Glue is poured into the tube and then a piston is pushed to force the glue out.

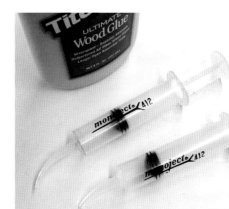

S

T-Bevel — See Sliding Bevel.

TEFC Motor — See TEFC.

T-Hinge — Also known as Cross Garnet. The T hinge has a butt leaf on one side of the knuckle and a longer triangular steel strap leaf on the other. The strap hinge in its smaller sizes may be used decoratively on cabinetry and, in its larger form, on entry doors, barn doors and gates.

T-Nut — The T-nut allows the woodworker to use metal bolts in woodworking. The workpiece is drilled to allow the threaded nut portion to be recessed. The prongs bite into it as the mating piece is pulled tight with a bolt. The T-nut is used in knock down furniture.

T-Slot — A slot cut into a cast iron saw tabletop that secures a miter gauge or other accessories. The T-slot may also be found on router tables, bandsaws and other tools. The T-slot is so called because of its shape. It is designed to allow the accessories to slide whilst keeping them secure on the tool. The accessories have a flat washer attached that rides in the T.

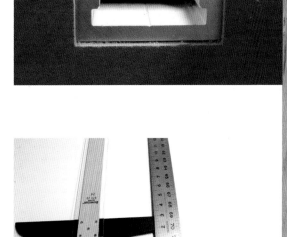

T-Square — The T-square was an architect's tool but as the architect's drawing tools have gone high tech, the T-square has ended up being a woodworking tool. The T-square has changed as well. The older types were made of wood, but now they are made of many materials. In fact, the table saw rip fences and miter squares are derivatives of the T-square.

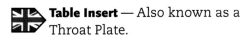 **Table Insert** — Also known as a Throat Plate.

Table Saw — See Saw, Table.

Tabletop Hinge — See Rule Joint Hinge.

Table Vise — See Vise, Portable.

Tack — The tack may be utilitarian or decorative or both. The tack is used by both woodworkers and upholsterers. The tack is a small sharp nail installed with a special tack hammer that has a magnetic head to hold the tack. The tack may be used to fasten upholstery to wooden frames or as a decorative addition to some furniture pieces.

Tack Cloth — The tack cloth is used by furniture makers just prior to

t

putting the first finishing coat on the workpiece. The tack cloth is saturated with a sticky (tacky) substance that dust clings to. The substance does not stain the raw wood or prevent the finish coat from adhering. The tack cloth is also used between sanding to remove all the sawdust.

Tack Hammer — See also Hammer. The tack hammer is, as its name implies, a hammer made specifically for hammering in tacks. Generally, *tack* means upholstering tacks. The tack hammer is also referred to as an upholsterer's hammer. The head is usually square in shape and split because it is a magnet designed to hold the tack and to save the upholsterer's thumbs. The user picks up a tack with the magnet and hammers it in. There is a narrow claw for tack removal.

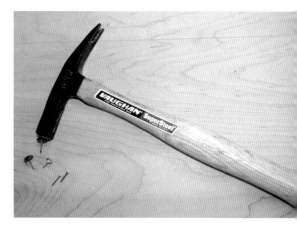

Tail Stock — See also Lathe. The tail stock is the left end of a wood lathe, the part that is not powered. A dead center (fixed) or a live center (free turning) is inserted into the tail stock. The tail stock can move along the lathe bed to facilitate the tightening of the workpiece on the lathe. An internal shaft can also be adjusted forward and locked.

Tambour — (tam-boor) A form of sliding cabinet cover or lid. The tambour is made up of a quantity of narrow wood strips mounted on a sheet of canvas. The ends are notched to fit into grooves (tracks) that allow the entire unit to slide open or shut. The tambour tracks are usually curved to allow the tambour door to be concealed within the cabinet when opened. The tambour door is made as a single unit or in pairs that meet

in the center of the cabinet opening. Typically, a roll-top desk is fitted with a tambour door.

Tang — a) This is what Neil Armstrong, John Young, Frank Borman and others used to slake their thirst when they were 150 miles up.
b) The steel protrusion of a file or rasp. Tangs are also found on carving tools, lathe turning tools and knives. These are the blade extensions that are fitted into a handle.

Tangential Shrinkage — See also Radial Shrinkage, Shrinkage. As wooden board dries, the moisture evaporates and the board shrinks. The way the board shrinks is dependent upon how the board was cut from the tree. If the board has been flat cut it will be subject to tangential shrinkage. This means that the board has been cut on a tangent to the growth rings of the tree. Left to dry uncontrolled this will probably result in seriously cupped boards.

Tannin — This is a Celtic word meaning *oak* and is an antioxidant. Oak trees and other plants contain tannin, but it is more prevalent in red oak. Tanning leather is done through the use of tannins, and tannin, when mixed with water, will create a chemical blue dye. Red oak is not used in cooperage (the making of barrels) because of this. The tannin in red oak furniture causes those black stains when water is spilled on it.

Taper — (tay-pur) Tapering is mostly done on furniture legs. Tapering is cutting a rectangular board and then making it narrower at one end. This is done by using a taper jig.

1482
2 Sided Taper
34½ x 3½ x 8

Taper Jig — (tay-pur) A taper jig is comprised of two square steel tubes attached by a pivot at one end. A scale and a locking screw maintain the desired angle opening. The taper of a board is made by placing one edge against a table saw rip fence with the board placed on the angle. The jig and the board are then pushed through the saw blade. The taper jig may be shop-made using hardwood as well.

Tape Measure — The conventional tape measure as we know it is a thin steel tape that is wound into a compact case. These are generally in the 6' to 30' lengths and are spring-loaded so that when extended they retract by themselves after pressing a release button. However, fiberglass is used for tape measures of 50' – 200' or more. These are not spring-loaded; they have to be wound back manually with a small crank handle built into the case. Although manufacturers strive to make their tape measures accurate, over a given span you may notice differences between them. It is best to use the same tape measure throughout your woodworking project.

Tear-Out — An undesirable situation that occurs mostly when crosscutting. The wood fibers of the board at the cut line tear rather than get cleanly cut. This could be the result of a dull blade or the type of wood. This tear-out can be prevented by clamping another thin sacrificial board on top of the cut line.

Teeth — The teeth we are talking about here are not the ones you soak in a glass at night, and they are certainly not the ones belonging to a beaver, even if it is an eager woodworker. These are the ones attached to saw blades. They are the teeth that do the wood cutting for a saw. Hand saw blade teeth are cut from hard steel as are bandsaw, hacksaw and some circular saw blade teeth. Most circular saw blade teeth today are made from tungsten carbide, a very tough compound. These teeth are brazed in place on the steel saw blade, although recent innovations have the teeth actually welded in place.

TEFC — An acroynym for totally enclosed fan cooled, refering to a type of induction motor used in stationary power tools. TEFC motors are sealed to protect them from sawdust infiltration and other contaminants. TEFC motors are used in dusty areas like those found in a tablesaw cabinet.

Template — A pattern usually made of a solid material that can be traced onto wood for multiple reproductions. For example, lettering kits are designed for duplication with a router. The router is fitted with a guide bushing that traces the pattern while the router bit cuts out the letters. Others might include difficult-to-duplicate patterns like cabriole legs or a specific lathe turning pattern.

Tempered Hardboard — See Masonite.

Tenon — As in mortise-and-tenon, the tenon is the male part of a joinery system. The mortise and tenon joint is very strong due to the large gluing area.

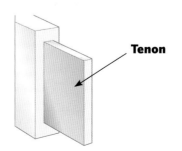

Tenon

t

Tenon Cutter — The tenon cutter is a tool that is fitted into a portable electric or cordless drill. The tenon cutter is much like a pencil sharpener. It has a sharp blade or blades. As it spins it is peeling and shaping the workpiece into a round tenon. There are various sizes available.

Tenon Saw — See also Saw, Hand. The tenon saw is a fine tooth saw (12 – 14 tpi) with a stiff body and a reinforced back. The back may be of brass or steel. The tenon saw has a full, enclosed handle. The tenon saw is also referred to as a backsaw and is used for general bench work as well.

Tenoning Jig — A tool that fits in the miter T-slot of a table saw and is designed to cut tenons for mortise-and-tenon wood joints. The workpiece is clamped into the jig at the desired shoulder width and depth for cutting. The workpiece is turned and measured for the desired cheek dimension.

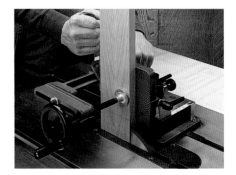

Thickness Planer Knives — These are narrow blades that are single- or double-edged and made in lengths to match the specific size of thickness planer. Generally, they are made from high speed steel, are sharpenable and are sold in sets. Installing these knives is usually done with a magnetic tool that sets them at a predetermined depth. Some are indexed and, although easier to install, they are not resharpenable.

Threaded Fastener — See also Screws. Threaded fasteners are screw-like fasteners used to join wood and other soft materials.

Thickness Planer Anatomy

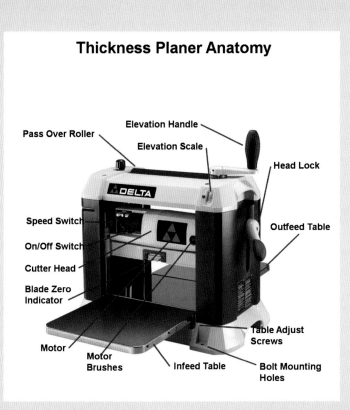

Pass Over Roller

Elevation Handle

Elevation Scale

Head Lock

Speed Switch

On/Off Switch

Cutter Head

Blade Zero
Indicator

Outfeed Table

Table Adjust
Screws

Motor

Motor
Brushes

Infeed Table

Bolt Mounting
Holes

Thickness Planer — The thickness planer is used to 'dress' lumber. Boards are placed on the infeed table and fed into the machine; high speed rotating knives plane or remove the surface of the wood. The cutter head is lowered in small increments to set the desired thickness of the board. The cutter head is locked after each setting to prevent 'snipe' at the beginning or end of the board. As an avid woodworker the purchase of a thickness planer can be an economical proposition as rough lumber is much less expensive than dressed.

Threaded Inserts — Hardware for connecting wood components with machine bolts. They have a threaded interior, and some are threaded on the outside as well. Other types may be pressure-fitted into pre-drilled holes. The threaded fasteners are inserted and tightened with a flat-head screwdriver or tapped in with a mallet. These are sometimes used in knock down furniture components.

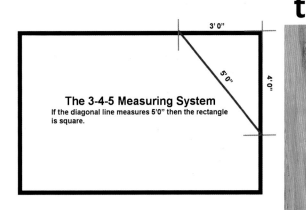

Three-Four-Five — The 3-4-5 system is a shortcut that checks a square or rectangular wooden frame for square. Using a measuring stick or tape, measure one leg of the frame and draw a line at the three-foot mark. Measure the intersecting leg and draw a line at the four-foot mark. Now, measure diagonally across both marks. If that measurement is five feet, the frame is square. This may be done in inches, millimeters, centimeters and meters as well.

3' 0"

5' 0"

4' 0"

The 3-4-5 Measuring System
If the diagonal line measures 5'0" then the rectangle is square.

t

Throat Plate — See Table Insert.

Through Dovetail Joint – See Dovetail Joint, Through.

Tilting Arbor — The mechanism in a table saw that allows the motor and the saw blade to be tilted to accommodate bevel (miter) cuts.

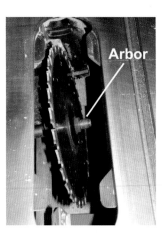

Arbor

Timber — A British term for board or lumber.

Timber Abbreviations — See Lumber Abbreviations.

Tin Snips — See Snips.

Tipped Saw — See Carbide Tipped Saw Blade.

Tire — See also Tyre. One would not normally think that a tire would be referenced in a woodworking encyclopedia, but you will soon understand when you open the upper or lower door of your bandsaw. Those wheels that the bandsaw blade is riding on have rubber tire inserts on them. The bandsaw tires have a slight crown on them, and the bandsaw blade rides on that crown.

Tire

Tyre

Toe Nail — a) The part of the anatomy that always gets stubbed against the leg of your workbench. b) Toe nailing is used mostly in construction but sometimes applies to woodworking. Toe nailing is the driving of a nail on an angle to secure a vertical member to a horizontal member. The method is called toe nailing because the vertical board is usually braced by the toe of a boot while driving the nail home. When driving the nail with a hammer (as opposed to an air nailer)

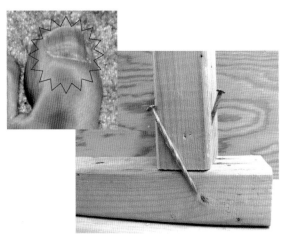

it is best to make an indentation in the wood with the nail head first. This makes a pocket in which to start the nail.

Tongue-and-Groove — A form of mortise and tenon joinery used quite commonly in construction. Tongue-and-groove joinery is used in the assembly of hardwood flooring and construction sheathing.

Tool rest — A long cast iron bar that fits into the banjo on a wood lathe. The too rest provides the turner with a pivot point on which to place his/her turning chisels and gouges.

Tooth Set — The tooth set refers to the way saw teeth are shaped or formed for circular saw blades, band saw blades and hand saw blades. In handsaws and band saw blades the teeth are bent out alternatively from the line of the saw blade. Circular saw blades also have a set to them, but being that most blades have carbide tips on them, it is varied positions of these that comprise a set.

Triple Chip Grind   Alternate Top Bevel

Torque — Simply, a rotational force. This is the power that a corded or cordless drill/driver applies to the turning of a drill bit or a screwdriver bit. The higher the torque the higher the power. Torque is shown in foot pounds (ft/lbs – torque = force X distance). Twisting strength is an example of torque.

t

Torx Screws — See also Spax Screws. Any wood screw with a torx head. The torx head is a star-shaped drive with six points. The shape was designed so that more torque can be applied without cam out. The torx screw was first designed for machine

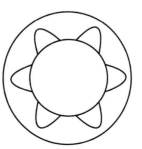

NOT SO FUN facts

Toxic Wood Species — There are a number of wood species that cause problems for woodworkers who use them. These problems may be as slight as a runny nose, or they may be downright carcinogenic. Handling this wood (with bare hands) may cause a reaction, but it is mostly the airborne sawdust that causes the trouble. An efficient respirator with the correct filter may relieve these problems. However, it is best to avoid contact with these species altogether.

Wood	Reaction	Site	Source	Incidence
Bald Cypress	S	R	D	R
Balsam Fir	S	E, S	LB	C
Beech	S, C	E, S, R	LB, D	C
Birch	S	R	W, D	C
Black Locust	I, N	E, S	LB,	C
Blackwood	S	E, S	W, D	C
Boxwood	S	E, S	W, D	C
Cashew	S	E, S	W, D	R
Cocobolo	I,S	E, S, R	W, D	C
Dahoma	I	E, S	W, D	C
Ebony	I, S	E, S	W, D	C
Elm	I	E, S	D	R
Goncalo Alves	S	E, S	W, D	R
Greenheart	S	E, S	W, D	C
Hemlock	C	R	D	U
Iroko	I, S, P	E, S, R	W, D	C
Mahogany	S, P	S, R	D	U
Mansonia	I, S	E, S	W, D	C
Mansonia	N	-	D	-
Maple (Spalted)	S, P	R	D	C
Mimosa	N	-	LB	U
Myrtle	S	R	LB, D	C
Oak	S	E, S	LB, D	R
Oak	C	-	D	U
Obeche	I, S	E, S, R	W, D	C
Oleander	DT	N, C	D, W, LB	C
Olivewood	I, S	E, S, R	W, D	C
Opepe	S	R	D	R
Padauk	S	E, S, R	W, D	R
Pau Ferro	S	E, S	W, D	R
Peroba Rosa	I	R, N	W, D	U
Purpleheart		N	W, D	C
Quebracho	I	R, N	LB, D	C
Quebracho	C	-	D	U
Redwood	S, P	E, S, R	D	R
Redwood	C	-	D	U
Rosewoods	I, S	E, S, R	W, D	U
Satinwood	I	E, S, R	W, D	C
Sassafras	S	R	D	C
Sassafras	DT	N	D, W, LB	R
Sassafras	C	-	D	U
Sequoia	I	R	D	R
Snakewood	I	R	W, D	R
Spruce	S	R	W, D	R
Walnut, Black	S	E, S	W, D	C
Wenge	S	E, S, R	W, D	C
Willow	S	R, N	D, W, LB	U
West. Red Cedar	S	R	D, LB	C
Teak	S, P	E, S, R	D	C
Yew	I	E, S	D	C
Yew	DT	N, C	W, D	C
Zebrawood	S	E, S	W, D	C

Reaction: I - irritant; S - sensitizer; C - nasopharyngeal cancer; P - pheumonitis, alveolitis; DT - direct toxin; N - nausea, malaise

Site: S - skin; E - eyes; R - respiratory; C - cardiac

Source: D - dust; LB - leaves, bark; W - wood

Incidence: R - rare; C - common; U - uncommon

screws but is now available for wood screws as well.

Torx Screwdriver — This is the tool used to drive torx screws and is available in several sizes that will match the screws.

TPI — Teeth Per Inch. This acronym refers to the amount and spacing of teeth in hand saws and band saws, sometimes referred to as points per inch (ppi) in the U.K. There will always be one more point per inch than teeth per inch. For example, a typical crosscut hand saw has 5 – 8 tpi or 6 – 9 ppi, a Rip Saw 3 – 4 tpi (4 – 5 ppi); a dovetail saw 16 – 22 tpi (17 – 23 ppi); and a hacksaw 24 – 32 tpi (25 – 32 ppi). Band saw blades have very broad ranges of tpi depending on the specific applications.

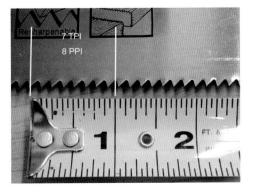

Tracking — The adjustment of the tracking wheel, knob or lever on a band saw to make certain that the band saw blade rides perfectly centered on the tire of the upper wheel of the tool.

Trammel Points — Trammel points are designed to clamp onto the edges of a steel ruler or a length of hardwood and are used as a compass to scribe or mark circles. Some trammel points allow you to install either a steel scribe point or a pencil lead.

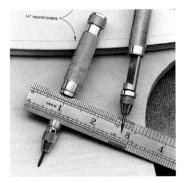

Transfer Scribe — The transfer scribe transfers (through a pencil line), the unevenness of a wall or other surface onto which the cabinet will be hung or placed. This allows for a truly flush fit of the cabinet. One leg of the scribe follows the wall contours while the pencil leg simultaneously transfers the contours to the sides of the cabinet for later cutting.

Tread — As in the tread on a wooden staircase. The staircase is made up of three parts: the stringer, the riser and the tread. The tread is the horizontal member that sits on the stringer.

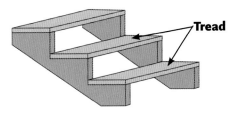

Tread

t

Tripoli Powder — See Rottenstone.

Truing — See Jointing.

Trunion — (trun-yun) The part of the table saw that raises, lowers and tilts the saw blade while connected to the electric motor, either directly or through the use of V-belts. Some trunions are bolted to the table saw top (as in contractor table saws) or frame-mounted (as in cabinet and some hybrid table saws). The frame-mounted trunions make it much easier to maintain alignment. Pictured is a table-mounted trunion.

Try Square — A try square is a precision tool use to "try" or check a workpiece for squareness. The try square is held tightly against the right angle cut of a board to verify that the cut is exactly 90°. As the square is held on the board edge it is held up to the light for verification. The try square is available in various blade lengths, the most common being 6" and 12".

Tungsten Carbide — This is an extremely hard chemical compound used in the manufacturing of cutting and drilling tools. There are a variety of compound mixtures that produce various results for specific cutting or

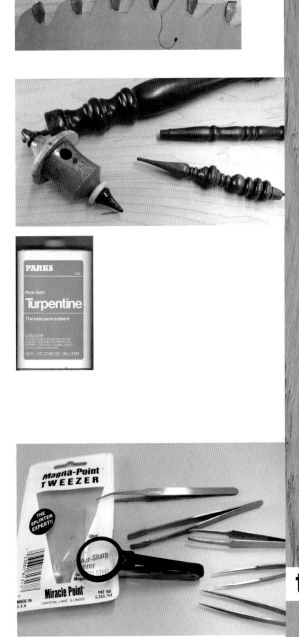

drilling operations. The most common use of tungsten carbide is in the tips of circular saw blades, router bits and drill bits.

Turner — This is the guy or gal who does the lathe turning.

Turning — This is the art of wood turning. The use of a lathe and various cutting tools to produce spindles, bowls, tops and other items that can be mounted on a lathe.

Turpentine — See also Mineral Spirits. This is a thinner for some types of paint and is made by distilling the resin from pine trees. Turpentine is also used as a cleaner for paint and oil stains. Turpentine is flammable and may spontaneously combust.

Tweezers — Aah, the life saving tweezers. There is little else that causes the woodworker as much stress as having a splinter stuck in his/her finger. Tweezers are the life savers, especially the ones attached to a magnifying glass. Tweezers are usually made from stainless spring steel. Two narrow pieces are layered and welded at one end. The pieces are curved outward and are tapered at the ends. The lengths may vary. The tweezers are squeezed in the middle to grasp that splinter and pull it out. Other types of tweezers are available as grasping tools for holding small wood parts.

Tyre — See also Tire. The British spelling for the rubber tire on the wheel of a band saw.

t

UHMW — Ultra-High Molecular Weight. A plastic used for various purposes in the woodshop. UHMW is used to make zero-clearance saw table inserts, table saw rip fences, bearings and others. UHMW is very smooth and almost slippery. The material may be cut and shaped with ordinary woodworking tools.

Undercut Saw — See Back Saw, Offset Saw.

Underground Burl — A burl in a log that has developed in the root of the tree and is fully or partially underground. These prized logs have to be dug out by hand in order to prevent damaging them. Underground burls are found in maple, myrtle, redwood, vavone and walnut.

Universal Motor — The type of electric motor found in most portable electric tools (such as routers). They are compact and can offer high speeds.

Urea Resin — (you-ree-ah) This is a chemical combined with formaldehyde which is used to make adhesives that are used in the making of products like particle board and chip board. The adhesive withstands the high heat and pressure used to form these sheets. This same adhesive is used to cement the plies in plywood.

u

Vacuum — See Dust Collector, Shop Vacuum.

Varnish — A protective finish traditionally used on furniture and other wood products as well as marine woodwork. Varnish is a combination of a drying oil, a resin and a solvent or thinner. The finish that varnish provides is traditionally a high gloss, but newer formulations of varnish may produce a satin or even a matte finish. It is not a totally clear product but has a light amber tone to it. Varnish is applied by brush. When applying varnish, bubbles (caused by the brush) will appear in the material. Don't worry. They will flatten out as the material settles.

V-Block — A rectangular piece of wood with a V-shaped groove cut

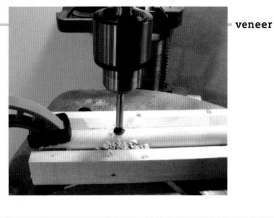

lengthwise into it. The V-block is meant to support a round dowel or other shapes for drilling. The V-block holds the dowel securely for cross drilling and holds a square bar for drilling into its edge.

De-barking the log

Flat Sawn Veneer

Half Round Veneer

Quarter Sawn Veneer

Rift Cut Veneer

Rotary Cut Veneer

Plain Sliced Veneer

Veneer — A thin sheet of wood that is chosen for its appearance. It is then glued to a substrate. Veneer is not considered a poor substitute for wood solids or even a synthetic plastic material with a printed wood grain appearance. When veneer is glued to a (usually) hardwood substrate it not only enhances the beauty of the piece but also adds to the strength as well. Veneer is produced by first selecting the desired tree. The tree is limbed and cut into log lengths (usually six feet) and then de-barked. The log then goes onto a lathe that slowly rotates the log. A sharp knife peels the log into thin sheets. The sheets are trimmed to the desired size and sequentially laid into a bundle called a flitch. The process is similar to unrolling toilet paper. The final log may be only a few inches in diameter. This process is called rotary cutting and produces the same grain pattern as the flat cut process. There are five basic ways of slicing logs to produce veneer: rotary cutting, flat cutting, quarter slicing, quarter flatting and rifting. Each type of cut produces a different appearance from the same log.

FUN facts

The use of wood *veneer* goes back to the days of Cleopatra in ancient Egypt. She was fond of many things, not the least of which was fine furniture made from exotic woods. Veneering continued but then was reborn in the eighteenth century by master craftsmen, who quickly understood its value compared to the cost of exotic wood solids.

During the Industrial Revolution, veneering became a shoddy form of furniture making that used poor quality veneer and substrates and that gave veneering a bad reputation that lingers. Today however, veneer is found on the finest cabinetry and furniture.

Veneer-Core Plywood – This is plywood that has solid veneer core where the plies are laid at right angles successively. What makes this different from standard plywood is that the inner plies are cut very thin like veneer, the advantage being that you can get many more plies into a given thickness and that makes for a stronger product.

Veneering — The art of applying veneer to a substrate, either plywood or a solid, less expensive species. The woodworker first applies a coat (or two) of contact cement to both the substrate and the back face of the veneer and allows it to dry until it is tacky. Next, sticks are laid across the substrate, and are evenly spaced every six inches or so. These sticks will prevent the veneer from contacting the substrate prematurely. The veneer sheet is aligned with the edges of the substrate and pressed down. From that starting point you start rolling with a rubber roller. As you progress the length of the veneer sheet you remove the sticks until all are removed and the entire veneer sheet has been laid. Using pressure, roll the veneer to make certain that it has full contact with the substrate. Should you be using solid wood, it is best to apply a veneer backing to balance the pressure.

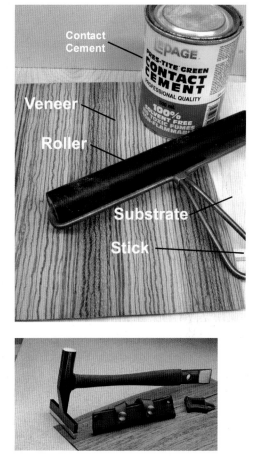

Veneer Hammer —A tool used to press veneer tight to the substrate and to remove any possible air pockets when applying veneer.

Veneer Patterns

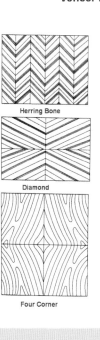

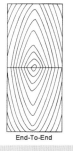

Herring Bone

Diamond

Four Corner

Mirror Matching

End-To-End

Veneer Patterns — The beauty of veneer is its versatility. Veneer can turn a bland-looking tabletop into a thing of beauty. This is done by carefully selecting the veneer and its application. A number of different patterns may be achieved by laying out the veneer in different ways. Herring bone, bookmatching, mirror matching, diamond, end-to-end matching and more.

Victorian Furniture

It was during the reign of Queen Victoria (1837 -1901) that comfortable furniture began appearing in the homes of the commoners. This was the ninteenth century, and as the years passed the designs became less formal. The upper classes still chose ornate styles with lots of carvings. Mahogany and rosewood were the species of choice for cabinetmakers. At the end of the century we saw designs by William Morris and the Arts and Crafts style that was totally devoid of filigree.

Veneer Saw — See Also Saws, Hand. The veneer saw is a specialized saw with curved edges meant for making clean cuts in veneer sheets. The teeth are very fine and have no set to them.

Vernier Calipers — (verr–nee-are kall-ip-pers) See Calipers.

Vise — See Vise, Bench.

Vise, Portable — A portable bench vise is one that may be moved around your shop or stored until needed. The portable bench vise may have thumb-screw clamps to secure the vise to your bench, or it may have fittings that are permanently attached to the bench.

VOCs — Volatile Organic Compounds. These components are found in some woodworking finishing products, but they are being substituted with less environmentally harmful components. Sorry, no photos, it's very difficult to photograph gasses and fumes.

Vises, Bench Type

Finished Bench Vise

Bench Vise Kit

Versa Clamp
Screws To Bench

Hold-Down
Bench Vise

Portable Bench
Vise

Surface Mount
Bench Vise

Drill Press Vise

Portable Bench
Viser

Vise, Bench — The bench vise is a clamping tool that is affixed to a work bench. The vise works by turning a threaded rod that opens or closes the jaws. There are hold-down types that use a compression lever as well as many other types, but their purpose is much the same.

Voids — This one we can photograph, or at least the surrounding areas of it. A void refers to a plywood defect. In some of the inner plies there may be instances where knots have fallen out prior to lamination. In higher quality (grade) plywood these areas are plugged with football-shaped patches. The voids may not show on a full sheet of plywood, but if the woodworker cuts the sheet the voids will become prominent. Generally, these will not affect the strength of the sheet, but if you are using it as a top then you will have to fill the gap.

V

Waferboard — See also Oriented Strand Board. Waferboard is another type of sheet goods material that is very similar to particleboard. It is made of wood shavings of a particular size and orientation that are heated, glued together and compressed.

Wainscott — (waynes-coat) 🇬🇧 wayne-scott). This is a decorative lower area of a wall that is separated by either a chair rail or some sort of moulding. The wainscott is usually 40" – 42" above the floor.

Walnut Oil — Walnut oil is a safe finish to use on wood products such as salad bowls, utensils, steak boards and cutting boards. Walnut oil should be heated prior to applying as it will dry faster. Several coats should be applied and rubbed in.

Wane — (wayne) A common defect found in all species of wood caused not by nature but by the sawmill. A wane is the presence of bark on the edges or ends of a board.

Wash Coat — (Or Spit Coat) Typically used as the thinned first coat of a finish. The wash coat is used to change the appearance or porosity of a surface.

Washer— An ingenious idea invented eons ago to help reduce friction on moving parts. The common washer is also used as a spacer and to prevent a bolt from damaging a surface.

    Flat Washer — The flat washer is used between a bolt head and the workpiece to prevent damage to the piece.

    Cup Washer — See also Screw Cup. The cup washer is a decorative washer. Combined with a matching wood screw it accents the fastener. This is a desired appearance in some applications.

    Lock Washer — A lock washer is, as the name suggests, a washer that helps secure a nut or bolt and prevents it from loosening if subjected to movement or vibrations.

Warp — The term *warp* can mean almost any type of twisting of a board. It is the distortion of boards away from being flat. This is usually caused by uneven drying.

Waterstones — Waterstones are used for sharpening blades. The advantage of waterstones over oilstones is that they don't leave an oil residue

W

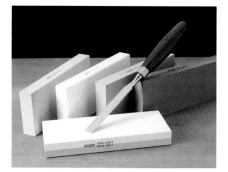

on the blade and they are easier to clean. Waterstones use water as the lubricant, and the stores are filled with water at the outset of your sharpening procedure. Waterstones are man-made and designed to be softer than oilstones.

Sharpening with waterstones should begin with 220 grit for major edge repair and then 1,000 grit to establish an edge. The 4,000 grit stone is used for maintaining an edge and the 8,000 grit stone is used for a mirror finish on the edge. Waterstones, because they are softer, require flattening on a regular basis, and a special flattening stone should be used.

Wax — See also Beeswax, Carnuba Wax. This entry refers to paste wax, such as a finishing wax, used as a final finish on turnings or cabinetry. The wax is applied with a soft cloth and then buffed dry. Paste wax is also used on woodworking machinery table tops to promote a smooth surface and help prevent rusting.

Web Clamp — See also Clamp, Strap. The web clamp is a nylon (usually) strap that is wrapped around your workpiece and then fed through a ratchet mechanism that pulls the webbing tight. The web clamp is the perfect clamp for assembling large round projects like tabletops and, with special corner pieces, is an excellent clamp for assembling boxes.

Wedges — See also Shims. Wedges are triangular or tapered pieces of wood of various sizes used in woodworking. Wedges may be used to lock tenons in the stretchers of a trestle table, or one may be used to secure an adze head to the handle.

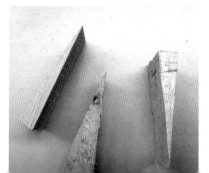

FUN facts

Willam And Mary Furniture
King William and Queen Mary ruled Britain from 1688 to 1702. William III of Orange was Dutch and was influenced by the Dutch furniture styles. Large numbers of Dutch cabinetmakers came to England, and their designs prevailed. Their style was graceful and decorative in appearance. Parquetry and marquetry became popular, and cabinetmaker Gerrit Jensen excelled in this art.

Wescott — A wrench with a solid (steel) handle and an adjustable jaw. The jaw movement is controlled by a helix-type screw that opens or closes to suit the nut or bolt size. Later types have an improved opening and closing slide mechanism that holds the jaws securely in any position.

Wet Dry Vacuum — See Shop Vacuum.

Wheel Dresser — A wheel dresser is a round dowel-like hard stone held in a tool that is used to flatten and re-surface a grinding wheel. The wheel dresser is held on the tool rest and pressed against the turning wheel.

White Glue — See also PVA. This is a form of woodworking adhesive that is made from polyvinyl acetate. White glue has a relatively short (3-5 minutes) open time. Squeeze-out should be immediately cleaned with water. White glue is considered an all-purpose glue.

W

Wing Nuts — Wing nuts are used in woodworking assemblies that need to be undone easily (without the use of a wrench or other fastening tool). Wing nuts are available in a number of sizes and are so called due to the large wing areas that facilitate hand tightening and loosening.

Wings — These are extensions to the standard saw table. Wings are attached to the right or left of the table saw to provide additional support while cutting large workpieces. These wings may also support a rip fence rail. The longer wings are usually supported by a set of legs. Wings may also be found on bandsaws.

Wire Wool — See Steel Wool.

Wonderbar — See also Pry Bar. The trade name for a pry bar made by Stanley Tools. The advantage of the Wonderbar over regular pry bars is that it is highly tempered and flat. This makes it easier to lever the tool between the workpiece and the floor or some other area. The Wonderbar is made in several sizes, some even small enough to remove staples and finishing nails.

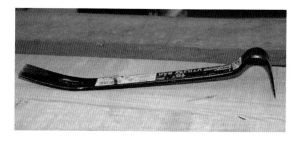

Wood Burning — Wood burning, also called pyrography, is art on wood. The artist uses an electric tool that heats the various types of interchangeable tips to burn lines, patterns and/or pictures on wood. The artist can vary the tone of the burn from light brown or tan to black to give varied effects such as that pictured. To preserve the work, the finished workpiece is then top-coated with a clear finish.

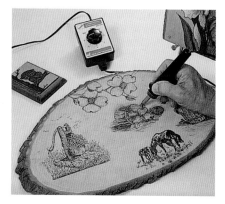

Woodcarving — Woodcarving can be likened to any type of sculpting by a fine master. Woodcarving may be very coarse through the use of a chain saw or very fine through the use of very sharp carving tools or even fine surgical knives. The woodcarver puts many long hours into his/her work, like this exquisite work by Canadian artist Dan MacLean.

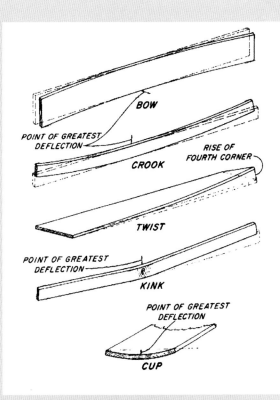

Wood Defects — These are flaws in a finished board, whether natural or man-made. These may be wanes, warping, cupping, twisting, checks or splits. All of these are undesirable traits that can spoil your woodworking plans for the day.

Wood Dyes — These are generally aniline dyes and are a synthetic tinting medium made from coal-tar products. These can be dissolved in water or alcohol and used to change the color of wood.

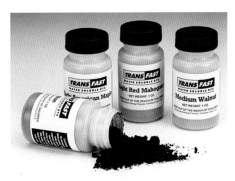

W

Wood Filler — Wood filler is like an eraser for woodworkers. Wood filler is a synthetic material in a paste form that can fill in nicks and dings. Most wood fillers are tinted to match various wood species or finishes. Some can also be stained to match surrounding areas.

Wood Lathe — See Lathe.

Wood Scraper — See Scraper.

Woodworker — That's me.

Wood Shavings — This is the part of the wood that you no longer require that comes out of the top of a hand plane or is expelled from a thickness planer or drill press. Your gerbil or hamster will appreciate as much as you can produce. (They prefer cedar.) Words of caution, however: never use walnut wood shavings to line the stall of your prized thoroughbred horse. The combination of oak and urine can be an irreversibly fatal combination for a horse.

Wood Stain — See also Wood Dyes. Wood stains are used to change or enhance the colour of wood and are usually applied prior to the finishing process of a workpiece. Your project may be made from pine, for example, but you would like it to be an oak colour. Wood stains of the proper type may accomplish this. There are oil-based stains (the most common), gel stains and water-based stains. The latter are free of VOCs (volatile organic compounds). However, these water-based stains are apt to raise the wood grain, requiring additional sanding work. Water-based stains penetrate deeper than oil or gel stains, so if you think that at some later date you might want to refinish the workpiece do not use them. Oil based stains blend better than water stains.

Workbench — While many woodworkers consider the table saw to be the central tool in any woodworking shop, the workbench is the central piece of furniture. Used for planing, joinery, assembly, finishing and many other aspects of woodworking a workbench is a versatile, essential (and personalized) part of any shop.

Workpiece — Any piece of work that you happen to be working on it is just an easier way of writing about a specific article of work.

Wormy — A somewhat desirous defect in some wood species. Wormy refers to pinhead-sized holes with dark edges in wood. Worm holes are quite commonly found in chestnut and considered an attractive feature.

Wrench — Any of several tools used primarily to tighten or loosen nuts and bolts. The most common, however, are the solid steel tools that are individually sized for specific fasteners. These wrenches may be single-ended, box-ended, open-ended or combinations.

W

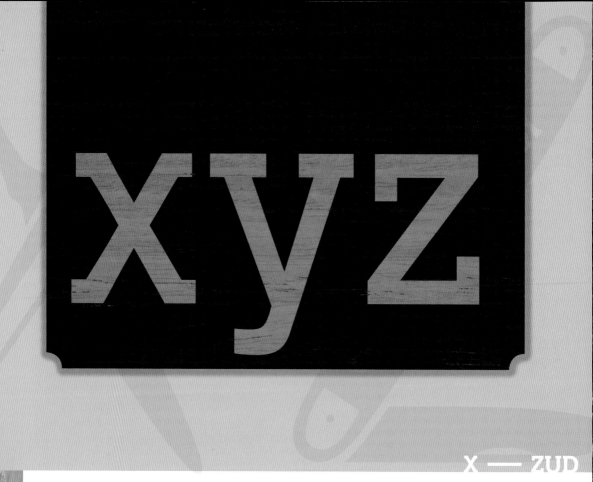

X — The drafting symbol for a cross section of an object.

Yankee Screwdriver — A combination screwdriver that is a ratchet as well as a spring-loaded double helix screw. As you press down on the handle the screw turns the installed blade (bit). The spring returns the bit to the top. The Yankee screwdriver has many bit types available including a flat blade, Phillips and Robertson styles. In addition, with the installation of special drill bits the tool becomes a twist drill. The tool is now a classic but was once considered a real time saver.

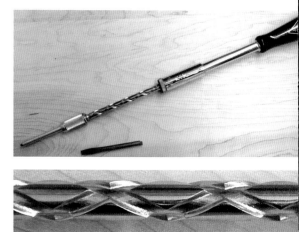

Yard — Three feet, or thirty-six inches fit into this, but for all of the details see our Conversion Tables at the back of the book.

Yardstick — See Ruler.

Yellow Glue — Also known as carpenter's glue. Yellow glue is an aliphatic resin product and is the most popular glue used by woodworkers. Yellow glue has a relatively short open time of five minutes. Yellow glue may be cleaned with water while still wet or with mineral spirits when dry.

Yellow Gum — An undesirable dark yellow patch found in american black cherry that remain visible even after surface treatment and finishing.

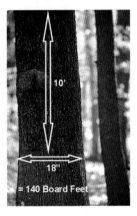

Yield — The net amount of useful lumber realized from a log or a tree. This is a 242' tall red creek fir tree on Victoria Island in British Columbia. It is the tallest standing tree in the country. The Yield? One heck of a lot of boards. The second photo shows the yield of another tree.

Zed — This is how we Canucks (and the Brits) pronounce the last letter in the English alphabet.

Zee — This is how the Yanks pronounce it. The term also refers to the occasional breaks that we woodworkers deserve.

Zero Clearance — A term used for table saw and miter saw inserts that have a kerf opening equal in width to the blade thickness being used. The purpose of a zero clearance insert is that it reduces tear-out.

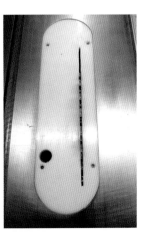

x
y
z

Zinc — A metal coating applied to fastening devices such as screws and nails for exterior use. These fasteners are galvanized with zinc.

Zirconia Alumina — A synthetic mineral that has a controlled breakdown that re-sharpens itself and is used as an open coat abrasive on sandpaper and other abrasive tools.

Zud — See Oxallic Acid.

Metric Conversion Chart

to convert	to	multiply by
Inches	Centimeters	2.54
Centimeters	Inches	0.4
Feet	Centimeters	30.5
Centimeters	Feet	0.03
Yards	Meters	0.9
Meters	Yards	1.1

Photo Credits

Although many of the photographs used in this book have been shot by the author, we would like to thank the following for their assistance in providing information and/or additional photographs in making this book possible. In particular, a special thanks to Freud, Lee Valley, Rockler and Woodcraft for their many photos (too numerous to recognize individually).

Accuride Drawer Slides – www.accuride.com

AccuScribe - www.fastcap.com

Adams Furniture Supply - www.adamsfurniture.com

Algonquin Wood Mouldings – www.algonquindirect.com

Always Victorian Woodwork – www.alwaysvictorian.com

Amana – www.amanatool.com

Amerock – www.amerock.com

Apter Fredericks – www.apter-fredericks.com

Bear Woods Supply – www.bearwood.com

Behlen - www.behlen.co.uk

Bessey Clamps – www.besseytools.com

Best Test Paper Cement – www.papercement.com

Black & Decker – www.blackanddecker.com

Bosch – www.boschtools.com

Bowclamp – www.bowclamp.com

BriWax – www.briwaxwoodcare.com

Busy Bee Tools – www.busybeetools.com

Cabinet Door Shop – www.cabinetdoorshop.com

Chipping Away – www.chippingaway.com

Classic Designs by Matthew Burak – www.tablelegs.com

CMT Router Bits – www.cmtusa.com

Colwood - www.woodburning.com

Constantines – www.constantines.com

Craeford School of Irish Dance –www.crawfordirishdance.com

Crown Chisels – www.crownhandtools.ltd.uk

CT Fine Furniture – www.ctfinefurniture.com

David R Webb Veneer – www.davidrwebb.com

Dap – www.dap.com

Delta Machinery – www.deltaportercable .com

DeWalt Tools – www.dewalt.com

Diefenbacher Tools – www.diefenbacher.com

Draper Tools – www.draper.co.uk

Dremel Tools – www.dremel.com

Elite Trimworks - www.elitetrimworks.com

Elmer's Probond – www.elmers.com

Famowood – www.eclecticproducts.com

Faux by Alissa - www.fauxbyalyssa.com

Fein Tools - ww.feinus.com

First Class Building Products - www.firstclassbp.com

Foredom – www.foredom.com

Freud – www.freudtools.com

Fuller Tools – www.fullertool.com

Gemini Touch Up Products - www.geminicoatings.com

General Tools - www.generaltools.com

Grizzly Tools - www.grizzly.com

Halifax Folklore Centre – www.hfxfolklorecentre.com

Herman Miller Inc. – www.hermanmiller.com

Hitachi Tools – www.hitachipowertools.com

House of Antique Hardware – www.houseofantiquehardware.com

Hudson River Inlay - www.hudsonriverinlay.com

Ikea - www.ikea.com

Inlay Product World - www.inlays.com

IPS Weld-On –www.ipscorp.com

Irwin Tools – www.irwin.com

Jacobs Chucks – www.jacobschuck.com

Jet Tools – www.jetequipment.com

Jorgensen – www.adjustableclamp.com

Kittinger Furniture - www.kittingerfurniture.com

Lee Valley Woodworking Tools – www.leevalley.com

Lie Nielson – www.lie-nielsen.com

LePage – www.lepageproducts.com

L. L. Bean - www.llbean.com

Makita Tools – www.makita.ca

Mertl, Peg - www.austincreekwoodwks.com

Milburn Guitars – www.milburnguitars.com

Miller Dowel – www.millerdowel,com

Miller Falls – www.oldtoolheaven.com

MinWax – www.minwax.com

Natural Resources Canada – www.nrcan-mcan.gc.ca

Norton Abrasives – www.nortonabrasives.com

Olson Saw Company – www.olsonsaw.com

Osborne Wood Products - www.osbornewood.com

Penn State Tools –www.pennstateind.com

Power Twist Plus 'V' Belts - www.fennerdrives.com

Rejuvination Hardware –www.rejuvenation.com

Robert Sorby – www.robert-sorby.co.uk

Rockler Woodworking Tools – www.rockler.com

Rolltop Desk Works – www.rolltopdesk.com

Ryobi – www.ryobitools.com

Sawbird.com - www.sawbird.com

ShopSmith - www.shopsmith.com

Skil Tools – www.skiltools.com

Snake Hollow Butcher Blocks - www.snakehollow.com

Soss Hinges - www.soss.com

Southern Pine Marketing Council - www.southernpine.com-

StairService - www.stairservice.com

Stiles & Bates Woodturning Supplies - www.stilesandbates.co.uk

Thomasville Cabinetry - www.thomasvillecabinetry.com

Traditional Tools - www.traditionalwoodworker.com

Varathane – www.flecto.com

Vaughan & Bushnell – www.vaughanmfg.com

Vermont American – www.vermontamerican.com

Wagner - www.wwwagner.com

Watco – www.rustoleum.com

Wychmere Woodworks - www.wychmerewoodworks.com

Woodcraft - www.woodcraft.com

Woodline USA - www.woodline.com

Woodstock International - www.shopfox.biz

Woodworker's Supply, Inc. - www.woodworker.com

Zinnser – http://www.zinsser.com

More great titles from Popular Woodworking!

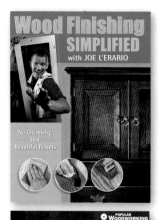

WOOD FINISHING SIMPLIFIED WITH JOE L'ERARIO

The author guides you to a great finish. Learn how to:
- Select the proper stain
- Prepare the wood for finishing
- How to apply stains and colors (use the technique of building layer upon layer to the big finish)
- Apply final top coats the RIGHT WAY

No other finishing book is this easy to follow and understand — and not nearly as fun!

ISBN 13: 978-1-55870-807-5
ISBN 10: 1-55870-807-3
paperback, 128 p., #Z0639

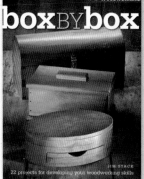

BOX BY BOX

By Jim Stack

Hone your woodworking skills one box at a time. In the pages of this book you'll find plans for 21 delightful boxes along with step-by-step instructions for making them. The projects include basic boxes that a novice can make with just a few hand tools to projects that will provide experienced woodworkers with an exciting challenge.

ISBN 13: 978-1-55870-774-0
ISBN 10: 1-55870-774-3
hardcover with concealed wire-o, 144 p., #70725

POPULAR WOODWORKING'S
ARTS & CRAFTS FURNITURE PROJECTS

This book offers a collection of twenty-five Arts & Crafts furniture projects for every room in your home. Some projects are accurate reproductions while others are loving adaptations of the style.

A bonus CD-ROM contains ten projects and ten technique articles to provide even more information on construction and finishing.

ISBN 13: 978-1-55870-846-4
ISBN 10: 1-55870-846-4
paperback, 128 p., #Z2115

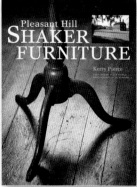

PLEASANT HILL SHAKER FURNITURE

By Kerry Pierce

Take a virtual tour through a restored Shaker community located in Pleasant Hill, KY. Study the history, the lifestyle and delve deeply into the furniture created by these gifted craftsmen. Includes painstakingly detailed measured drawings of the original furniture pieces and hundreds of beautiful photos. Learn the secrets of Shaker construction while learning about the Shaker's themselves.

ISBN 13: 978-1-55870-795-5
ISBN 10: 1-55870-795-6
hardcover, 176 p., #Z0564

These and other great woodworking books are available at your local bookstore, woodworking stores, or from online suppliers.